MONTICELLO

Thomas Jefferson, by Thomas Sully, c. 1822—*Jefferson Society*

Elizabeth Langhorne

MONTICELLO

A Family Story

Algonquin Books of Chapel Hill 1987

To the memory of
Catherine Drinker Bowen
kind mentor and generous friend

published by
Algonquin Books of Chapel Hill
Post Office Box 2225
Chapel Hill, North Carolina 27515-2225

in association with
Taylor Publishing Company
1550 West Mockingbird Lane
Dallas, Texas 75235

LIBRARY OF CONGRESS CATALOGING-IN-PUBLICATION DATA
Langhorne, Elizabeth Coles.
  Monticello, a family story.

  Bibliography: p.
  Includes index.
  1. Monticello (Va.)   2. Jefferson, Thomas, 1743–1826—
Homes and haunts—Virginia.   1. Title.
E332.74.L36   1987   975.5'482   86-20630
ISBN 0-912697-58-x

Contents

Illustrations

Preface

JEFFERSON, THE PUBLIC man, is a familiar figure; the private Jefferson has been little studied, and even less revealed. It was, in fact, a strictly guarded privacy. Between a husband and wife so often separated by the call of public duty we may assume that there were intimate letters; none can now be found. In all probability Jefferson himself destroyed them. There are, however, other opportunities for a close-up view. It is the object of this book to show the private Jefferson, the man behind the public image. We rely not on wild supposition, but on whatever his own letters and the direct observation of his contemporaries may bring to light.

The one observer who never fails us was his favorite grand-daughter, Ellen Wayles Coolidge. To an earlier biographer Ellen wrote: "You are inquiring, as you are bound to do, most minutely and particularly into all the details of private life. In order to understand him you must understand those by whom he was surrounded." I have made great use of Ellen's observations, many never before published, and of a whole chorus of other observers on the Monticello scene.

Monticello, the home, was an extremely personal creation. In the following chapters we will see Jefferson the architect and landscape designer at work on his ideal country house. We will see the master of a great plantation, and of that extraordinary black family, the Hemingses, Monticello slaves.

In my picture of Monticello the figure of Jefferson predominates. He affected the character of every one of those who surrounded him, and to some extent they affected him. The support of his family was, indeed, essential to the public man. That it did not come without cost is the story that we are about to tell.

E. C. L.
Charlottesville, Virginia
June 1, 1986

Acknowledgments

FIRST OF ALL my thanks must go to those who have made me feel at home at Monticello, beginning with Director Daniel Jordan. For special information I am indebted to James Bear, Charles Grandquist, and the unfailing help of William Beiswanger, nor can I fail to mention Sondy Sanford, Lucia Stanton, Peggy Newcomb, and William Kelso. Equally cooperative have been the hostesses and the secretarial staff; a special bow goes to my good friend Cenie Re Sturm.

This book would have been impossible without the help and cooperation of my home library, the Alderman, at the University of Virginia. Special thanks go to Michael Plunkett, R. A. Hull, and Gregory Johnson in the manuscript department, and to Mildred Abraham and the rest of the staff in the department of rare books. Photo credits appear elsewhere, but I would like to mention Pauline Page, my mainstay in the printing department of the library. Among other librarians who have offered their time and facilities are those at the Southern Historical Collection of the University of North Carolina-Chapel Hill, at Duke University, the Library of Congress, the Massachusetts Historical Society, the Virginia Historical Society, and the State Library in Richmond.

At the University of Virginia I am also indebted to Frederick D. Nichols, K. Edward Lay, William D. Rieley, and Charles Purdue. Dumas Malone has been an inspiration for many years. Particular thanks go to Merrill Peterson, whose scholarly reading of my manuscript has been of the greatest assistance.

Finally a salute to the memory of two great ladies, Miss Olivia and Miss Margaret Taylor, who made me welcome to their own personal shrine to Thomas Jefferson. Thanks also to my son, John Coles Langhorne, whose interests run parallel to mine, and to Joan Baxter, whose willingness to type manuscript has helped me over many a tight spot.

MONTICELLO

Chapter 1

Monticello Begins

THE HOUSE THAT YOUNG Thomas Jefferson was planning to build on his mountaintop was not like any house that had preceded it in the Piedmont. Nor did this young lawyer and rising politician mean to slavishly copy the finer houses familiar to him in the Tidewater. Just as his father, Peter Jefferson, had moved westward to establish himself in the new land at the foot of the mountains, so was the son determined to break new ground, set a new pattern, even in something as apparently everyday as the house in which he planned to live.

Peter Jefferson had been a younger son, who rose mostly by his own effort, but also through his friendship with William Randolph of Tuckahoe. Randolph, whose plantation stood on the James just above Richmond, was one of the great Tidewater clan of that name. From this association sprang the tale of Peter Jefferson acquiring the land in Albemarle (then Goochland) County in return for a bowl of Henry Wetherburn's best punch. This famous punch from the Raleigh Tavern in Williamsburg did change hands, or more likely was consumed by both parties to the deal, when Randolph gave Jefferson two hundred acres of undeveloped land north of the Rivanna River. Peter Jefferson considered this Randolph land more suitable for a house site than the mountainous tract he had patented the year before. He later acquired additional land, and at the same time paid his friend in full for the two hundred acres exchanged for a bowl of punch.

Peter's house site was on the river, nearer to crop land than the mountaintop later chosen by his son Thomas. His house was placed where the Rivanna flows out of the mountains on its way to join the James, very near to the present site of Charlottesville.

Jefferson tells us that the trail past the house was already in use by parties of Indians making their way downriver. As the youngest son of a not too prosperous family Peter himself had little education, but he made sure that his son should have the best available. In his own case great physical strength and natural gifts made up for the lack. He was a leading man in the up-country, who could count among his friends such figures as Colonel Joshua Fry of Viewmont and Dr. Thomas Walker of Castle Hill.

Peter Jefferson had put the final touch on his Randolph connection by marrying Jane, daughter of Isham Randolph of Dungeness. Dungeness was not far from Tuckahoe, and indeed not far from Peter's native place at Fine Creek, south of the James. Jane brought her husband no additional land. It may have been a love match, but clearly the large Randolph connection, one of the most powerful in Virginia, was no handicap to the future career of her son.

Thomas was the eldest boy in the Jefferson household. When the boy was only three years old Peter had moved his family from the simple frame house he had built on the Rivanna at Shadwell to the more elaborate home of his friend William Randolph at Tuckahoe, on the James River above Richmond. William's death and Peter's role as guardian had occasioned the move; young Thomas's most impressionable years were therefore spent in a fine house. Tuckahoe was architecturally sophisticated and boasted some of the finest interior woodwork in the colony. There were books at Tuckahoe, and no doubt books were available to the boy after he had returned to Shadwell. Books and more books, and time to spend in study, were what Thomas sought. It was this that he explained to his guardian, Dr. Walker, after his father's death, asking that he might go to the College of William and Mary.

It is not recorded when young Thomas Jefferson first came upon an illustration of the classical orders of architecture, but it was surely a moment pregnant with great things. It seems that the buildings he saw around him failed to impress the young connoisseur. Though often at the Governor's Palace during his student years at Williamsburg, he could speak scornfully of local buildings as "brick kilns," or as "boards plastered with lime . . . impossible to devise things more ugly."[1] His own taste was formed upon his reading. He was already thinking of a new world, a world still unknown in what was then Great Britain's uneasy colony. Philosophically and politically it would owe much to his reading in the French and British philosophers. Even physically it should show a totally new face. The house he was to build for himself was adapted from the work of the Italian master, Palladio. It was his cousin Edmund Randolph who wrote of this young man: "He panted after the fine arts, and discovered a taste in them not easily satisfied with such scanty means as existed in a colony, for it was a part of Mr. Jefferson's pride to run before the times in which he lived."[2]

Williamsburg, of course, had more to offer than books. While still a student young Thomas played the violin with a choice quartet at the Governor's Palace; he visited at the great house of his young friend Mann Page at Rosewell across the York River in Gloucester County; and he even courted his fair Belinda, in the guise of the sixteen-year-old Rebecca Burwell. When told that she must wait until her suitor had taken time out to see the world Rebecca had not unnaturally preferred the more ardent suit of Jacquelin Ambler. Jefferson, in fact, was a late bloomer, in a day when the young generally wasted no time in going about the business of life. Consciously or unconsciously, he was preparing himself for a career unlike any other in the colony, where study should lead to action, and theory take its place on the national scene.

One cannot escape the thought that at home the affairs of the plantation took second place, while the young man pursued politics and the practice of law. Nevertheless Jefferson had inherited land; there was no escaping the fact that almost by definition he must be a planter. As early as 1768 he was planting tobacco at Monticello with one W. Hickman, who made the crop on shares, and the following year he was laying out an extensive plantation of fruit trees on the southeast slope of his mountain.[3] A letter from Mrs. Drummond of Williamsburg tells of his obtaining grafts through his neighbor John Coles "from the choicest Englis fruite Green Springs afforded."[4] Natural enough, but all this assumed the position of the house to be, not like that of any sensible planter near to his barns and crop land, but on a mountaintop! He drew for the plans of his future home not on any existing models, and surely not on the resources of the local builders. "There is scarcely one to be found," he said, "capable of drawing a [classical] order."[5] Instead he turned to the Italian Renaissance architect Palladio, whose work he owned in the four-volume Leoni edition. It was here that he found what he sought, ideal form related to a personal philosophy: "Palladio . . . exemplifies the ideal life of the villa [a sort of Virgilian dream]. The ancient sages commonly used to retire to such places, where being oftentimes visited by their virtuous friends and relations, having houses, gardens, fountains and such like pleasant places, and above all their virtue, they could easily attain to as much happiness as can be attained here below."[6]

This was the ideal. When it came to its practical implementation even Palladio had relied somewhat on his own imagination, for his knowledge of "the antients' designs of country houses was limited to the descriptions of Vetruvius and Pliny."[7] Palladio may well have overdone the use of the portico in domestic building on the Roman model. However that may be, the Palladian portico suited the taste of the young man who wished to dominate a mountaintop, and to impose a rational order on the sprawling effect of the typical plantation village.

Virginian fortunes, like those of the Venetians for whom Palladio built, had originally been made in trade, but like the Venetians Virginians required plans for a productive estate, in which service quarters were grouped with the owner's dwelling. In Virginia the design had lagged far behind the more formal efforts of Palladio. Jefferson's design of offices in L-shaped terraces, with rooms along the corridors, incorporates the full Palladian scheme. The pavilions that stand upon the ends of the terraces at Monticello restore some of the visual support that such houses normally received from adjacent outbuildings.

This and many other modifications show us that Jefferson was no slavish copier of published designs. Bending over a drawing board at Shadwell, and later in the South Pavilion when that single chamber was finished at Monticello, the young architect was feeling his way, producing a series of designs for his future home.

These early drawings already show recessed stairs, a Palladian touch, and of course the use of the portico. We see with what care and precision Jefferson recorded the necessary measurements, and the mathematical proportion with which he worked. This was in line with Palladian theory, for the Italian master believed, as did Jefferson, that Nature herself was governed by mathematical law.

For recreation from this exacting work he had his garden plans. The delightfully discursive work of William Shenstone, "Unconnected Thoughts on Gardening,"[8] must have particularly struck • his fancy, for Shenstone's ideas related to the problems on his own mountain. There are those who believe that the young man's imagination ran away with him. His notebook for 1771, the year before his marriage, is filled with schemes for Greek temples, Chinese pagodas, and sylvan grottoes complete with recumbent nymphs. At first it was thought that none of these plans were actually realized, but now the uncovering and restoration of the garden pavilion south of the vegetable garden has brought at least one of them to life.

If we can credit Jefferson's political imagination with, as Garry Wills has it, inventing America, then surely we can credit him with the invention of that other ideal, Monticello, the perfect country house. It was, of course, to be subject to all sorts of modification, rebuilding, and extension, but if it were not for the conception of 1771 we might have lost more than a fountain here or a pagoda there. Without that heroic thrust, Monticello might not have existed at all.

One thing, to be sure, was lacking. A Virginia plantation needed a mistress. Seventeen seventy-one became the year of courtship, in which Jefferson found the widow Skelton. Martha Wayles Skelton was the eldest daughter of the Charles City County planter John Wayles. Wayles, an extroverted and energetic gentleman, had acquired a large legal practice and considerable land. Although the land was somewhat encumbered by debt, Martha might expect to inherit a substantial fortune. Her first husband, Bathurst Skelton, had died young, after less than two years of marriage. Martha was still only twenty-four, five years younger than her future husband, when Jefferson had gone courting at the Forest, Martha's home.

As an attractive young widow she was naturally besieged by suitors. The story goes that two of these arrived at her door at the same time, only to find that Thomas Jefferson had arrived there before them. Met by the sweet sounds of a duet in the voices of Martha and Thomas they both retreated, leaving Jefferson in command of the field. He played the violin, she the pianoforte. Although Monticello was not yet really ready to receive a bride, and certainly was not calling for the care of a mistress, Jefferson was impatient to wed his Martha. By August he was interrupting his architectural drawings and his work on his fruit trees to write his future brother-in-law Robert Skipwith: "In every scheme of happiness she is placed in the foreground of the picture, as the principal figure. Take that away, and it is no picture for me." Mrs. Drummond, his correspondent in connection with the fruit trees, found his description of Martha the most "Romantic, Poetical one I ever read."*

* This is Julian Boyd's reading of Mrs. Drummond's letter. An alternative reading might refer to Jefferson's description of his mountaintop.

Chapter 2

A Bride Comes to Monticello

JEFFERSON AND MARTHA SKELTON were married at the Forest, on the first day of the new year of 1772. When at last the festivities at the Forest had come to an end, the young couple set out for Monticello. As they left a light snow was falling. By the time that they reached Blenheim, the home of Col. Edward Carter, a heavy snow covered the mountain. The family were away, but the overseer and servants made them welcome for the night. Jefferson would not stay, he was impatient to have his bride at home. They left their carriage at Blenheim and went on horseback through the silent forest, over the track of unbroken snow. On the mountaintop they found the little pavilion empty, the servants gone back to their quarters. Jefferson lit a fire, and pulled a bottle of wine from its hiding place behind the books on a shelf. The young couple had it all to themselves, the mountaintop and their future happiness, together on that January night.[1]

In the years to come they complemented one another: she was lighthearted where he was serious; social by instinct, she was an admirable link to the country society around them. We know so little about her now because, deliberately, Jefferson is supposed to have destroyed every letter that ever passed between them. Even letters to others, such as their Coles neighbors, were later sought out, apparently with the same object. In reply to a request for these letters from her brother Miss Betsy Coles wrote that the last she had seen of Mrs. Jefferson's letters "they were in Mama's cap drawer." Their whereabouts after their disappearance from this depository is unknown. Aware of his own inevitable role as a public figure Jefferson took pains to keep his personal life private, at least in connection with this its most intimate aspect. What these letters may have revealed it is now too late to speculate.

It is clear that his wife's place was totally separate from his political career. When he was absent in Philadelphia Patty wished for him at home, but did not join him. It was to be, unhappily, a recurring theme, for she was increasingly either unable or unwilling to follow her husband in his political career. Jefferson had been a member of the House of Burgesses meeting in Williamsburg in 1769, but in the two years immediately following his marriage calls for attendance had not been frequent. By mid-1774 this situation had abruptly changed. The march of events, of rebellion, in short, from the mother country, was leading to the great declaration of 1776. It inevitably drew Jefferson from home.

Clearly Martha Jefferson was no Abigail Adams–type of helpmate. Nor had there been any model in Jefferson's past for that sort of relationship. His mother had brought him the Randolph blood. "They trace their pedigree," her son said, "far back in England and Scotland, to which let everyone ascribe the faith and merit he chooses."[2] He much preferred the self-made-man image projected by his father. Peter Jefferson had turned for companionship not to the feminine figure of his wife Jane, but to the male companion of his active days. Peter and his friend Joshua Fry had divided the week between them, Peter spending half with Fry at Viewmont, and Fry spending the other half with his friend at Shadwell. The world of men and women were thus early defined, in Jefferson's experience, as separate. Nevertheless, there were occasions when a wife's place was at her husband's side. All too often Martha Jefferson was at home, or at her own old home, the Forest. It is clear that Jefferson sorely missed her presence. Even worse, when illness did keep her at home, she often failed to write. To Jefferson, so fluent with his pen, this was always hard to understand.

At home at Monticello it was quite a different story. She had put herself completely in his hands on the honeymoon journey, when they had ridden up the snow-covered mountain to the single little brick pavilion waiting for them at Monticello. Did Martha share in those exciting plans for their future home? Very likely she did.

Dreams of "landskip" apart, there was plenty of a practical nature to engage a young bride's attention. Jefferson himself set about the serious business of planting tobacco, the single money crop on which their livelihood depended. Martha must endeavor to keep the accounts that her husband deemed so important. One such early effort at bookkeeping has survived, decorated halfway down the column of figures by an addition all Martha's own, a sketch of a little bird.

As the plantation village expanded she must "carry the keys." Far from a euphemism, this meant supervising the production of all that the family ate and all that the army of slaves used for food and clothing. There was, of course, a smokehouse for meat, a dairy, and a garden for vegetables, herbs, and flowers. At the time that Martha came to the mountain in the new year of 1772 the garden was already well established. For such details as these Jefferson took the same care that he did for the plans of his house, nor was his passion for figures lacking. For example, Martha could count on cucumbers; as early as 1769 her husband had noted that "Millar's [sic] Garden Dict[ionary] sais that 50 hills of cucumbers will yield 400 cucumbers a week."[3] By the first summer in their new home the Jeffersons were enjoying, in addition to all those cucumbers, "our peas," snap beans, and Irish potatoes. There were chickens, hams, and beef in plenty.

Isaac Jefferson, in his "Memoirs of a Monticello Slave," gives us a picture of the young housekeeper. "Mrs. Jefferson would come out there [to Isaac's mother Ursula, who was pastry cook at Monticello] with a cookery book in her hand and read out of it to Isaac's mother how to make cakes, tarts, and so on." The observant little black boy remembered in old age the sight of this lady; her figure he later described as "low," in other words she was short and slender—a "pretty lady." Martha presided skillfully over such a household, and Jefferson could be most proud of her when foreign visitors such as Chastellux came to stay. She retired early, leaving the men to quote the poems of Ossian to each other over a punchbowl, but this was only the proper thing for her to do.

At this time Jefferson was a considerable landowner, possessing more than 5,000 acres in Albemarle. At the death of his father-in-law, old John Wayles, the young couple inherited an additional 11,000 acres, of which they retained 5,000 in Bedford County. The remaining 6,000 acres were sold to meet payments on the Wayles debt. The Jeffersons now met the qualifications named by Heather Clemson as constituting in England membership in the "upper gentry." They were, and considered themselves to be, well off. They could scarcely have realized that the Wayles debt was to remain a never lifted incubus on the Monticello estate.

Land and debt—it was not an uncommon Virginia heritage, but old John Wayles had left his daughter and son-in-law an even more sensitive inheritance. A warm-blooded, popular gentleman, Wayles had run through three wives in his lifetime. His first wife, the mother of Martha Jefferson, had been an Eppes. As part of her marriage settlement she had brought Wayles a slave woman and her mulatto daughter by an English sea captain named Hemings. The captain wished to buy the pair, but Wayles refused. The mixed blood was rarer than it later became, and Wayles declared that he wanted to observe the result in the person of this child. Her name was Betty Hemings. One result that soon became evident was that there was no question as to Betty's fertility. She had four children by a black father or fathers before, at the death of his third wife, she became Wayles's concubine. There followed the five Wayles-Hemings children who were to play such a part in Jefferson family life. At Wayles's death Betty and all her progeny went to his daughter Martha, for the fortuitous reason that Betty had originally been an Eppes family Negro, belonging to Martha's mother. It so happened that now five of Mrs. Jefferson's half brothers and sisters were Jefferson slaves at Monticello.

Winthrop Jordan and others have believed Martha to be ignorant of this relationship, but this was not likely in the close-knit plantation society. Everyone, both black and white, would be fully aware of such a situation. There might be anguish of heart among planters' wives and slave husbands, but by and large one accepted what could not be helped. Human nature being no worse than it is, there was often a closeness, an added sense of responsibility, in such a relationship.

Whatever the tensions that might occur, we know that with Jefferson the problems posed by slavery were real. It was not his custom to speak passionately, or to reveal with freedom any depth of feeling, but this subject was the exception. He wrote: "I tremble for my country when I reflect that God is just; that his justice cannot sleep forever; that considering numbers, nature and natural means only, a revolution of the wheel of fortune, an exchange of situation is among possible events; that it may become probable by supernatural interference! . . . But it is impossible to be temperate and pursue this subject." These were the words that made him hesitate to have his *Notes on the State of Virginia* published in his home country, but they reflect his unchanging conviction.

The situation at Monticello must of necessity have been a delicate one. Whether or not related by blood, the Hemingses were as much a part of Monticello as the Jeffersons themselves. It would have been unthinkable to have banished them, as some have suggested would have been the more expedient course, to the Bedford land. They fell naturally into the category of house servants and craftsmen, closest to the white family. In the course of this book we may see how both families fared in the home conceived and created by Jefferson to provide "as much happiness as can be attained here below."

Chapter 3

Mrs. Jefferson

In a situation in which I would not wish to leave her.

IN AUGUST OF 1775 JEFFERSON was elected to the Continental Congress meeting in Philadelphia. He traveled by phaeton, with two spare horses ridden by Bob and James Hemings. He did not leave home until September 25, so that the death of his second daughter, baby Jane, must have occurred shortly before, or immediately after his departure. The eldest, Martha, had been born in 1772. In the midst of the stirring times that met him in Philadelphia he was never completely free from anxiety about conditions at home. The British, he wrote his brother-in-law Francis Eppes, were reacting vigorously to their defeat at Bunker Hill. "The plan is to lay waste all the plantations on our river-sides." [1] Jefferson too was reacting vigorously. "By the God that made me I will cease to exist before I will yield to a condition on such terms as the British Parliament propose, and in this I think I speak the sentiments of America." [2]

In the meantime Patty, as he called his wife, was not answering his letters. When for nearly six weeks he had heard nothing, he wrote again to Francis Eppes at the Forest, where Patty was staying. "The suspense under which I am is too terrible to be endured." [3] By the end of December he received special permission to go home to Monticello.

Mrs. Jefferson was perhaps in better health than he had feared, but a new trouble lay in wait. He was never to leave any record in writing of his feeling for his mother. There is only that laconic entry in his Account Book: "March 31 [1776]. My mother died about 8 o'clock this morning in the 57th year of her age." But the body is not so easily controlled as the pen. It was after this loss that Jefferson suffered his first prolonged attack of migraine headache. It is impossible to know what his feelings were, except that they were violent, and the reaction prolonged. He had long helped his mother to manage her affairs, but did he now feel the whole weight of the family descend upon his shoulders? Whatever the cause he was certainly *hors de combat* during five weeks of this time so pregnant with the march of events.

By the middle of May he had returned to Philadelphia, but there is no question that even in the area of public affairs his concern remained in Virginia. In Williamsburg they were busy framing a constitution for the new state government. Jefferson could hardly contain his desire to be present; it was a chance to create a state in the image of his own thought. In the airy second-floor rooms that he had rented at Seventh and Market streets he set to work; he would lay out his own plan for such a government. Although his plan as a whole was not adopted in Williamsburg, the final document was in effect close enough to his own draft.

When time came for Congress itself to seek a declaration of independence for the nation, Jefferson's pen was already warm. When the course of events called for his eloquence, it was ready; it poured inevitably from the pressure of long and serious thought. The famous document was intended as its own justification, an expression of the American mind in its thrust for freedom. He spoke, as he believed, for an entity which he called "the people" and which he declared had "an inalienable right" to claim their own government. This belief, central to Jefferson's thought, was to be the driving force behind the American Revolution, the great principle on which the future nation was to rest. "Posterity," cried John Adams, "will triumph in that day's transaction."[4] Indeed we have been triumphing ever since.

To Jefferson himself at the time, the changes made by Congress in the original document—stressing as they did the concept of merely individual freedom—vitiated his vision of a free people. His distress had been so obvious that Franklin had to comfort the younger man with his story of the hatter. This tradesman had spent some time devising an elaborate sign announcing his readiness to supply hats, but after the criticism of his friends this fine sign had been reduced to his name and the picture of a hat. All very well, but Jefferson may have thought that even a part of his own hat had been lost.

Added to these public distresses were disquieting reports from home. On July 30 he wrote from Philadelphia: "I propose to leave this place the 11th of August. . . . [E]very letter brings me such an account of the state of her health, that it is with great pain I can stay here till then."[5]

What was wrong? Mrs. Jefferson's ailment was not described, but as all her health problems seem to have been related to child-birth she may possibly have had a miscarriage. It was not until early September that Jefferson was at last able to leave Philadelphia, arriving home on the ninth. A month after his return he received a most tempting offer. Patty was better, but even so he turned down the appointment then offered to go as a commissioner to the Court of France. For three days he fought with his conscience over this matter before sending his refusal: "But circumstances very peculiar in the situation of my family, such as neither permit me to leave nor carry it, compel me to ask leave to decline a service. . . ."[6] Less than nine months later Patty bore them their only son. The infant survived for scarcely more than two weeks. Mary was born in 1778; she and her sister Martha were the only Jefferson children to survive to adulthood.

In spite of the loss of two children and of Mrs. Jefferson's frail health, life at Monticello was not dull. Quite the contrary, for as always the improvement of Monticello offered its master constant occupation and amusement. He made barometrical observations from the top of the house, and he was busy stocking his deer park. The elk, he had once remarked, should be kept shy, the Monarch of the Glen. He should not be too commonly visible. In 1777, in the serious matters of building, he was burning bricks in a kiln located, as it happened, in the deer park on the southwestern side of the mountain. Here the deep red clay was most suitable. He was also sawing planks for flooring, and of course setting out an abundance of fruit trees. The following spring he planted "calycanthus from the Green mountain"—an evidence of his interest in native as well as imported plants.[7]

During all this activity Mrs. Jefferson must have become quite used, and one hopes resigned, to the sound of hammering. How much of her own things she had brought with her we do not know. We know that the musical young bride had possessed a spinet, and that Jefferson had ordered a very special pianoforte for her as a wedding gift. For some years after their marriage they both took lessons from the Italian musician Alberti, whom Jefferson had persuaded to come to Albemarle.[8] Books, of course, were being constantly acquired; in 1774 Jefferson already possessed a library of over 1,200 volumes. His Account Book shows that he owned a Chippendale bookcase capable of holding 500.[9]

Almost all the furniture that Jefferson might have inherited had been lost in the Shadwell fire. The only piece of his mother's at Monticello is the little candle stand that stands by his bed, and presumably always stood there. Jefferson was always to be an indefatigable, even reckless, buyer of furniture. For their new home on the mountain the young couple were soon taking advantage of the sophisticated cabinetmakers then working in Williamsburg, often from English pattern books. In the early seventies they bought tables and a handsome clothes press.[10]

Their social life was also active at this time, so that the furniture was no doubt needed. In the spring of '79 Major General Phillips (in command of the Hessian prisoners held near Charlottesville) requested Mr. and Mrs. Jefferson's "company at dinner on Thursday next at two o'clock to meet General and Mme. de Riedesel." After the custom of the day the Baron de Riedesel, commanding officer of the Hessian troops, was not confined, but was allowed to live quite comfortably at Colle, the place owned by Jefferson's friend and neighbor Mazzei. This breezy baroness appears to have appealed to Martha, as did the two Riedesel daughters. Frederika de Riedesel wore boots, and rode astride in the masculine fashion. When they moved into Colle, the baroness's horses ate up all the vines planted by Mazzei. Nevertheless the Jeffersons enjoyed their company. Mrs. Jefferson accompanied the baroness's lusty soprano on the pianoforte. For some unexplained reason, unless it was indeed due to Mrs. Jefferson's declining health, the piano was sold to the de Riedesels when they left Colle.

The Revolution brought Jefferson other contacts with the world of European culture. The German officers, prisoners of war in the county, were held under virtually no security other than their word of honor. So gentlemanly was the war of the day that Jefferson and his erstwhile enemies could discuss philosophy together at Monticello.

There were other bonuses from this association with a European world. Jefferson took advantage of the presence of English deserters in his neighborhood who were craftsmen of greater skill than those available at home. Among them were Billy Orr and Davy Watson. They boarded on the plantation. When a job was done they were paid in kind, always including liquor, either rum, whiskey, or brandy made on the place. Billy and Davy would then take a week off, singing and drinking until the liquor was gone. It was these cheerful craftsmen whom Jefferson later engaged to build a phaeton to his own design. Billy did the iron work, and Davy built the body.[11]

Meanwhile men were dying in the cause that was Jefferson's own. In June of 1779 when the assembly elected him governor of the state there was no turning down that call to duty. Once again the exigencies of war drew the master from home. When Jefferson took office as governor he rode to Williamsburg in the elegant vehicle built by Billy and Davy. There was one little black boy, Isaac, who looked on excursions to the capital as occasions of pure pleasure. When later the whole staff moved, Isaac described the safari. Jefferson went ahead in the phaeton. Bob Hemings drove. Jim Hemings was the body servant, Martin Hemings the butler. These two rode on horseback. Jim and Bob, who were Wayles-Hemingses, were bright mulatto. Martin was darker. The family followed in a coach and four driven by Jupiter, who had been Jefferson's body servant when the governor had been a young student at William and Mary. John Hemings rode postillion, that is, he rode on the rear wheel horse of the four drawing the coach. According to Isaac, Jupiter and John wore caps and gilded bands, a display of elegance that Jefferson was to tone down in later years. The women servants—none were ever called slaves—rode behind in a wagon. These were Mary and young Betty Hemings (later called Betty Brown), seamstress and house woman, and Sukey, Jupiter's wife. Sukey was the cook. Although Isaac does not mention himself, we assume that he too rode in the wagon.

It must have been like a picnic in that bright autumn weather. Certainly it seemed so to Isaac. This major move did not occur until the fall after Jefferson's election, for Mrs. Jefferson, we know, did not accompany him until then. He had left her, as he had done so frequently before, with her sister Eppes at the Forest, joining her later for the last weeks of summer at Monticello.

Jefferson, as wartime governor, was not content with Williamsburg as the state capital. He envisioned a great city, centrally located, convenient to the west as well as to the eastern sections of the state. Williamsburg had another and even more immediate disability: it was hardly defensible from an attack by sea. In the spring of 1780 Jefferson and his family, as usual accompanied by the Hemingses, all moved to the new capital at Richmond. Isaac remembered seeing in this new location a detachment of soldiers drawn up, with fife and drum corps playing, to salute the governor. Isaac knew a white fifer and a black drummer; the latter, who was "sort a-makin' love to Mary Hemings," would come into the kitchen. He taught Isaac how to beat a drum.

It is hoped that Mrs. Jefferson, sitting upstairs in the parlor, also enjoyed the society of Richmond, although it was not to be for long. In November another little daughter, Lucy Elizabeth, was born. Rumors of a British attack were already circulating in the city; on the last day of 1780 a British fleet was sighted in Chesapeake Bay. It seems that Jefferson, no military man, discounted the seriousness of the threat, and that there was about a two-day delay in calling out the militia. By January 2, 1781, it was evident that a fleet of twenty-three British ships, containing among other forces those of the traitor Benedict Arnold, was sailing up the James, presumably toward Richmond. The capital's defenses were not only inadequate, they were virtually nonexistent. By the fourth the enemy forces had landed at Westover and were marching toward the city. At half past seven that evening Jefferson sent Mrs. Jefferson with the two little girls and the month-old baby to their cousins at Tuckahoe. He himself spent most of that night and the following day moving military stores and arms across the river to safety. The enemy marched into Richmond, burned a few buildings, and then retired toward Westover.

Jefferson had left the command of what small force could be assembled entirely up to Baron Steuben. As that officer complained, there was no organized force; whatever militiamen assembled appeared to lack not only arms, but even clothes, tents, camp kettles, and shoes.[12] This was surely the nadir of Jefferson's public career, but just as certainly there was no trace of personal cowardice. He was simply not a military man, nor did he ever think of a governor as called to act in that capacity.

For the next three months, a lull between invasions, Jefferson tried desperately to organize a reasonably effective force from the Virginia militia. It was apparently an effort doomed from the start to failure. The militia, inexperienced and not very effective even when present, usually failed to appear when needed. British pressure, on the other hand, could not be discounted. The theater of war was moving to the south; Cornwallis, who had been entrenched at Charleston, had begun his move into Virginia, where he was later met by the American forces under Lafayette.

In the governor's mansion, a simple brick house not nearly as grand as the old Williamsburg Palace, a private grief had once again struck this beleaguered family. On April 15 the latest baby, little Lucy Elizabeth, died. On the sixteenth Jefferson excused himself from attendance at the Council: "Mrs. Jefferson in a situation in which I would not wish to leave her."[13] Three days later the word came: the British fleet had again passed through Hampton Roads and was on its way up the river.

This time Jefferson acted swiftly; within the hour he had called out the militia. Some days later the Council, not unreasonably, voted to evacuate Richmond. Council and Assembly members retired to Charlottesville. Jefferson first sent his family, refugees for the second time, to Elk Hill. Unable to leave himself, he put them in the care of Jupiter, oldest and most trusted of the Monticello servants. The way from there back to Monticello was not easy; most of the usual means of transportation had been commandeered for the army.[14] On May 10 Jefferson went to pick them up, and returned with them to Monticello. Martha Jefferson could not have been sorry to be back home. Out of six children, counting little John Skelton from her first marriage, she had lost four. Where little Lucy Elizabeth was buried is unknown.

By the end of April Lafayette's troops had entered Richmond; the tide of defeat in the south had begun to turn. It was only a beginning. Not until the long-expected arrival of de Grasse with a French fleet from the West Indies was Cornwallis trapped at York-town. Washington marched rapidly southward, so that the Americans on land and the French at sea finally did in Cornwallis.

Monticello proved to be anything but a safe refuge; Cornwallis had detached Banastre Tarleton and his dragoons with the express purpose of taking the governor prisoner. We need not repeat here the story of Jack Jouett's all-night ride through the Virginia forest to bypass Tarleton's troop and bring the warning to Monticello. Again Jefferson sent Martha and the girls on ahead, while he himself set about collecting important papers. Dumas Malone suggests that these probably included notes taken for his *Notes on the State of Virginia*. Any author will appreciate this concern. Martin Hemings was in charge of the silver, which he buried under the front portico. Jefferson himself did not leave the mountain until he could actually see redcoats in the Charlottesville streets. Seeing no reason to remain in order to become a prisoner of the British, he too departed. His good horse Caractacus took him down the Thorofare Gap road around Carter's Mountain to join his family for dinner at Colonel Carter's Blenheim. They then went on to the Coleses at Enniscorthy, where the family stayed until departing for their own Poplar Forest in Bedford County.

Back at Monticello a trooper pointed his pistol at Martin Hemings's chest, but Martin revealed nothing, neither the whereabouts of his master nor that of the silver. His helper, a slave named Caesar, at the last moment had not been able to leave the silver's hiding place before Martin had closed the opening. For eighteen hours Caesar made no sound, remaining hidden with the plate.

Jefferson was sick of his role as wartime governor. Moreover it seemed to him that he was no longer needed. With the arrival of Lafayette in Richmond and of the French fleet in the Chesapeake, Cornwallis was safely bottled up in Yorktown. The acute phase of the war was indeed over. But this alone was not the cause of his decision to withdraw from public life. It came only after a conflict of will and desire as severe as he was ever to undergo.

Martha Jefferson was exhausted, both physically and, one expects, psychically. His term as governor had officially ended on June 2, at which date the Assembly, meeting at Charlottesville, would have elected his successor. June 2 fell on a Saturday. The legislators voted to put off action on this important matter until the following Monday. Too late! For on that day, June 4, Jack Jouett sent governor and legislators alike fleeing from Tarleton's dragoons.

There followed a rather awkward interregnum. Jefferson was not about to expose his wife's situation to the world. It was something that lay between themselves. In his state of emotional tension he did not take kindly to the demands of some members of the Assembly that he return to office. Out of touch at Poplar Forest he felt relieved of responsibility; apparently some of his colleagues did not agree. One totally undistinguished member, George Nicholas, whose name might otherwise have been lost to fame, moved a resolution that inquiry be made into the governor's conduct, or misconduct, in office.

Jefferson did not receive notice of this unfortunate resolution until his return to Monticello in late July. He had been detained at Poplar Forest due to injuries from a fall from the faithful Caractacus. To the man who was always to feel his sole reward to be the trust of his countrymen this was, perhaps out of all proportion, a shattering blow. At about this time he was informed through his friend Lafayette of his appointment to a peace commission to be sent to Europe. His reply to Lafayette of August 4 gives full rein to his feelings, and a view of the personal struggle in which he was then engaged:

[The appointment] that I cannot avail myself of has given me more mortification than almost any occasion of my life. I lose an opportunity, the only one I have ever had and perhaps ever shall have, of combining public service with private gratification, of seeing countries whose improvements in science, in arts, and in civilization it has been my fortune to admire at a distance but never to see, and at the same time of lending further aid to a cause which has been handed on from its first origination to its present stage by every effort of which my poor faculties were capable. These however have not been such as to give satisfaction to some of my countrymen . . . the independence of private life . . . will I hope yield me that happiness from which no slave is so remote as the minister of a Commonwealth.[15]

We may take these as expressions used under emotional stress, but we may also assume that in later life the mature, highly self-disciplined Jefferson would never have used them thus freely. At this point he could still attribute his decision to the necessity of testifying before the Assembly. By September he was forced to admit that there were other considerations. Twice in little more than two spring months Mrs. Jefferson and the two little girls had been forced to take refuge, traveling over roads often nearly impassable, sleeping as they might, sometimes with friends but often in the noisy, dirty lodgings then available. The lady too was in poor health, frail and never at the best of times of an independent temperament. In the middle of September Jefferson could have known that his wife was again pregnant. Clearly temporary measures would not do; his commitment to retirement must be complete, and to all intents and purposes, permanent. So he put it to Monroe: "Before I ventured to declare to my countrymen my determination to retire from public employment I examined well my heart to know whether it were thoroughly cured of every principle of political ambition, whether no lurking particle remained which might leave me uneasy when reduced within the limits of mere private life. I became satisfied that every fibre of that passion was thoroughly eradicated." [16]

We must believe him. His self-will had been tried, and at last utterly subdued. About two weeks previous to this letter to Monroe, Mrs. Jefferson had borne their last child. At the end of a long self-justifying letter he barely mentions this fact, which was his real justification. "Mrs. Jefferson," he says, "has added another daughter to our family. She has been ever since and still continues very dangerously ill."

During all this there was a little girl present, able to observe. She saw the devoted care that Jefferson gave his dying wife. "For the four months that she lingered," the young Martha remembered in later life, "he was never out of calling; when not at her bedside, he was writing in a small room which opened immediately at the head of her bed." Jefferson could not be idle. He was working on his *Notes on the State of Virginia*. At the same time his deepest feeling centered on the room that opened just off his own, where that dearest life was slipping away.

They had been reading Laurence Sterne together. One day Martha had started to copy a special passage:

> Time wastes too fast: every letter
> I trace tells me with what rapidity
> life follows my pen. The days and hours
> are flying over our heads like
> clouds of windy day never to return—
> more everything presses on—
> [Here Martha's hand stops and Jefferson's takes over]
> and every
> time I kiss thy hand to bid adieu, every absence which
> follows it, are preludes to that eternal separation
> which we are shortly to make.

Years later the young Martha found this sheet among Jefferson's papers: "A lock of my dear Mama's hair enclosed in a verse . . ." [17] This alone he had not brought himself to destroy.

As the end drew near the servants filed in to say goodbye, Betty

Hemings at their head. She had been Martha's personal maid. The entry in Jefferson's Account Book simply read: "September 6, 1782. My dear wife died this day at 11 : 45 A.M." This entry could not have been made immediately, for its author lay unconscious in the next room in a state of symbolic death.

Chapter 4

Bound for France

WE HAVE THE SCENE now as Martha, the little girl present at the time of her mother's death, remembered it in later life:

A moment before the closing scene he was led from the room almost in a state of insensibility by his sister, Mrs. Carr, who, with great difficulty, got him into the library, where he fainted, and remained so long insensible that they feared he never would revive. The scene that followed I did not witness; but the violence of his emotion, when almost by stealth I entered his room at night, to this day I dare not trust myself to describe. He kept to his room three weeks, and I was never a moment from his side. He walked almost incessantly, night and day, only lying down occasionally when nature was completely exhausted, on a pallet that had been brought in during his long fainting fit. . . . When at last he left his room, he rode out, and from that time he was incessantly on horseback, rambling about the mountain, the least frequented roads, and just as often through the woods. In those melancholy rambles I was his constant companion, a solitary witness to many a violent burst of grief. . . .[1]

What happened on that mountainside was the complete bonding of the child to the man. How completely Jefferson had separated himself from the world and how difficult was his return is expressed in a letter to his friend Chastellux: "A single event wiped away all my plans and left me a blank which I had not the spirits to fill up."[2] Jefferson, the devoted husband who had given up all for his wife's sake, had had to die before Jefferson, the man that we know, could rise from the ashes.

He could only wonder at how little the children seemed to feel the catastrophic event. About a month after their mother's death, he wrote to his sister-in-law Elizabeth Eppes: "They are in perfect health and as happy as if they had no part in the unmeasurable loss we have sustained. Patsy rides with me 5 or 6 miles a day and presses for permission to accompany me on horseback to Elkhill whenever I shall go there." [3]

Patsy, indeed, had assumed a new role; she was doing her best to take her mother's place. Jefferson could comfort himself with the thought that there was at least one angel in heaven who viewed with pleasure his attention to the children. Nevertheless he could write his sister-in-law: "This miserable kind of existence is really too burdensome to be borne." In a long, productive life such a thought was never again to occur to Thomas Jefferson. No apocryphal deathbed promise to his wife was needed, only the violence of his reaction assured that never again would Jefferson take a wife, never again would he risk such a conflict.

It was not long before Jefferson was again in public service. It would have been a natural course to send all three surviving children to Eppington, home of their devoted aunt, Elizabeth Eppes. Mrs. Eppes was more than willing to be a surrogate mother, and so she became and was always to remain in the life of the little Maria Jefferson. Martha, the "solitary witness," already saw herself as her father's companion. Without perhaps fully realizing what it would mean in the life of this child so like himself, he determined to keep her with him.

The first journey was to Philadelphia, where Jefferson was once more to serve in the Continental Congress. Martha was not his only companion. James Hemings, born in 1765 and then a lad of eighteen, the son of Betty Hemings and John Wayles, had been Jefferson's body servant. He had ridden behind his master's carriage on the governor's first journey to the capital at Williamsburg. Now once again he occupied the same privileged position; father and daughter rode in a two-horse phaeton, and James rode behind. For this trip Jefferson chose the westernmost route he was ever to take from Monticello to Philadelphia. Accustomed as he was to looking ahead, this trip by way of the upper Potomac was probably no accident, for he was already interested in potential waterways to the western territories; yet his reaction to the scene at Harper's Ferry went far beyond the practical.

Much has been made of Jefferson's rationality, of his lack of religious feeling. Before or at about the time of Wordsworth, Jefferson poured a very high voltage of emotion into his feeling for nature. As father and daughter approached from the west the range of mountains that separated the eastern seaboard from the western plain they were met by what looked like an impenetrable wall. The Potomac and the Shenandoah had met west of the mountain range to break through the barrier, not as though seeking some easy path through an already prepared gap, but as though forcing their way, tearing "the mountain down from its summit to its base." "The first glance of this scene," he said, "hurries our senses into the opinion that this earth has been created in time, that the mountains were formed first, that the rivers began to flow afterwards . . . that continuing to rise they have at length broken over at this spot . . . the mountain being cloven asunder, she presents to your eye, through the cleft, a small catch of smooth blue horizon, at an infinite distance in the plain country, inviting you, as it were, from the roar and the tumult roaring around, to pass through the breach and participate in the calm below." [4]

In these words the intuitive scientist in Jefferson has seized in a sentence the operation of nature; he has been conducting a dialogue, if you will, with nature's god.

Martha accompanied her father to a great rock, a stand from which he could point out the Shenandoah on her right and the Potomac on her left, coming down to their epochal meeting. On this climb they had passed the new stone house of John Harper, built the year before. They engaged with him for a passage on his ferry. Crossing the Potomac above the junction, Jefferson described their passage "through the base of the mountain for three miles, its terrible precipices hanging in fragments over you." They spent the night at McMahon's tavern. Indefatigable, he had climbed the heights on the Maryland side, whence the view is most stupendous. From here he could stand like Moses, looking westward to the Promised Land.

Did Martha, and perhaps even James, clamber over these forbidding rocks on the Maryland side? Whatever she did made an indelible impression on the child, who was to hark back in later years to this journey with her father. Her presence enhanced Jefferson's own pleasure. He was later to write her of "The delight with which I recall the various scenes through which we have passed together."[5] As for James, he was already a seasoned traveler. Whether or not he climbed the heights, no doubt he missed little to be seen in McMahon's kitchen, perhaps instructing his host as to the tastes of his master.

Pursued, it appears, by mobs of unpaid Continental soldiers, the Continental Congress was at that time pretty much a peripatetic affair, moving from Philadelphia to Princeton and from there to Annapolis. Jefferson decided to leave Martha in a more stable situation with friends in Philadelphia, where she could be exposed to the best cultural amenities and receive the maternal care of his old friend and former landlady, Mrs. Hopkinson.

Jefferson, who characteristically expressed an opinion on every subject under the sun, had little to say in general on female education. Martha, of course, was an exception. Just as he always interested himself extensively and intensively in the education of the many young men who turned to him for advice, so he applied himself to the education of Martha. He wrote a French friend: "The plan of reading which I have formed for her is considerably different from what I think would be most proper for her sex in any other country than America. I am obliged in it to extend my views beyond herself, and consider her as possibly at the head of a little family of her own. The chance that in marriage she will draw a blockhead I calculate at about fourteen to one."[6] But we may doubt if his concern was entirely one of preparation for her hypothetical blockhead. He himself was the much nearer and present companion. The schedule of studies sent to the good lady in whose care he had left her was formidable indeed:

> from 8 to 10 o'clock practise music
> from 10 to 1 dance one day and draw another
> from 1 to 2, draw on the day you dance, and write a letter the next day.
> from 3 to 4, read French

from 4 to 5, exercise yourself in music
from 5 to bedtime read English, write, etc.

For Martha the challenge was explicit: "The acquirements which I hope you will make under the tutors I have provided for you will render you more worthy of my love. . . ."[7]

It was his settled, and perhaps humorless, belief that had the Almighty not formed man for a rational life in society He would have been but a "pitiful bungler." It followed, therefore, that Martha should exert herself not to disappoint the expectations of either her earthly or her heavenly father. Fortunately Patsy took in stride precepts that could and did crush weaker spirits. However, we may be reasonably sure that French and drawing were not allowed to interfere with Mrs. Hopkinson's bountiful dinner.

The long-awaited commission as minister plenipotentiary and peace commissioner finally came through, so that the three travelers, two Jeffersons and one Hemings, once more set out together, this time on the good ship *Ceres* from Boston, bound for France.

Chapter 5

Paris

"THE VOYAGE WAS AS PLEASANT as fine weather, a fine ship, good company, and an excellent table could make it."[1] Their nineteen days at sea were improved by the indefatigable Jefferson, who learned Spanish on his way across the ocean. Like any American tourist, Martha later remembered, he had been overcharged by the people who moved their baggage from Le Havre-de-Grâce to Paris. Here at least one can empathize, if not with the man who could learn Spanish in nineteen days!

One of Jefferson's first acts on arriving in Paris, after the purchase of some necessary clothes, was to place Martha in the Abbaye Royale de Panthemont. This was the fashionable convent school, where Martha was introduced by the Marquise de La Fayette. Jefferson visited the school daily, until his resilient Martha had recovered from her initial homesickness.[2] The little girl from Virginia was soon to become as much at home in Paris as was her cosmopolitan father.

In Paris Jefferson saw and came to know at first hand the civilization of which he had so long dreamed. In this decade immediately preceding the French Revolution, Paris was building, expanding physically, and alive with ideas. Not now through books alone, Jefferson took part in the intellectual feast. There were conversations with Buffon, the great French naturalist, to whom Jefferson later sent animal specimens from America in order to disprove Buffon's theory that species had declined in the new world. At a dinner in the home of the venerable Franklin, then the American minister, the Americans were seated on one side of the table, and the French on the other. When the guests were invited to rise, the Americans were seen to stand on average a good six inches taller than their French opposite numbers.[3] *Quod erat demonstrandum*.

Eighteenth-century science was not compartmentalized as science is today. In these studies the two men were attempting to penetrate, as Jefferson put it, "into ages past." To Jefferson the fossil bones displayed at Monticello were not mere curiosities; they were a source of intellectual excitement, calling up visions of a geologic past.

Jefferson's delight in natural phenomena was always accompanied by a search for rational explanations. His God was a rational God, the creator of an orderly universe. The mammoth bones dug up in what is now West Virginia represented for him a hitherto unknown link in the great chain of being. "If one link be lost," he told the American Philosophical Society in a paper delivered from the chair in 1797, "another and another might be lost, till the whole system of things would evanish by piece-meal."[4] That every species was distinct and must be a permanent element in the population of the earth was part of his philosophy. To have thought otherwise would have been to go against his sense of order in a Newtonian universe.

While in France he had sent to America for the largest bones he could find to use as a tool in his dispute with the French naturalists who were claiming the degeneration of species in the North American climate. He had already treated this subject in his *Notes on the State of Virginia*. Closer to present-day science was his conclusion that fossil shells found fifteen thousand feet above sea level in the Andes may have been heaved to these great heights by some convulsion of the earth. In other words, he anticipated the theory of the movement of the earth's crust, but writing almost two hundred years before anyone had conceived of tectonic plates he was careful to point out that there was no evidence of any such convulsion in historic time.[5]

This was Jefferson the scientist. That he could occupy himself with such concerns in the midst of public and private cares speaks to the extraordinary fertility of his mind. More immediately useful, perhaps, was his passion for architecture. Mme. de Tessé was the intimate friend with whom he shared his love of architecture and landscape gardening. This great lady of the *ancien régime* was both a political liberal and a female *philosophe*. Jefferson wrote her: "While at Paris I was violently smitten with the Hôtel de Salm, and used to go to the Thuileries [*sic*] almost daily to look at it. The loueuse de chaises, inattentive to my passion, never had the complaisance to place a chair there; so that, sitting on the parapet, and twisting my neck round to see the object of my admiration, I generally left it with a torticollis."[6] That is to say, a stiff neck.

It was his own Monticello that engaged Jefferson's mind as he sat upon his parapet. The Hôtel de Salm gave the effect of a single story, and, perhaps most exciting of all, it broke all precedent with domestic building. It had a dome! It was lighter, and more sophisticated, than the house he had left behind him. Undoubtedly the great remodeling of Monticello came to birth in those hours so vividly described to Mme. de Tessé. He was later to describe the new ideas gained in Paris: "All good and new houses are of a single story. That is of 16 or 18 ft. generally, and the whole of it given to rooms of entertainment; but in the parts where there are bedrooms they have two tiers of them of from 8 to 10 ft. high each, with a small private staircase."[7] This was exactly the scheme he used when he began the rebuilding of the first Monticello. The alcove bed was another French idea highly thought of by Jefferson, if not equally appreciated by family and guests who were to find them used throughout the remodeled Monticello.

In the liberated atmosphere of Paris, Jefferson's political ideas were welcomed in the most advanced intellectual circles, but one may wonder if he spoke as freely of the one moral question that could have concerned him most. Of private conversation we cannot know, but in a formal letter to the editor of the *Encyclopédie Méthodique* he revealed to a remarkable extent his own feeling in regard to emancipation in America. The time, he said, was not ripe. The legislature in Virginia was not prepared to consider any such proposal; it could only rivet still closer the chains of bondage. At the same time he did not conceal his own opinion: "What a stupendous, what an incomprehensible machine is man! Who can

endure toil, famine, stripes, imprisonment or death itself in vin-
dication of his own liberty, and the next moment be deaf to all those
motives whose power supported him thro' his trial, and inflict on
his fellow men a bondage, one hour of which is fraught with more
misery than ages of that which he rose in rebellion to oppose." [8]

Jefferson was not the material of which martyrs are made,
certainly not in a hopeless cause. He had been willing to endure all
that he had described to obtain the liberty of his countrymen; he
had made it abundantly clear that he believed this liberty should
also be given to those of his countrymen who were black, but if his
country would not support such a measure, then, quite frankly, it
would be left to the "workings of an overruling providence." Even
such a statement as this could only be made between scholars. As a
public servant representing the United States, Jefferson refused an
invitation to become a member of the society for the abolition of the
slave trade. "Those whom I serve having never yet been able to give
their voice against this practice, it is decent for me to avoid too
public a demonstration of my wishes to see it abolished." [9]

Instead, Jefferson comforted himself with the optimistic and, as
it turned out, illusory thought, that the task of emancipation could
be left to the young. It was this belief that accounted for his perhaps
imprudent plan to place a copy of his *Notes on Virginia*, with its
impassioned denunciation of slavery, in the hands of every student at William and Mary. Discretion later prevailed; thirty-seven
copies were sent to George Wythe "to be given to such young
gentlemen of the College . . . as Mr. Wythe shall think proper." [10]

As an individual planter and private man, Jefferson meant to
take stronger steps. He was planning a liberal experiment which
would surely have shocked his Albemarle neighbors: "I have decided on my final return to America . . . to endeavor to import as
many Germans as I have grown slaves, on farms of fifty acres each,
intermingled, and place all on the footing of the metayers [tenant
farmers] of Europe. Their children shall be brought up as others
are, in habits of property and foresight, and I have no doubt they
will be good citizens." [11]

This would have been a bold experiment, in line with Jefferson's belief that the small, or yeoman, farmers, not the great agricultural capitalists of his own plantation world, were the chosen people of God. That blacks, even as tenants, could be absorbed into such a social pattern was easier to believe among the philosophes of France than it later became at home on a Virginia plantation.

In his personal household at the Hôtel de Langeac there were two former slaves. James had recently been joined by his little sister, Sally. They were legally free, but this fact could be judiciously ignored, and there is no contemporary evidence that the subject ever came up between Jefferson and his black servants in Paris. They were paid for their services,[12] but this practice was not un-known at Monticello. There was nothing really to show that their position was any different than it had always been. James's presence in Paris had been deliberately planned; Sally was there quite by accident.

When Jefferson had left for France he had taken Martha with him; the two younger girls had stayed behind in Virginia, in the motherly care of their aunt Elizabeth Eppes. When word had come to the family in Paris of the death of the youngest, little Lucy Elizabeth, of whooping cough, Jefferson determined that Maria must join them. From the Virginia side this course was delayed as long as possible. Maria's answer to her father was the essence of simplicity:

Dear Papa,
    I should be very happy to see you, but I cannot go to France, and hope that you and sister Patsy are well. Your affectionate daughter. Adieu.
                                                    Mary Jefferson [13]

The Eppeses at last succeeded in getting Maria aboard ship, but only by the ruse of allowing the child to go on board with a black playmate, as though merely visiting, and not as passengers. After the children had fallen asleep the Eppeses departed, leaving Maria and her playmate to wake up at sea. The good captain made Maria his special charge, but at the end of the voyage she had again to be torn from the arms of this latest friend. Landing in England the two children were delivered to the care of Abigail Adams, wife of Jefferson's colleague then in London.

Mrs. Adams did her best, but quite frankly wrote to Jefferson that she regretted the absence of "the old nurse whom you expected to have attended her . . . the girl who is with her is quite a child, and Captain Ramsay is of opinion will be of so little service that he had better carry her back with him." [14] She did not conceal her opinion that Jefferson should have come himself to pick up his daughter. He had sent his maître d'hôtel Petit, a responsible man who unfortunately was not reassuring to Maria. He did not speak a word of English, and she, naturally, did not understand French.

We know very little of Sally during her time in Paris other than that she received a small salary, less than James, and that in April of 1789 she was outfitted as a maid and sent out to board for five weeks, presumably to be trained in the exacting role of lady's maid to a debutante. [15] Martha was now a young lady about to go out in society. Of James we know a good deal more.

If the *haute cuisine* of France may be considered an art, James was soon to become a skilled and disciplined artist, for Jefferson lost no time in apprenticing him to the finest chefs in Paris. This was no last-minute inspiration. The new American commissioner had, as usual, laid careful plans in advance. On the very day that he heard of the overseas post he wrote to William Short: "I propose for a particular purpose to carry my servant James with me." [16] James had been chosen as most apt for the sensitive post, chef to the American minister, and later to be the bearer of the authentic art to America.

After a few months of "seasoning," during which James suffered an undiagnosed illness, he entered on his apprenticeship with the restaurant-keeper Combeaux. James's education was no hit-or-miss affair. He received special instruction in *pâtisserie*, and later served an apprenticeship in the Prince de Condé's kitchens, which Jefferson said came at "great expense." In little more than a year he was speaking passable French, and by late 1787 his great moment arrived: James became *chef de cuisine* at the American ministry, that is to say, Jefferson's residence at the Hôtel de Langeac. He was paid twenty-four livres a week for his services. Apparently on his own, independently of Jefferson, he was taking lessons in French grammar from one Perrault. When this unfortunate man presented his bill, James attacked him with kicks and blows.[17]

By now James was speaking fluent French, and no doubt was getting around the town. He had always been accustomed to freedom of movement and to making small, necessary purchases for the household. Surely he would have heard the words then on everyone's lips: "liberté, égalité, fraternité." Even if James did not, at this time, ask for his freedom, the new ideas around him did take root in his mind.

Jefferson could easily have left his two black servants as free individuals in Paris. He may well have thought that both were better off in his household than either would have been on his or her own. Sally was barely sixteen, and James had been educated "at great expense" for a special and important task. Obviously Jefferson felt quite comfortable with the Hemingses as they were, and had no desire to change the position.

Martha, of course, echoed her father. In a letter to him, which she had done her best to fill with fashionable gossip, she remarked that she wished that all the poor Negroes could be free.[18] She meant it sincerely, in a general way. It may not have occurred to her that the wish could include Sally and James. The claim, later to be widespread, that the little mulatto maid was her father's mistress, would indeed have made an interesting subject of Parisian gossip. Unfortunately for such a claim, it was never so much as hinted at by the many contemporary observers.

Martha, meanwhile, had concerns of her own to consider. She was becoming a young lady, not perhaps always in the way Jefferson would have wished for her. To her dying day the Republican matron was to retain something of the style, the *savoir faire*, and even a touch of the caustic wit she had acquired during her life in France. The thing most deprecated by her father was the position of women in that advanced society. Martha's own countrywoman, the beautiful Mrs. Bingham, for example, had been seduced by the greater liberties taken by her sex in France. The former Anne Willing of Philadelphia had not hesitated to speak her mind. "The women of France," she wrote Jefferson, "often give a decided turn to the fate of Empires. . . . They have obtained the rank and consideration in society which the sex are entitled to, and which they in vain contend for in other countries." Jefferson enjoyed crossing swords with this holder of advanced opinion. "Our good ladies," he wrote, with an unusual teasing thrust, "have been too wise to wrinkle their foreheads with politics. They are contented to soothe and calm the minds of their husbands returning ruffled from political debate." He challenged her opinion that a Parisienne is happier than an American. "You will change your opinion, my dear Madam, . . . compare them with our own countrywomen occupied in the tender and tranquil amusements of domestic life. . . . As for political news [had she been rash enough to ask him for it?] . . . I will not detail them to you, because you would be less handsome after reading them."[19] Clearly Martha was not encouraged to discuss politics, or even, as it later unfortunately turned out, that other masculine concern, family finances.

Studies of a cultural sort were a different matter, and here Jefferson continued to encourage, not to say push, his daughter. Perhaps not above a little teasing herself Martha wrote him: "Titus Livius puts me out of my wits." This brought on a lengthy lecture. "Idleness begets ennui, ennui the hypochondria, and that a diseased body. No laborious person was ever yet hysterical, etc., etc." Martha replied with aplomb that she would have another go at her Livy, but "As for the hysterics, you may be quiet on that head, as I am not lazy enough to fear them."[20]

Now, in that gay summer of 1789, the last blaze of glory of the *ancien régime*, Martha was out in society. Naturally she was meeting young men, to Jefferson a cogent threat. There was one dashing and attractive young man called Tom in the British embassy in Paris. A schoolmate of Martha's, the Lady Elizabeth Tufton, when asked if she were in love with Tom replied no, but that she "knew an American young lady who admired him above all things in the world."[21] At the same time Mrs. Adams was promoting her son,

John Quincy; she hinted broadly that she would not object to exchanging a son for a daughter: "I am all in favor of a federal union."[22] Jefferson had taken alarm. Martha may not have been aware of it, but these young men were one of the strong reasons for the American minister's wish to leave his post for home. He had no wish to lose Martha either to London or to Boston. To Elizabeth Eppes at home in Virginia he wrote that "Patsy will have to learn from you the things which she cannot learn here." But the anxious father was a little late. Eager as she always was to please him, Martha had already learned to be an independent person.

Chapter 6

Mr. Jefferson, Tourist

AS A DIPLOMAT IN EUROPE, Jefferson had as his official charge the negotiation of treaties favorable to American trade, a matter of great importance to the new nation. However, he was never out of touch—mainly through correspondence with Madison—with an even more important effort taking place at home: that of building a constitution fitted to the government of free men. It is difficult to realize today how blank was that page, how everything had to be created anew before a nation could be born. The United States was still without a national capital, almost without a native culture, which must depend upon centers of art, music, and intellectual society still, to put it kindly, in their infancy. Jefferson was reveling in all that Europe had to give, and what is more, he intended to bring back to America all that he could possibly ship on a boat or carry in his ever-fertile brain.

In this regard Mr. Jefferson, the indefatigable tourist, was even more useful to his country than was Thomas Jefferson, the official envoy. He certainly did not limit his attention to Paris. Even his kindest critics occasionally noted a slight stretching of diplomatic duties in favor of his desire to see more, to learn more, and to cover as much as possible of the fascinating European world. When on his travels, he wrote to William Short: "Architecture, painting, sculpture, antiquities, agriculture, the condition of the laboring poor fill all my moments."[1] Manufactures he could afford to ignore, as "all knowledge of them would be useless."

True, he had not had to leave Paris to fall in love with the Hôtel de Salm, but equally important sights lay ahead. At the same time that Jefferson had succeeded Franklin as American minister to France, his old friend and colleague, John Adams, had gone to

London to serve as minister there. In the spring of 1786 Adams called upon his friend to come over to England to help negotiate various trade agreements in London. This journey in no way improved Jefferson's already low opinion of the English. He wrote of his reception at court: "On my presentation as usual to the King and Queen at their levees, it was impossible for anything to be more ungracious than their notice of Mr. Adams and myself."[2] In fact, the king had turned his back. It was not a reception calculated to encourage "falling in love," even architecturally, with anything British.

However, Mr. Jefferson and Mr. Adams did decide on a tour of the landscaped gardens, about which Jefferson had already read so much. He toured the English gardens with a copy of Whately's *Observations on Modern Gardening* in his hand. Of the dome at Chiswick House Jefferson could only remark that it "has an ill effect, both within and without," and yet it is the octagonal shape of the Chiswick dome that we see repeated at Monticello. However, there is a difference. The shape of the Monticello dome was predetermined by the walls of the semi-octagonal parlor beneath it. It is also lower than the one at Chiswick, more in harmony with the total effect of the building. As usual Jefferson was bringing back ideas from his travels, which, typically, he would freely adapt to the needs of his own designs at home.

At times his landscape designs exceeded the original models in scope and daring. The roundabouts at Monticello are on a grander scale than the more modest paths that he had once admired in Shenstone's plan for the Leasowes near Birmingham. On his visit there in '86 Jefferson enjoyed the ninety-degree prospects, which recalled his own blue mountains. Also, although he does not mention it, he copied a Latin inscription from an ornamental urn. This tender inscription to the memory of a young woman who had died young Jefferson kept by him, and later enclosed it in the box of mementos of his own dear Martha, lost to him four years before.[3]

At another of these romantic gardens, Esher Place, he particularly admired the use of trees: "heights rising one beyond and above another, with clumps of trees."[4] Hagley was another romantic favorite, where Jefferson was at last to encounter a nymph, "in a small, deep hollow, with recesses of stone in the banks on every side. In one of these is a Venus pudique, turned half round as if inviting you with her into the recess."[5] Even here his observations end on a practical note: "The ponds yield a great deal of trout."

In Paris that summer Jefferson's sense of romance was not obliged to wait on marble nymphs. It was then that he met Maria Cosway, the wife of an English artist. For Jefferson this lovely lady was the epitome of all that was charming in the City of Light, and for him it was a whirlwind affair. The Cosways' stay in the city was brief. Just before their departure this serious American envoy attempted to leap over a low wall while strolling with his lady. The result of this most untypical exuberance was a fall and a seriously broken right wrist. Sadly, and with aching wrist, Jefferson had put the Cosways into a carriage for their return to London.

The fall may have had a cautionary effect. In any case Jefferson sat down and wrote with his left hand an extraordinary letter: a dialogue between the Head and the Heart, in which the Head, in effect, exhorts the Heart to break off this burgeoning romance.[6] The reason given is a rather ambiguous one: the distress of the inevitable parting—a distress that few lovers would dwell on, especially as Maria intends to return.

Maria was quite unable to answer in this elevated style. She took refuge in Italian, but in any language her feelings are clear, and they are considerably warmer than Jefferson's. "Night Thoughts," she exclaimed, "before the fire, and when the imagination is well warmed up, one could go cool off in a river."[7] Clearly the Head took alarm at this letter. Jefferson found nothing very cheerful to say in reply; he was still very much aware of the hazards of this relationship.

In the following spring he set forth on a tour of the south of France, from which he wrote several letters to his daughter and one to Mme. de Tessé, but none at all to Mrs. Cosway. On a journey the following year through the Netherlands and Germany he was equally remiss, but after his return he wrote what may have been the most revealing letter of that whole painful correspondence:

"At Strasbourg I sat down to write to you. But for my soul I could think of nothing at Strasbourg but the promontory of noses, of Diego, of Slawkenburgius his historian, and the procession of the Strasburgers to meet the man with the nose. Had I written to you from thence it would have been a continuation of Sterne upon noses. . . ."[8]

What exactly had Sterne said about noses? One has only to read his cautionary tale of the fate of the Strasburgians' infatuation with Diego, the man with the outsize nose, to discover what it could have meant to this dilatory lover. The whole population of Strasbourg had rushed out of the city gates to view this remarkable organ, leaving their city exposed to the attack of their enemies. Mrs. Brodie in her *Intimate History* has leapt to some extraordinary conclusions; she believes that it was Maria, not Jefferson, who broke off their affair. At the risk of out-psyching Mrs. Brodie one may substitute a rather similar organ for Diego's nose, and come up with a very severe warning against sexual dalliance of any kind.

Whether or not Jefferson was aware of the import of this story, it could hardly have boded well for his affair with Maria. "How," she exclaimed, "could you . . . think of me, have Many things to say, and not find One word to write, *but on Noses?*"[9] Maria returned to Paris, but the affair, the only one that threatened to involve Jefferson with a woman after his wife's death, came to a gradual but definitive close.

It was, of course, not only noses that had occupied Jefferson on these tours. The southern tour in particular was motivated by his passionate interest in the architecture of Rome. Once again he wrote to Mme. de Tessé of a love affair, not with a woman, but with a building. It was the Maison Carrée at Nîmes that evoked this enthusiasm and that he was later to use as a model when he designed the capitol building in Richmond. Even here, although he spoke of his model as "the most perfect and precious remain of antiquity in existence,"[10] Jefferson and his consultant, the French architect Clérisseau, made several adaptations in their design for the Richmond capitol. They simplified by substituting the Ionic order for the Corinthian, and they made the portico only two columns deep, in that way lengthening the building and affording more light without changing the proportions.

Houdon's full-length statue of Washington stands in the entrance hall of the capitol. It was commissioned by Jefferson, and it is perhaps the finest example of his not always happy ventures in bringing art to America. Jefferson shared the common eighteenth-century view that copies of old masters were to be preferred to less famous "originals." The walls of Monticello were covered with copies of Biblical scenes and other edifying subjects, all the more to be regretted when we learn that the fine French artist David was a personal acquaintance, familiar with Jefferson's home in Paris. Jefferson did in fact admire this artist: "I do not feel an interest in any pencil but that of David," he wrote a friend.[11] Perhaps it was expense that prevented a purchase. More fortunate were the purchases of Houdon's plaster busts. These sculptured likenesses of Jefferson's contemporary heroes had perforce to be "originals"; like so many tutelary deities they adorn Monticello.

It was not painting, but the decorative arts that engaged Jefferson's principal attention. It is hard for us to imagine the brilliance of the decor and how it must have struck American eyes. That unabashed Yankee, John Adams, could complain to his diary: "I am wearied to death with gazing wherever I go. . . . Gold Marble, Silk, Velvet, Silver, Ivory and Alabaster make up the scene everywhere."[12]

When Jefferson furnished the Hôtel de Langeac, the house that he occupied as American minister to France, he went all out. The inventory made when his furniture was shipped to America shows fifty-nine chairs and numbers of sofas and tables, among them four of his favorite tables with brass-bound marble tops. Curtains for the Paris home included "six large blue damask curtains [later to hang in the drawing rooms at Monticello], eight medium size of the same, six crimson curtains and eight cords with crimson tassles" as well as twenty-two bell pulls. Armchairs were also upholstered in crimson and blue, colors appropriate to the setting of eighteenth-century Paris. There were the painted *boiseries*, unfaded tapestries and carpets, gleaming ormolu, etc., which illuminated that brilliant scene. Jefferson's taste was relatively restrained; expense alone, if not his actual taste, would have forced him to patronize dealers who catered to the bourgeoisie rather than to the great aristocratic houses. Certainly guests at the Hôtel de Langeac did not find the decor inferior or dull.

The eighty-six crates of his belongings shipped from Paris went not to Monticello, but to the Market Street residence in Philadelphia used by Jefferson on his return to America, as Washington's secretary of state. So long as he remained in public life Jefferson retained something of this elaborate decor, greatly modified upon his retirement to Monticello. Here the "simple" country gentleman favored the plainer English or Philadelphia style, but a French flavor remained. Nothing could be more elegant than the fine pier glass mirrors still hanging in the parlor, or more pleasing than his use of mirrors opposite windows to enhance both the lighting and the size of his handsome downstairs rooms, a decorating innovation in America at the time.

His taste for gadgetry and invention is also displayed in these rooms. No one but Jefferson would have designed his own revolving chair to fit a revolving tabletop for writing, and an extended Windsor couch to support the writer's outstretched legs. Although this ingenious seating arrangement was manufactured in America (Thomas Burling, a New York cabinetmaker, made the chair), the idea was originally French. Who but a radical republican, exclaimed his Federalist opponents, would have thought of such a thing! "Who has not heard from the Secretary of the praises of his wonderful Whirligig Chair, which had the miraculous quality of allowing the person seated in it to turn his head without moving his tail?"[13] One may say that Monticello captures it all, the many sides of this many-sided man, who preferred use to display, yet who nevertheless managed a high style all his own.

"I am but a young gardener," Jefferson wrote from the President's House, but we need not take him seriously. He may have meant that he was "young," new to the practical care of flower beds, but he was by no means new as a botanist. We know that his interest in landscape and planting dated from the first clearing of his mountaintop. With his intimate friend Mme. de Tessé, the charming and highly cultivated aunt of Lafayette, he carried on a lifelong correspondence on garden matters, and an equally long exchange of botanical specimens. Among the many professional gardeners that Jefferson counted as friends was "my old friend Thouin of the National Garden at Paris," who continued during a long life to keep Monticello supplied with seeds of "all the fine flowers of France."[14]

Nothing useful in the way of agricultural experiment escaped his attention. A brief trip was made to the north of Italy for the express purpose of smuggling out some of the superior rice of the Piedmont. Jefferson filled his pockets with this rice; export was strictly prohibited. His experiments included planting of the fig, the olive, and the sugar maple; with the exception of the fig, none throve at Monticello. His imported Scotch broom, on the other hand, throve so well that it has remained a curse to Albemarle farmers. Not everything succeeded, but surely he would be happy to see Albemarle hillsides today, again planted with the fine vines that he had so admired on his journey through Burgundy and the Bordeaux country.

Mr. Jefferson, tourist, was bringing home the fruits of his travels, but on this journeying there could also be occasions of pure pleasure. His voyage down the Canal de Languedoc combined business with pleasure. He was taking notes on the construction of the canal with "the possibility of opening water communication between the Potomac, the Ohio, and Lake Erie" in mind.[15] At the same time he stressed the pleasures of boating. "I write to you, dear Patsy, from the Canal de Languedoc, on which I am at present sailing, as I have been for a week past, cloudless skies above, limpid waters below, and on each hand, a row of nightingales in full chorus."[16] Jefferson had his carriage mounted on a boat, from which he could sit comfortably watching as the countryside rolled leisurely by. "Of all the methods of travel I have ever tried this is the pleasantest." When tired of his observation post in the glassed-in carriage, he could walk along the towpath. On each hand, also, were the vineyards of this superb wine country. In Burgundy his favorite wine had been the Montrachet Chardonnay, selling at 48 sous the bottle. Grapes from this vineyard were grown at Monticello; this and other imported wines were kept there in constant supply.

Hampers of fine wine were also included in his shipments to friends and colleagues in America. To Washington, as he pointed out, he sent wine straight from the vineyards he himself had visited. "The vigneron," he said, "never adulterates his wine." [17] Madison received no wine, but many books, and a complete set of the medals struck in Paris to commemorate American Revolutionary War heroes. A set of these also hung on the walls at Monticello. These sets were in tin rather than the original silver, but Jefferson assured his friends that they were "in fact more delicate than the medals themselves." [18] These, and the Houdon busts, were part of Jefferson's efforts to create an American canon, to give to the new nation figures of its symbolic heroes.

On a more personal level was music, "the favorite passion of my soul." As early as 1778 he had dreamed of importing craftsmen from Italy who might also form a wind band. The chosen instruments were two French horns, two clarinets, a hautboy, and a bassoon.[19] Unfortunately even Jefferson was unable to realize this unique combination of the useful and the aesthetic. The band failed to appear. In Paris he made sure that both his daughters had lessons on the harpsichord from the noted master Balabastre. Martha's instrument was purchased from Kirckman in London in 1786, and another Kirckman was ordered for Maria in 1798.[20] Maria also played the guitar. That Martha played with feeling we know from a story describing the family scene. Jefferson and Maria were listening to Martha at the harpsichord. Seeing that Maria was in tears Jefferson asked, "My dear, what is the matter." "Nothing," answered Maria, "only the music is so mournful." [21]

We cannot doubt that Jefferson strove to create at Monticello a home fit for the Palladian sage, his family, and friends, and to an extraordinary extent he succeeded. Certainly he neglected nothing that could be imported from that vaunted scene of Europe.

Chapter 7

The Travelers Return

IN THE MIND OF at least one member of the party who now returned to America the dangers of a journey, any journey, remained uppermost. Only the prospect of a return to Eppington sustained Polly, and even this seemed far ahead and fraught with difficulties. Martha, confident traveler as she had long been, journeying at her father's side, was in a sunny mood as the three Jeffersons and two Hemingses set sail from Le Havre on their way back to America in the fall of 1789. Jefferson's request for accommodations on board ship specified "three master berths and berths for a man and woman servant, *the latter convenient to that of my daughters*" (italics added).[1]

No doubt the black members of the party also carried a few mementos of Paris home with them, but if so no record was kept. James almost certainly had seen to the packing of some items of culinary equipment. The archaeological work now taking place at Monticello has turned up one small china mug in the area once occupied by the slave quarters. It is inscribed "Tessier Ps. la Rue de Richelieu visavis le Café de Foi Paris." It requires no stretch of the imagination to see James buying this in Paris and carrying it home for his own use in Virginia.

The voyage home was a pleasant one. Autumn sunshine sparkled on the high seas; anticipation of the landfall increased for each in his own way. Jefferson was anxious to see how his plantation business had fared in his absence. He may have already wondered if his idea of importing German tenant farmers to work beside his own slaves would succeed. The part of his plan that outlined the treatment of his slaves was already in operation on his own farms. That it was a prescription for financial ruin, in the tobacco market then obtaining, did not occur to the born optimist who regularly paced the deck of the returning vessel, with Martha at his side, and Polly loitering behind.

The *Clermont*, with its freight of black and white passengers, landed at Norfolk on November 23, 1789, one month and a day after its departure. The last leg of the voyage was exciting. Dense fog and then a high wind impeded the landing, but Captain Colles finally brought his ship safely to port. Jefferson was met with news that must have been only partially pleasing to a man intent on getting on with his own affairs. He was Washington's nominee for secretary of state.

To Polly in particular the formalities at Norfolk—the greetings by the mayor and aldermen—were irksome, as they kept her from beloved Eppington. Finally the girls got off. There was, we believe, a stopover at Tuckahoe, Col. Thomas Mann Randolph's plantation on the James above Richmond. Tuckahoe was a familiar stopover to all the family party. The girls, especially Martha, had known Tuckahoe since childhood, and felt naturally at home there. It was a house not out of touch with Europe; the two sons, at any rate, had been educated abroad in the colonial fashion, in Edinburgh. On the occasion of this visit the oldest son, Thomas Mann, Jr., was absent. That December, "in a hurry and in bad weather," he had stormed out of Tuckahoe—". . . you were disgusted," his father wrote him, "not only with the world, but I fear your father." [2]

Throughout his life Tom Randolph was given to these sudden flare-ups, to departing in high dudgeon.

The return of this son could not have been easy for "Colonel Tom," *bon vivant*, racing man, and as confirmed a political conservative as any grandee of the Tidewater. While in Edinburgh Tom had been one of Jefferson's numerous young protégés, and the young man had been a ready recipient of the older man's democratic theories. Jefferson saw in Tom a shining opportunity. "Few persons in your own country," he wrote him in May of 1786, "have started from as advantageous ground as that whereon you will be placed." He assured him that "Honesty, knowledge and industry are the qualities which will lead you to the highest emploiements of your country and to its highest esteem."³ True, but Jefferson had apparently failed to notice that his protégé had written: "As yet I have entered on no pursuit immediately relating to my intended profession [politics], being convinced that to begin . . . before a proper foundation had been laid . . . [would] tend to create an unwillingness to prosecute further a subject which exhibited at first view such apparently insurmountable difficulties."⁴

This sounds convincing, but a closer reading might have discouraged his adviser. It was perhaps Randolph's misfortune that he could write so plausible a letter. At any rate it brought in reply an outline of proposed studies as formidable on its own level as the schedule Jefferson had once sent to his eleven-year-old daughter in Philadelphia. He advised natural history, botany, and physics as subjects for specialization. History to be read for relaxation after dinner. The history of Greece and Rome should be read in the original authors. After that, Gibbon, then a general history of Europe, particularly England, then America. "An author who writes of his own times, or of times near his own, presents in his own ideas and manner the best picture of the moment in which he writes." Then the study of the law, "which like history can be read on one's own. I would propose you doing it in France."⁵

The only trouble with this program was that Tom scarcely followed any of it. It may not surprise us that he did not answer this letter for nearly a year, but when he did he showed that he had embraced the goal while skipping the preparation. In April of '87 he wrote Jefferson that "Ambition; perhaps I ought to be ashamed to confess it, as it must allways be mixed in some degree with vanity, hindered me from fixing on a knowledge of Natural Philosophy or Mathematics as the sole end to which I should wish to attain. Being certain that Politics was a science which would lead to the highest honors in a free state, and the study of which by many of its members would be of the greatest utility to the community in an infant one, I resolved to apply chiefly to it."⁶

Jefferson, of course, approved, while continuing to stress the importance of the study of law to a career in politics. Tom, however, was not heard from again. Shortly after this letter he had returned to Virginia, where he managed to include a trip to the capital in New York as an easier approach to politics than the study of law. Although there is family tradition to the contrary, it is now clear that Tom Randolph never saw his future bride in Paris, but went directly from Scotland to Virginia. He had left Edinburgh, in fact, without receiving a degree.

No doubt Tom's younger brother and sister spoke admiringly of him to Martha. If they did not meet at Tuckahoe, they met very soon thereafter, for Tom was on his way to Monticello in pursuit of his mentor and friend, the great Mr. Jefferson. There was the man, he felt, who truly understood his political ambitions. The journey up-country was interrupted as usual at the home of kinfolk, this time at Rock Castle, the house belonging to his uncle Tarleton Fleming. So the young Randolph and Martha, his soon-to-be bride, were moving north at about the same time, and at the same pace. The Jeffersons arrived at Monticello just two days before Christmas.

The two black members of the party had a family reunion to look forward to. What would their mother, the redoubtable Betty Hemings, think of French airs and graces? They may have expected to shine in the reflected glory of their master, whom they had seen greeted everywhere as a man high up in the new government, and if so they were not disappointed. In fact, perhaps nothing in the life of Jefferson or his family equaled this moment of greeting by his own slaves. Martha described it:

We reached Monticello the 23rd of December. The Negroes discovered the approach of the carriage as soon as it reached Shadwell and such a scene I never witnessed in my life. They collected in crowds around it and almost drew it up the mountain by hand. The shouting, etc., had been sufficiently obstreperous but the moment it arrived at the top it reached the climax when the door of the carriage was opened and they received him in their arms and bore him to the house crowding round and kissing his hands and feet, some blubbering and crying, others laughing. It seemed impossible to satisfy their anxiety to touch and kiss the very earth which bore him.[7]

Among the little black children present were Wormley and Burwell, both Hemings grandchildren, who were later to play such prominent parts in the household. They were among the youngest of twenty-two Hemingses, headed by Betty, still strong and in her prime, with four husbands and twelve children behind her. Even James, showing off in the kitchen, must have respected that rapid tongue. Betty was noted for her long words, picked up from the white folks, and used in a freewheeling style all her own.

Jefferson's sister, Aunt Carr, and her boys had been keeping house at Monticello while the family was away, and the house was spruced up and prepared for their arrival. Martha, just turned seventeen, had barely revisited familiar sights when her cousin Tom Randolph arrived from downriver. The Carr boys, Martha's own age and much given to romping, faded into the background. It was the visitor, tall, dark, and romantic as an Indian with his tawny complexion and black hair, who absorbed her attention. No untutored local, he—like Martha—had been educated abroad. He had come to visit his patron, the man in public life, his political ideal, but it did not escape Tom that the hero had a daughter. It was the fair-skinned, red-headed Martha, with her merry and active temperament polished by Parisian society, who captured him completely. Nor was Martha far behind in their mutual attraction. Tom was certainly not dull or in the least crude. She observed his conversations on serious subjects with her father. The combination of dash and intelligence was irresistible. He may also have been the first of Martha's young men to actually propose marriage. Tom knew what he wanted. It seems to have been the one passion in which he never vacillated, the one decision that he never regretted. In a matter of weeks Martha was engaged.

Jefferson was needed in New York. It suited the young people perfectly that there was no time for a prolonged courtship—or opportunity, one imagines, for Jefferson to notice Tom's uncertain temper, or that he was changeable as the wind. One suspects, however, that part of Tom's attraction for his prospective father-in-law was geographical. As distances went in Virginia, Tom's home was just down the river. His father even owned land adjoining Shadwell in Albemarle. "He would have been my own first choice," Jefferson wrote Mme. de Corny in Paris, "yet according to the usage of my country, I scrupulously suppressed my wishes that my daughter might indulge her own sentiments freely."[8] As to that, Martha certainly acted freely, but one cannot suppose that she was unaware of her father's wishes.

The wedding date was set for February 23, 1790. Although the time was so short, the house was ready. It was to be, in fact, the last time for many years that the house was not torn up and in the process of remodeling. The master already had plans for enlarging, for opening up the east front and rebuilding after the latest fashion he had seen in France, but this would have to wait. At the time of Martha's wedding the family had a roof over their heads, hams in the smokehouse, and no doubt James in the kitchen astonishing if not outraging the incumbents with his French desserts.

As the father of the bride Jefferson had the financial settlement on his mind, always important in a plantation marriage, particularly in the case of a young heir to large estates. Both fathers were rightly considered wealthy men, but both were burdened with debt. Jefferson had not succeeded in paying off the large debt that had come with the Wayles inheritance, and Colonel Randolph too had mortgaged property. Both hastened to dower the bride and groom. Colonel Randolph made over the farm at Varina, with its mortgage of $2,900, to Tom, and Jefferson gave Martha a portion of his Bedford County land inherited from her mother.

Although the young couple were well provided for, Jefferson was not at all happy with the Varina land. He even advised Tom not to accept it, for he had his heart set on a much more accessible part of the colonel's property. Back in 1736 when Colonel Tom's father, William Randolph, had sold Peter Jefferson two hundred acres north of the Rivanna for a bowl of Henry Weatherburn's best arrack punch, he had kept a larger piece adjoining it on the northeast. This was the Edgehill farm. It would have been a natural enough gift to a Randolph son marrying a Jefferson bride; to

Jefferson it would mean an inestimable boon, keeping Martha as near as might be to his side. Colonel Tom, however, had different plans. He declared that he had to keep Edgehill in order to make provision for his younger children. Another, and perhaps more persuasive reason, was that he was about to take a second wife. Tom's mother had died shortly after his return to Virginia; his father's new wife was to be Gabriella Harvie, a girl young enough to be his daughter. Her father's land lay on the other side of Edgehill, and John Harvie wanted to buy it, or the portion of it adjoining his own land.

Gabriella, in short, had an interest in it. In fact without it, John Harvie might not have approved the marriage, and this was enough for the infatuated Colonel Tom. His position was reasonable: he had given his son Varina—what more could be desired? But he knew little about the man with whom he had to deal. The boy he had grown up with was now a trained lawyer, a skilled diplomat. "My father," said Martha in later life, "was never known to give up a friend, or a point." The colonel, it appeared, did know his friend well enough to take alarm; even before the wedding he was digging in his feet. When invited to Monticello to discuss matters, he replied that "My coming up to Monticello to pay my respects to you depends on the weather, having had . . . two slight attacks of gout."[9] The eighteenth century was happier in its excuses than our time, for the gout, unpredictable in its comings and goings, could be a better excuse than the flu! From Jefferson's reply on February 4 it is clear that the colonel had not yet made a contractual commitment. Jefferson assured him that the pains of the journey "may be lessened by making short stages. The last must be from Point of Fork, where you can be well lodged, and from thence the road is good." He remarks that "Your letter to me [of January 30, offering the Varina plantation] and this to you [offering Bedford County lands] could be good against you and me; but nothing can be good against all the world but a deed duly executed and recorded. Come then, my dear Sir, and let us place them in security before their marriage."[10] Thus adjured, the colonel had come to the wedding, presumably breaking the journey at Point of Fork. Although the deeds in Bedford County and to Varina, with its $2,900 mortgage, were executed, the question of Edgehill remained suspended. This land, named after an ancient battle on a Scottish moor, was to be a source of contention for many years to come.

Chapter 8

Edgehill

"I, MARTHA, TAKE THEE, THOMAS . . ." In that day it was for life, unless indeed some unforeseen disaster separated those whom God had joined together. This time God had acted rather hastily. No one at that time imagined that a newly married couple required any special treatment, or time to themselves. At Monticello Martha frolicked with her Carr cousins, sliding on the ice while her serious young husband looked on. After all she was just eighteen.

The obligatory round of visits to Tom's family was a somewhat different matter. To Martha, accustomed as she was to the temperate and rational company of her father, the household at Tuckahoe must have come as a shock. Old Colonel Tom was about to marry a young bride, a circumstance that Tom resented, on his mother's account and on behalf of his young sisters at home. Thus were always the Randolphs. In the words of one of them, "Clever we may be, eccentric we often are," but peaceful never! In comparison with the rest of his family, Tom shone all the brighter in Martha's eyes.

Jefferson had been absent since March 1, when, as planned, he had gone to take up his duties in Washington's cabinet. The president had hoped to hand down to his successor a profoundly united nation. He failed, because two divergent interests were already firmly represented in his own government. Hamilton, as secretary of the treasury, led the "money men" who had profited by cornering the state certificates depreciated after the Revolution, which were later redeemed by the Treasury at their full value.[1] Jefferson himself had suffered heavy losses due to these certificates, but even more upsetting than the monetary loss was his colleague's bland statement that corruption was an essential aspect of effective rule. Hamilton believed that federal financial institutions would stabilize the government by cementing rich men to the federal power.[2]

There was an even more profound difference in the view that these two men took of the future of their country. Hamilton was all for the growth of northern industry and of capital to develop it. Jefferson still believed that America might remain an agricultural country; he favored an open exchange with Europe of farm products for manufactured goods. This was a long-range goal; in the meantime he advocated commercial discrimination against the British trade monopolies. Hamilton, on the other hand, wished to allow nothing to interfere with the flow of English trade, which required the funding of the English debt.

It was indeed a complicated situation that faced the new secretary of state. There was incipient conflict here between regional interests, which were to have later repercussions on Jefferson's own financial affairs. Speculation and fluctuation in the value of the currency had not been favorable to the plantation economy. The extent to which he had been disturbed by the "money men" may be seen in a letter to his son-in-law: "Here the *unmonied* farmer, as he is termed, his cattle and crops are no more thought of than if they did not feed us. . . . Scrip and stock are food and raiment here, . . . the credit and fate of the nation seem to hang in the disparate throws and plunges of gambling scoundrels."[3]

By "scrip and stock" the secretary referred to the notes issued by the newly chartered Bank of the United States. This was an extreme statement, made, as it were, in the bosom of the family. It need not be taken as a wholesale condemnation of banking. He saw it as a tool devised by Hamilton to subvert the legislative branch of the government by what amounted to bribery. The bank was to be "under a *private* not a *public* direction—under the guidance of *individual interest*, not of public policy."[4] The opportunity thus afforded for the concentration of power seemed to Jefferson to be unlimited and he was correct in recognizing that this, in fact, was Hamilton's avowed object. Jefferson's opposition to Hamilton ran far deeper than a mere difference in regional interest, although this, of course, was also present. Basically he feared what he called Hamilton's "monarchical views."

Hamilton made no effort to conceal his admiration for the British system of government. He believed in government by the rich and powerful; he had no faith whatever in Jefferson's reliance on the plain people. In his "Report on Manufactures" he could even speak admiringly of the British cotton mills, where "4/7 nearly (of the workers), are women and children, of whom the great proportion are children and many of them of a tender age."[5] Whether or not he was familiar with Blake's "Dark, Satanic mills," the human being in Jefferson must have revolted at such a concept of the benefits of industry. The man fresh from the counsels of France's most liberal intellectuals feared above all the threat to those inalienable rights for which his own revolution had been fought.

The conflict within the cabinet made Jefferson miserable. To Martha he wrote of "the toils and inquietude of my present situation" and of his "desire of being home once more, and of exchanging labor, envy, and malice for ease, domestic occupation, and domestic love and society."[6] He had hoped to leave the capital at the beginning of the new year, 1793, but under attack, as he then was, he determined to stay on. It was to Martha that he turned in his need: "Continue to me your own love which I feel to be the best solace remaining to me in this world."[7]

Exacerbating public worries were private ones. Jefferson had expected the return from his Poplar Forest plantation to retire the Wayles debt, but no such thing had happened. His land, he felt, had been mismanaged, and now the affairs of state and political conflict left him no time for needed reform, much less for the bold experiment of importing German labor that he had outlined to his friend Bancroft in Paris.

No longer, in fact, did he breath the purely intellectual air of Paris. His experience of political maneuver had taught him, first, the importance of Southern or agrarian solidarity, and second, that feeling in Virginia would forbid any measures taken with an announced purpose of leading to emancipation. He might freely apprentice his own slaves, particularly of course the Hemingses, to white craftsmen; this was common enough, and did not need to be overtly related to the ultimate freedom of the apprentice. He might, and did, attempt to lease as much of his own land in Albemarle as he could, eliminating to some extent his dependence on the system, but this was not very successful. The plain fact was that the small farm, particularly on run-down land, could not compete with the large single-crop plantations in Virginia. Tenant farming, under such a system, had little appeal to a man who might move to better land of his own in the West. Jefferson the private man might detest slavery with all his heart, he might and did find it unprofitable, but economic and political reasons were alike overwhelming. He was stuck with it.

At home at Monticello Martha had picked up the reins of housekeeping with black servants. It presented difficulties un- dreamed of in Paris. James had departed for Philadelphia with the secretary of state, leaving Martha to cope as best she could. She wrote her father: "I took account of the plate, china, etc., and locked up all that was not in immediate use . . . by which means the china was preserved entire except our beautiful cups which being obliged to leave out are all broke but one. . . . I visit the kitchen, smoke house and fowls when the weather permits. . . . I can give but a poor account of my reading having had so little time to myself."

Jefferson thoroughly approved: "Nothing is so engaging as the little domestic cares into which you appear to be entering, and as for reading it is useful for only filling up the chinks of more useful and healthy occupations."[8]

Tom was not quite so industrious. He was always attracted by anything of scientific or mechanical interest, which of course he shared with Jefferson. "I must trouble you to communicate to me in your next letter the method of making the mould board [plow] which we admired so much at Monticello. The necessity I am under of turning my attention to the cultivation of my little farm, has inclined my thoughts toward agriculture. To one as fond as I am of Physical research, and so much accustomed to exercise, such an inclination might be dangerous: but however enticing the subject, however pleasing the employment, I am resolved that it shall never seduce me from the study of the law, and the attempt to acquire political knowledge."[9] Brave words, and although Tom meant them sincerely, they did not represent his true tastes. His real enthusiasm was reserved that summer for an exercise in "Physical research," which involved breeding a wolf to a dog.

These exertions had taken place at Varina, where, naturally enough, Tom had planned to turn his attention to farming. Jefferson responded immediately. For the first time in her life it had become clear that separation from Martha was a real possibility. A month after his departure for the capital he was writing her words of fatherly advice. "The happiness of your life depends now on your continuing to please a single person. To this all other objects must be secondary; even your love to me, were it possible that that could ever be an obstacle. But this it can never be. . . . Cherish then for me, my dear child, the affection of your husband, and continue to love me as you have done."[10]

Even in this letter of advice, evidently written in good faith, there is a subtle, and perhaps not so subtle, overtone of concern for himself. Martha responded with an answering fervor: "I received yours My Dearest father with more pleasure than is possible to express. . . . I have made it my study to please [her husband] in every *thing* and do consider all other objects as secondary to that *except* my love for you. . . . Mr. Randolph has some thoughts of settling at Varina for a little while until he can buy a part of Edgehill. I am much averse to it myself but shall certainly comply if he thinks it necessary. . . ."

Jefferson had already expressed himself on this subject. In fact their letters had crossed; he had anticipated the problem: "I hope Mr. Randolph's idea of settling near Monticello will gain strength; and that no other settlement will in the meantime be fixed on. I wish some expedient may be devised for settling him at Edgehill." To effect this he was determined to come to Virginia in the fall, but so impatient was he that he did not wait for fall to bypass his son-in-law and to enter into direct negotiations with TMR, Sr. At the same time he took care to conciliate the potential adversary, John Harvie: he wrote Harvie offering him favors on behalf of his friend, a Mr. Austin. On the same day, July 25, 1790, he wrote his fellow father-in-law outlining a plan that should enable TMR, Jr., to buy out his sisters' interest in Edgehill:

If it be possible to save for him so valuable and convenient a tract of land, he paying the daughters' portions, I think it desirable for all parties. And this I think can be arranged among us on my return, without deranging any view you have as to those lands. I think that Mr. Randolph, occupying the house and appendages at Monticello, furnishing his table, etc. from the farm I have proposed he should purchase from you immediately, and his other expenses from his plantation at Poplar Forest, would be so much at his ease, that he could appropriate all the profits of Varina to the accomplishment of our wishes respecting Edgehill. Think of this, my dear Sir, and write me a line on the subject. . . . I set out to Virginia . . . pretty certainly by the beginning of September.[11]

A copy of this was sent to Tom, with the following enclosure: "You see that I have taken great liberties in hazarding ideas on which you ought to have been previously consulted: however I do it in such a way as to leave them open for your correction, and when we meet at Monticello, the arrangements may be finally put into such a shape as may suit all."[12]

If the Randolphs had only known it, the battle of Edgehill had just begun. Poor Colonel Tom will be persuaded that his daughters may depend upon the exertions of their brother for their portions, exertions which he may already have had cause to doubt. What Randolph, Jr., made of the enclosure we do not know, beyond the fact of his desire "to gratify Patsy," as he too called his wife.

The plot, however, did not thicken until Jefferson went down to Tuckahoe in October. There, in the beautifully paneled room that he remembered from boyhood, Jefferson sat down at "a short table" opposite his old friend. Prudently this former lawyer had brought with him a prepared form of contract, with only the figures left blank. The sale had been agreed upon, but not the terms. Jefferson was offering 1,700 pounds, in payments of 500, 600, and 600; Randolph held out for 2,000 pounds in payments of 500, 750, and 750. As Jefferson later described the circumstances:

. . . finding that you would not abate in the sum, I agreed to it, but urged that the additional 300 pounds should make a fourth paiment. You objected to it, but, as it seemed to me, not very positively. I declared I would fill up the blanks for paiment with 500, 600, 600, and 300 pounds. . . . You still declared against it. But I so filled up the blanks before your face; you were sitting at the other end of the short table on which I did it, and within reading distance; and you signed before you rose from the table, which I considered to be meant as finally assenting. I mentioned these circumstances to your son on my return, and observed to him that if you should require to have these particulars altered back to what you had insisted on, it would be better to comply with your desire. He did not hesitate to say that they should be arranged as you pleased. . . . As for the contract, be it off, if you wish it, no matter what the laws of the land are. Nature knows no laws between parent and child, but the will of the parent. If you desire to keep the land, your son decided in the first moment to comply with your desire. But if you are only dissatisfied with any particular articles, model the whole to your own mind. . . . If the contract can be adapted to your mind, I confess I have it much, very much at heart.[13]

One cannot help observing the subtlety of this letter. Whether or not Jefferson planned it that way he has employed the old lawyer's trick of pushing for more than the minimum acceptable, so that that minimum will appear like a concession, which it would be ungenerous to reject.

But when father and son met face to face all this lawyerly subtlety and Jeffersonian calm had gone by the board. On their meeting the colonel had obviously exclaimed that he had been bamboozled, and that he would not live up to the contract unless "compelled." At the word "compelled" Tom had "taken fire" and had stormed out of the house, a form of exit not unusual with him. He had then taken a lofty stand; expressing doubt that a man "so remarkable for his accuracy should have committed such a capital error as it is incredible that one who had spread the fame of his integrity through half the globe should have intended to insert a fraudulent article in the contract."

This grandiloquent praise of Jefferson could not have sat well with the colonel, who had probably not welcomed an intermediary in the first place. In the meantime Tom had sent back to Monticello for a copy of the contract, without again seeing his father. Almost as impulsive as his son, the colonel had fired off a letter calling Tom "not only undutiful, but insolent," nor would he honor the contract "unless COMPELLED." Tom replied with conscious virtue, "There are few men, I believe," he wrote his father, "who would have supposed that the consideration of a pitiful advantage in a bargain would have compelled me to such a breach of honor and duty as the compulsion you feared." The colonel by now had had time to cool off. "My last letter to you," he wrote, "was perhaps rather warm. . . . I wish, if you are not too much irritated, to speak three or four words to you—and after that, your impetuous temper may renounce your father forever, if it is your choice—I wish you to have the 1600 acres of land at Edgehill on the terms I mentioned to Mr. Jefferson."

Jefferson, back at Monticello, had already correctly interpreted the colonel's attitude. He wrote to Tom: "You are certainly right in deciding to relinquish the purchase if Col. Randolph desires it. But I rather suppose he means nothing more than that he will not abide by the agreement if all the articles are insisted on." But Tom had gone too far to back down now. Randolph "warmth" had caused the loss of this preliminary skirmish, but the battle was not yet lost. Meanwhile Edgehill remained unclaimed.[14]

Chapter 9

Bizarre

THE ALARUMS AND EXCURSIONS over Edgehill had not precluded one happy event: Martha had become pregnant. Polly, left in charge of an older sister so recently married and so absorbed in her own pressing affairs, seems to have felt somewhat left out. In a letter to her father, dated February 13, 1791, Polly describes the birth with her usual straightforward simplicity: ". . . In my last I said that my sister was very well, but she was not. She had been very sick all day without my knowing any thing of it as I stayed upstairs the whole day. However she is well now and the little one also. She is very pretty has beautiful deep blue eyes and is a very fine child." [1]

Jefferson, with his usual care to anticipate Martha's problems, had sent her a copy of Dr. Gregory, the Dr. Spock of the day, on advice to young mothers.

As soon as the infant comes into the world, our first care is to cram it with physic. . . . The medicine which nature had prepared for this purpose is the mother's first milk. This indeed answers the end very effectually, but we think some drug forced down the child's throat will do it much better. The composition of this varies according to the fancy of the good Woman who presides at the birth—It deserves to be remarked . . . that calves . . . are treated in the same manner. They have the same sort of physic administered to them, and often with the same success, many of them dying under the operation. . . .

Notwithstanding the many moving calls of Natural Instinct in the child to suck the mother's breast yet the usual practice has been, obstinately to deny that indulgence till the third day after birth. By this time the suppression of the natural evacuation of the milk, usually bringing on a fever, the consequence proves often fatal to the mother. . . . [2]

These commonsense counsels had not arrived until after the event, but Martha had managed very well on her own. Tom had not been present. He had gone to Rock Castle to fetch his aunt Fleming to preside at this important occasion and, typically, had not gotten back in time. Martha's own aunt, Mrs. Lewis, seemed an adequate substitute. Martha assured her father, "I have read Gregory and am happy to tell you it was precisely the plan who [sic] we had followed with her for her birth by Mrs. Lewis's advice."[3]

Jefferson, one feels, would have liked to have borne the child himself if such a thing were physically possible. He did unbend enough to answer his younger daughter's letter: "I congratulate you my dear aunt on your new title. I hope you pay a great deal of attention to your niece and that you have begun to give her lessons on the harpsichord, in Spanish, etc."[4] We hope that Polly enjoyed the joke. It must have been a brave effort on Jefferson's part, for things were not going well for him at the seat of government. The secretary of the treasury continued to carry out fiscal policy that appeared to enhance unduly the executive power. Even John Adams, friend and colleague of the Paris days, was taking up the federalist cause of a strong central government, to Jefferson scarcely different from a return to monarchy. Separation from his daughters had never been more trying. The news from Monticello must have been welcome indeed.

Martha refused to refer to their first child as anything but "the infant" until her father should give her a name. Jefferson, with exquisite tact, chose Anne Cary, the name of Tom's beloved mother. In the same letter he congratulated the father: "Happy is the man whose quiver is full of them." Tom was to have no worries on that score. Eleven more were to follow in rapid succession; only one died in infancy, and every one was named by the grandfather!

Neither childbirth nor farming appears to have distracted the young Randolphs from extensive visiting and traveling. Not, surely, to Martha's unadulterated distress, Tom had found that the climate at Varina did not agree with him. The hot sun on the low grounds caused his skin to break out painfully, in what was then called a "miliary eruption." That this was a psychosomatic illness we may assume today, for, although complying, as she had assured her father, with Tom's wishes, Martha's aversion to Varina must surely have shown through. Jefferson himself seems to have suspected a psychosomatic source, for his letters to his son-in-law are full of exhortations to rise above illness. In Jefferson's words, "[Nature's] efforts would indeed be immensely aided if you could by the force of reason and confidence in her, counteract the mechanical effect of this disease on your spirits."[5] Tom and Martha continued to rely on journeys for improved health—at least it deferred the critical decision: Varina versus Albemarle.

Jefferson was never in any doubt: "It is essential to my happiness," he wrote Tom, "our living near together." If it could not be at Edgehill, on one side of Monticello, it might as well be as near on the other side. Mr. Randolph, he wrote his sister Bolling, "will now endeavor to buy some of Mr. Carter's land,"[6] mountainous as much of this land must have been. Fortunately, this became unnecessary when in 1792 Tom finally succeeded in purchasing Edgehill from his father.

Tom's family, much larger of course than Martha's, also kept them from home. He felt very responsible for the younger brothers and sisters, especially his sisters, for the girls were not getting on at all with their new stepmother. A disconsolate letter from Martha to her father early in that same year of '92 refers to "a journey of three months in which I have not had it in my power to write to you." They had been "at Dick Randolph's," at his ill-fated home, Bizarre. Ill-fated indeed, for thereby hangs a tale as startling as any that ever rocked Virginia society to its foundations. No family could have been more of that foundation sort than the Randolphs, but Tom's branch of it was showing serious signs of decline. It was often said of the Randolphs that they married one another because no one else was good enough, and indeed three of Tom's sisters married men of their own name. Judith had married her handsome cousin Richard of Bizarre, the "Dick Randolph" of Martha's letters. Unhappy at home, Virginia (Jenny) and Anne Cary (Nancy) had both visited their brother at Monticello. Nancy had gone to her sister Judith at

Bizarre, and there Tom and Martha were visiting when this last and most outrageous of the Randolph scandals began to unfold.

The members of the house party were young, but not particularly happy. How much did Martha notice when, in Judith's phrase, Nancy and Richard "were only company for themselves"? Probably she noticed a good deal, although she retailed no gossip to her father. Judith's husband, the charming Richard, had become a bone of contention between the sisters. Richard was a favorite of the beautiful Mrs. Bingham, whom we have met before in Paris. Richard's brother, poor Theoderick, whom Nancy had once wished to marry, was also at Bizarre. Wasted with tuberculosis to a mere skeleton, he had come home to die. John Randolph, the third brother, and many other young men who were not Randolphs at all were also in love with Nancy. She attracted young men like flies to her honey. Unfortunately the honey was tainted, for Nancy appears to have been a first-class bitch, second only to her cousin John when it came to stirring up trouble. More than twenty years later John and Nancy were at it again, reviling each other's part in the ancient scandal. Here is a letter, lately come to light, in which Nancy describes the scene. It is addressed to the Randolph boys' stepfather:

I left home to avoid a marriage hateful to me, having visited my father's excellent Sister, and my Brother at Monticello, I accepted an invitation to Bizarre. Dick entered my apartment one morning, threw himself on his knees, and begged that I would listen to him and not alarm anyone. He declared his own unhappiness, that he knew his wife did not love him, that the first night of their marriage she made him sit up altogether in a corner of their apartment at Presque Isle (this she had boasted of) to shew her power, he endeavored to shake my principles. I said I would be silent because Polly, the woman who waited on me in 1791, would soon be up with water and she had better find him in the room than meet him coming out of it. He proceeded to tell me that he had once entered the chamber of Miss Betsey Talliaferro, afterwards Mrs. Call, at old Mr. Wythe's, the house now Mr. Skipwith's, in Williamsburg, that she received him to her Bed, and that the same reception had been given him by a Miss Kitty Ludlow in New York. I burst into tears and exclaimed 'Oh my poor father what has your wretched marriage brought on your children I will write and conjure him to send for me. I am engaged to your brother.' The tears streamed from Dick's eyes, mine fill, with a recollection of the heart rending scene, Polly came with water who had witnessed much anguish at Tuckahoe, she was daughter to the faithful creature who nursed all my mother's family. I made the best appearance that the case admitted by turning to her and saying Polly I wish my mother had lived. Dick left the room professing Friendship with me. I wrote to pray my father would send for me; his wife answered that the horses were too lame to travel, but, it was no secret that she set out with them to meet Frank Corbin at old Colonel Basset's. I had no home to receive me. It was a winter of extreme misery to me, but I might in the spring have married Genlo Lee, Ben Harrison, or Archy Randolph.[7]

With all this reputed choice of husbands Nancy chose to stay on at Bizarre.

"Dick repeated the frantic kind of scene already described, and conjured me not to marry anyone, that the Idea distracted him." It was at this time, and apparently with every justification, that Judith reproached Nancy with being "the blaster of my happiness."

A young man dying of tuberculosis and illicit love upstairs. It must have happened before in Virginia, but anything happening to the Randolphs always seemed to be magnified a hundred times. Martha, missing her father, was delighted to be back at Monticello, but Tom's concern constantly turned to his motherless, and virtually fatherless, younger sisters. In September they were back at Bizarre, where things had certainly not taken a turn for the better. It was generally believed now that Nancy was pregnant. An inquisitive relative, Mrs. Page, was present in the house and offered to examine her niece. Miss Nancy refused, but her aunt peeked through a crack in the door and overheard Nancy asking her maid whether she thought she was smaller. No, replied the maid, she thought she was larger. Miss Nancy looked down at her waist, and then cast her eyes up to Heaven in silent melancholy.

Judith and Martha discussed the practical aspects of this dilemma, and Martha recommended gum guiacum. We wonder whether it was one of Dr. Gregory's prescriptions. It was an excellent remedy for the colic, said Martha, but was dangerous as it often produced an abortion. Nancy was present, but made no comment.

Later Mrs. Page asked Martha if she could get some of this potent gum for Nancy, and Martha did send some back to Bizarre after she and Tom had returned to Monticello. Martha herself was approaching her second childbirth; she was happily delivered of a boy very soon after their return.

Nancy must have tried everything, including gum guiacum, without result. On October 1, 1792, a cavalcade of Randolphs set out from Bizarre to visit their cousin Randolph Harrison and his wife at their new house, then being built, at Glenlyvar. The party included Judith and Richard; John Randolph, Richard's youngest brother; Archibald Randolph, one of Nancy's suitors; and Nancy. Nancy was feeling very unwell, and retired to her room as soon as they reached Glenlyvar. The house was under construction; piles of lumber were stacked in the yard, and only two bedrooms were finished on the upper floor. One opened across from the other, with a stairs in between. Nancy occupied the inner room. Sometime in the night screams were heard from the upper floor. At first Randolph Harrison and his wife believed them to come from Judith, but then discovered that they were Nancy's. Laudanum was applied for, and sent up by a servant. On going upstairs to her guests Mrs. Harrison found Judith sitting up in bed, apparently untroubled by her sister's condition. She observed that Nancy had colic, and often suffered from the hysterics. Richard had gone to Nancy's room to administer laudanum. Mrs. Harrison had then tried to enter the inner room, and had found the door locked from within. This she attributed to the fact that the spring lock was broken, and that there was no other way to keep it closed. Richard opened the door, and requested her to leave her candle outside, as Nancy had taken laudanum and the light hurt her eyes. After a brief conversation in the dark, Mrs. Harrison had found Nancy easier, and had returned downstairs to bed. Later in the night they had heard footsteps descending the stairs; by the weight of the tread they inferred it to be Richard. Subsequently the footsteps returned the way they had come. Mr. and Mrs. Harrison supposed that Richard Randolph may have gone to send for a doctor to attend Nancy, although they did not inquire further. The next morning, rising early, Mrs. Harrison found tracks of blood on the stairs, and later found blood on one side of Nancy's pillow and further stains on the mattress, where an ineffective effort had been made to wash them out.

All this had occurred on a Monday night. By Wednesday Nancy was up and about, although feeble. Her cousin Archibald had almost to carry her up the stairs after dinner. There had been a noticeably unpleasant smell in her room, which had lingered, but the Harrisons had noted no other change in the behavior of their guests, which seemed entirely normal. This was all that ever could be formally reconstructed of the events of that week at Glenlyvar, but the story would not lie down and die. It offered, certainly, all the ingredients of a full-blown scandal. Servants had seen a fetus, or possibly a stillbirth, or even the body of an infant, stuffed down between two logs near the house, under some blood-stained shingles. Such a heap of building material did in fact remain there for some weeks, undisturbed. Word spread from servants to masters, that there had been at the least a miscarriage there that night, possibly infanticide, but the testimony of slaves against whites could not be taken in court. It transpired that Randolph Harrison had noticed a blood-stained shingle, but had forborne to look further. To this discretion Nancy and Richard may have owed their lives; for at Richard's own request a hearing did take place, to determine whether criminal charges should be brought against them.

Such a hearing, before no fewer than sixteen magistrates, and with the two greatest luminaries of the Virginia bar as counsel for the defense, was surely calculated to prolong the life of what might, in connection with any other family, have been a ninety-day wonder. It did seem that there was a curse upon the Randolphs of Bizarre! [8]

The story had spread like wildfire through the plantation society, not the least among the Randolph connection. Sorely pressed, Richard had demanded the hearing on the rather naive principle that an acquittal would end the gossip. He had engaged his cousin John Marshall, and even routed old Patrick Henry out of retirement, to make that acquittal doubly sure. The old warrior was known to be at his best in a criminal case; the charges could have been murder and incest, as relations between a man and his wife's sister were considered at that time. It is all there still in a document called *Notes of Evidence*,[9] taken by John Marshall and copied in John Randolph's hand. Martha and Tom were both present at the hearing, and Martha was called as a witness.

Before the hearing Nancy, in her desire to clear Richard, had prepared a written confession naming Theoderick as the father of whatever had been buried beneath the shingles at Glenlyvar. Tom was beside himself. It was, he cried, an open confession of his sister's dishonor, and he would not allow it. There were high words that winter at Bizarre. Tom told Richard, "I will wash out with your blood the stain on my family."[10] He clearly meant it. Richard held the written confession in his hand, and perhaps with some feeling of shame, dropped the incriminating paper in the fire.

Still, no one knew how the hearing would turn out. The verdict when it came hinged partly on Randolph Harrison's discretion in never looking under the shingles at Glenlyvar, but mostly it depended on Judith. Through the lengthy preliminaries she sat grimly silent, even during Patrick Henry's interrogation of Mrs. Page. When Mrs. Page had finished her testimony about her observation through the crack in the door, the great orator asked his witness: "Madam, which eye did you peek with?" When even the magistrates must have smiled, Judith sat on, unbending.

Silence fell on the courtroom when at last Judith rose to her feet. Her demeanor was superb, almost arrogant. She knew, and they knew, that she held the lives of the accused, her husband and her sister, in her hands. Nothing that she had witnessed, she declared, gave the slightest support to anything out of the way happening that night at Glenlyvar. Yes, Nancy had had hysterics, but she was often subject to them. No one could have left Nancy's room or descended the stairs without her knowledge, and Mr. Randolph had not gone down until morning.

After this the verdict was inevitable: for lack of conclusive evidence they would not be brought to trial. Although, as Martha wrote her father, "but a small part of the world and those the most inconsiderable people in it" believed them innocent.

Martha was admirably loyal to her husband's family. Before the hearing she had relayed no gossip, even to her father, but the rumors had reached Philadelphia without her assistance. Although, Jefferson wrote his daughter, it had long given him "great uneasiness," it was some time before he brought himself to attack the subject head on. His object was, as always, to guide his daughter toward the rational view of whatever irrationalities might assail her. "The world has become too rational to extend to one person the acts of another. Every one at present stands on the merit or demerit of their own conduct. I am in hopes therefore that neither of you feel any uneasiness but for the pitiable victim, whether it be of error or slander. In either case I see guilt in but one person, and not in her." [11]

Tom's feelings were less restrained. He had suffered agonies over the attack on his sister's honor, which he could do nothing to defend. A duel might have eased his feeling of helpless rage. As it was the hearing only amounted to a further trial; Martha's appearance on the stand had harrowed the feelings of her sensitive young husband. Martha herself was sufficiently moved to take issue with her father. "I am sensible," she wrote, "of the illiberality of extending to one person the infamy of another . . . yet the generality of mankind are weak enough to think otherwise. . . . As for the poor deluded victim I believe all feel much more for her than she does for herself. . . . Amidst the distress of her family she alone is tranquil and seems proof against any other misfortune on earth but that of a separation from her vile seducer." Jefferson had urged her "never throw off the best affections of nature in the moment that they become most precious to their object." In reply Martha is able to say "In following the dictates of my own heart I was so happy as to stumble upon the very conduct you advised me to." Nevertheless, although she has sometimes "*doubted* the truth of the report," she confesses, "I would to heaven my hopes were equal to my fears but the latter often too often presides." [12]

She remarks that "The divisions in the family increase daily. . . .

There is no knowing where they will end. The old gentleman [Tom's father] has plunged into the thick of them governed by the most childish passions." Tom alone appears to her as the pillar on which the family leans: "He is the link by which so many discordant parts join." As they are now once more at Monticello she can relax, telling her father of the new baby. This second child, Thomas Jefferson Randolph, was born on September 12, 1792. Martha must have been quietly chatting with Judith about gum guiacum very near to the date of her own confinement. Perhaps fortunately she was never put to the test of sheltering "your afflicted friend," as Jefferson called Nancy, for the victim of all this disorder preferred to remain at Bizarre.

We can only guess at the Gothic scene that prevailed there. Certainly there was no peace between the sisters. Nancy wrote to St. George Tucker of Judy's frequent reproaches "for my too great fondness for Dick. . . ."[13] She characterizes her sister in these letters as a proud, malignant and haughty woman. Proud and haughty Judith may well have been, but for all that Nancy stayed, and stayed. Only Richard's death, under mysterious circumstances, rang down the curtain at Bizarre. It looked suspiciously like poison, but which, if either, of the sisters was responsible will never be known. Only Tom never abandoned Nancy. He continued to support his unhappy sister with a regular allowance, long after he himself had ceased to have money to spare.

Chapter 10

The Plantation

Bad year or good year, crop or no crop . . . these dependents must be clothed and fed.

IN THE SAME MONTH that his daughter Nancy was acquitted of murder and incest "Old Colonel Tom" Randolph, failing rapidly and bethinking himself, perhaps, of his children's future, finally conveyed the deed to Edgehill to his eldest son. The price was that originally asked, 2,000 pounds.[1] Tom had already wondered if it were a wise move to burden himself with such a large slave estate, 1,152½ acres, but Martha's obvious satisfaction must have settled this question without real discussion. She simply took it for granted that now they would settle on land so conveniently situated, adjoining her father's.

Neither Randolph nor his father-in-law were free from financial problems. Jefferson relied a good deal on the younger man to supervise affairs at Monticello while he himself was engaged in "the drudgery of business," that is to say, the affairs of state. Nevertheless, this secretary of state was also finding time to study the methods of the good Pennsylvania farmers, such as his friend James Logan of Stenton. Tom agreed with him that the northern states produced better farmers, although he did not feel that their methods necessarily suited conditions in Virginia.

Some sort of reform was overdue, for Jefferson's returns from his own farms were still inadequate to settle the Wayles debt. In the fall of '92 he even resorted, against all his principles, to the painful necessity of selling Negroes to raise money. "In Albemarle," he explained, "I have concluded to sell Dinah and her younger children, and wrote to my brother to find a purchaser in his neighborhood, so as to unite her to her husband. . . ." Surely this was approaching the necessity of a sale as humanely as possible! Publicly as well as privately it was an uneasy subject. Jefferson preferred to keep his own name out of such transactions, and to sell through an intermediary, a position he made clear in a letter to Bowling Clarke: "I do not (while in public life) like to have my name annexed in the public papers to the sale of [this form of] property."[2]

Inevitably Jefferson's attitude toward slavery complicated his position as an individual planter. At the same time that he was forced to sell slaves to make ends meet, some of his neighbors were making money in the traditional way. Years before when the colonists had petitioned the Crown to send ministers of the Gospel to the colonies, the Lords of the Plantation, as the Colonial Office was called at the time, shot back the unequivocal answer: "Souls! Damn your souls. Make tobacco!" And so it had been ever since. To Jefferson tobacco was the source of all evil. "It is a culture," he had written in his *Notes*, "productive of infinite wretchedness. Those employed in it are in a continued state of exertion beyond the powers of nature to support. Little food of any kind is raised by them; so that the men and animals on these farms are badly fed, and the earth is rapidly impoverished."[3]

At Monticello only one-third of the work force were employed on the farm. The majority were house servants, or worked in the stables or garden, or were apprenticed craftsmen and builders. Field hands alone were employed in the culture of tobacco.

We may ask what this tobacco culture, so misprized by Jefferson, actually entailed. The plants were raised in beds, then replanted in the fields in early spring. When the stalk began to grow, and the broad green leaves were starting to form, the hoeing began. A row of slaves, women and men together, moved down the field, with probably an overseer, or at least a driver, as the black foremen were called, making sure that the work rhythms did not falter. Then came the "topping," cutting of the head to check the upward growth and produce a broader leaf. Cutting off the ground leaves was called "succoring," also a necessary process. When finally the stalks were cut, they were placed on racks to dry, and later carried to the tobacco shed for further seasoning. This was the lengthy process before the dried leaves were ready to be stripped, packed or "prized" in hogsheads, and rolled perhaps many miles to where they might be loaded on batteaux and shipped downriver.

Merchant traders then took over the crop to ship to the London market. Naturally under this system much of the return went to the middlemen, and indeed was so low that the planter could not have made a profit without a rigid adherence to the system of slave labor. We see that the yeoman farmer was abandoning Virginia in droves, and even sharecropping, as Jefferson's experience showed, was unable to compete.

Circumstances had forced Jefferson to give up the idea of mingling German sharecroppers with his slaves; but he had not yet abandoned hope of setting up a system of tenant farmers. In the winter of '92 he took pains to describe alternatives to the tobacco culture to a prospective overseer, one Samuel Biddle from Maryland. He was attempting, in fact, to set up a less onerous system of agriculture. Even his botanical imports had been experiments with that object in mind. A sugar maple on the west lawn of Monticello still marks his unsuccessful attempt to substitute maple for cane sugar. "What a blessing," he wrote in 1790, "to substitute a sugar which requires only the labor of children for that which it is said renders the slavery of the blacks necessary."[4] From the same motive, he had tried to import the olive tree, but it had also refused to flourish.

In the letter to Biddle, the prospective overseer, he described the Monticello farm:

The farm is about 5 or 600 acres of cleared land, very hilly, originally as rich as any highlands in the world, but much worried by Indian corn and tobacco. It is still however very strong, and is remarkably friendly to wheat and rye. These will be my first object. Next will be grasses, cattle, sheep, and the introduction of potatoes for the use of the farm, instead of Indian corn, in as great a degree as possible. You will have from 12 to 15 laborers under you. They will be well clothed, and as well fed as your management of the farm will enable us, for it is chiefly with a view to place them on the comfortable footing of the laborers of other countries [this had been a major object of his research in Europe] that I came into another country [Maryland] to seek an overseer for them, and also to have my lands a little more taken care of. . . .⁵

The most arresting part of this letter is Jefferson's hope for bettering the situation of the slaves. It was a very real factor in his desire to get out of debt. It was all part of his effort to prepare some of his slaves, at least on an individual basis, to make their way as free men in a white world.

Jefferson also hoped that Biddle would find him white tenants from Maryland. Obviously they were very difficult to obtain in Virginia, and the same seems to have been true of Maryland. No tenants appeared. The small farmer had been largely forced out by the heavy expenses of shipping, but even the greater volume permitted by the tenant system failed to succeed. Only the large *slave* plantations prospered, and tobacco, as in colonial times, remained the most profitable crop. Jefferson might try as he would to escape the system; his efforts could only lead to his own eventual ruin.

James Hemings was surely an example of one who might be expected to move successfully into that white world of freedom. This young man, now twenty-nine years old, had been a city dweller for the greater part of his adult life. In Paris he had lived for some months, in the servants quarters at least, in one of the most magnificent palaces, that of the Prince de Condé. He had no wish to return to "the mountain," and to his rustic slave family. He had his reputation as the chef of the secretary of state to maintain; he was familiar with tavern life, and must have felt that good jobs could be his for the asking. But Jefferson had not taken him to France and paid for his expensive training for nothing. Just as Jefferson had brought what he considered the best of painting and sculpture with him when he returned to the new land, so he expected James to bear the art of French *cuisine*. He now promised this Hemings his freedom on the condition that he would train a successor as cook at Monticello. This was to be the position of a younger brother, Peter. James, manifestly unwilling, had no choice but to return to Monticello.

Next we may come to the eldest of the Wayles-Hemingses,

Robert, called Bob. It was at this time that Bob purchased his own freedom, so that he might join his wife and child in the service of a certain Dr. Straus, then living in Richmond. Dr. Straus had put up the money for Bob's purchase. Martha reported to her father that she had seen "Bob frequently while in Richmond. He expressed great uneasiness at having quitted you in the way that he did . . . but could not prevail himself to give up his wife and child."[6]

There was, certainly, no lack of other Hemingses to take his place. Martin, Betty Hemings's son by a black father before her connection with John Wayles, was also a trained coachman. Neither was there any lack of Hemings women. Betty's first daughter was Mary, born 1753, a pastry cook, sold by her own desire in 1792 to Col. Thomas Bell. She had been Jefferson's seamstress during his time as governor in Richmond. Mary was the mother of Joe Fosset, born 1780, by one of the white craftsmen at Monticello. Joe later became the plantation blacksmith, although as will appear later Joe too was restless at Monticello.

Bett, called Betty Brown, was the second of Betty's daughters, followed by Nance, both by black fathers. These three women and the boy Martin were all born before their master's liaison with their mother. Betty Brown became the mother of seven, among them Wormley and Burwell, both important members of the later household at Monticello. Betty Hemings's six children by Wayles followed in rapid succession: Robert, James, Thenia, Critta, Peter, and Sally. Thenia was sold to James Monroe, the only Wayles-Hemings ever to be sold, in 1794. Thenia was followed by Critta, born in 1769, a favorite mammy, and by Peter, now starting a career as James's pupil in the kitchen. Sally was the youngest of the Wayles-Hemingses, born in 1773, the year of John Wayles's death.

The indestructible, indefatigable Betty produced two more children after her arrival at Monticello: John, by an Englishman, a carpenter called Nielson, and Lucy, who died while the Jeffersons were in Paris.[7] John, or Johnny, as he was affectionately called by the family, was—next to James—the star of the Hemings clan. He was apprenticed to the master builder James Dinsmore, and became in later years himself the chief builder at Jefferson's Bedford

County retreat, Poplar Forest. Unlike his brother James, John Hemings remained a slave until freed by Jefferson's will in 1826. In the course of the Monticello story there is not a single one of the craftsmen and house servants who does not emerge, to some extent, as an individual in his own right. Nevertheless, they also appear as integral units in that plantation society.

House servants and artisans did not normally work in the fields, although there might be some exceptions at harvest time. Women and men worked together on the crops. Jefferson's meticulous records show how carefully work was apportioned to the strength and ability of the worker. Children under ten years of age served as nurses; from ten to sixteen, the boys worked in Jefferson's nailery and the girls were spinners; at sixteen they went into the field or learned trades.

The following entry in Jefferson's Farm Book shows the arrangement of the wheat harvest for 1799:

> Cradler: 12 males [John Hemings led the cradlers
>   in this list]
> Binders: 9 females, 3 boys
> Loaders: 7 males
> Stackers: 1 male, 1 female, 1 boy
> Cooks: 3 females
> Water tenders: 2 boys
> Liquor and a grindstone was in a cart, tended
>   by one old man.[8]

Jefferson was quite solicitous of his "breeding women." In a letter to the overseer Joel Yancey he takes care to set forth his position: "The loss of five little ones in four years induces me to fear that the overseers do not permit women to devote as much time as necessary to the care of their children. . . . I consider the labour of a breeding woman as no object, and that a child raised every two years is of more profit than the crop of the best laboring man. In this, as in all other cases, Providence has made our interests and our duties coincide perfectly."[9]

Although to modern ears this may sound like self-interest, not to say hypocrisy, we must consider that this hard-nosed approach was for the benefit of an overseer. More significantly, if Jefferson's concern had really been solely economic, we would have had much more comprehensive figures on the cost of raising and training a child plus the loss of the mother's labor against the purchase price of a new slave, etc., etc.

Most of our knowledge of the life of the Monticello slaves comes from these and similar documents from Jefferson's Garden Book, his Farm Book, or his accounts. There are at present no reconstructed slave cabins on the property, but an insurance record of 1796 does describe 5 servants' houses on Mulberry Row. One was 20½ feet by 12 feet, made of wood, with a wooden chimney and earth floor. Three others of similar construction were 12 by 14 feet.[10] Recent archaeological work shows that some of the later slave houses, particularly those of Hemingses and other upper servants and craftsmen, were distinctly superior to this early model. Whenever free from affairs of state Jefferson made a real effort to improve living conditions. Excavations show that some of the slave houses were built of stone, and that they were furnished, perhaps in unofficial ways, with odd bits of china and other amenities. There is even the mug, described earlier, that James may well have brought with him from Paris.

There were always routine supplies. When John Hemings married Priscilla, he was supplied with "a pot and a bed" as well as blankets, clothes, sifters for flour and meal, hats, stockings, and shoes. As John was literate we may suppose that he knocked together a bench or a table on which to write. Compared to the luxury of Monticello it sounds poor enough, but we should not forget that the young Abe Lincoln fared no better than this on the frontier.

Medical care was regularly supplied, as indeed was true on most Albemarle plantations. A recurring problem, certainly in Martha's eyes, was the slaves' own preference for African medicine. One sad example was the fate of Jupiter, faithful body servant and coachman who had so long cared for the family. Although ill he had insisted on accompanying his master on a trip to the capital. As his condition grew worse on the way, Jefferson arranged for him to rest

at a tavern, but even this Jupiter refused to do. When at last he
returned to Monticello, Martha wrote her father of the sad event.
He seemed "as well as he had been for some time past," but
subsequently took "a dose from this black doctor who pronounced
that it would kill or.cure." The doctor had not exaggerated. Two
and a half hours later Jupiter fell down "in a strong convulsion fit
and was never heard to speak again." [11] Martha was indignant. In
her view African medicine was a real hazard on the plantation,
although obviously Jupiter had preferred it to white doctoring.
"With all his defects," Jefferson wrote to his daughter, "he leaves a
void in my domestic arrangements which cannot be filled." [12] There
were, in fact, a number of Hemingses ready to fill the gap.

Considering the volume and detail of Jefferson's farm records it
strikes us with all the more astonishment that he never in his life
was to add up the profit and loss at the end of any calendar year.
The reason is, perhaps, not far to seek. It was in his granddaughter's
mind when she explained: "Bad year or good year, crop or no crop,
these dependents were to be clothed and fed—well clothed and
well fed. . . ." [13] There was rarely any profit to record!

In spite of debt, in spite of tobacco, the absentee farmer in
Philadelphia was yearning for home. He wrote to his "dear daughter," Martha: "When I shall see you I cannot say: but my heart and
thoughts are all with you until I do." [14]

To Randolph he sent elaborate plans for the eight-year rotation
of crops, accompanied by appropriate charts and figures. Such
playing with charts seems to have been his favorite relaxation from
the cares of state. He proposed to divide his four Albemarle farms
(Shadwell, Lego, Tufton, and the home farm) into fields of sixty
acres each, each farm to contain seven fields. "So," he calculated,
"these fundamentals being laid down, the laws of combinations
decide inflexibly that the number of fields and number of years
constituting the complete rotation must always be equal." [15] Even
Dumas Malone, Jefferson's most complete and one of his most
admiring biographers, wonders if farming can be quite as mathematical as Jefferson supposed. Randolph, who was becoming an
excellent practical farmer, carefully pointed out the flaws in his

father-in-law's theory. Different crops matured within different periods of time; harvests should then be staggered without regard for the inflexible laws of combinations, thereby producing a more constant use of the labor force; different soils required different treatment. Randolph made many other sensible comments of the same kind. On one thing both men were agreed, that wheat, as far as was economically feasible, should replace tobacco.

This was a step in the right direction, although even here Jefferson sacrificed private profit to the public good. He built not one, but two most uneconomical grist mills—one solely, as he told Randolph, for the benefit of his neighbors. In 1796 seven thousand man hours of labor were consumed in the construction of these mills, and the canals needed to channel water from the Rivanna to turn the mill wheels. Even so they were vulnerable to flood water. Ultimately they cost Jefferson $18,000. This tremendous effort did encourage the cultivation of wheat, but it did not help to pay off the Wayles debt.

Randolph was, in fact, a good farmer. Jefferson called him the best in the United States, and in this role, certainly, he shone to better advantage than he was ever to do in later life as a politician. But somehow there was a fatal flaw: he could raise a crop, but few men had less success in getting a crop to market. Indecision, and perhaps a lurking contempt as well as a fear of business, dogged this Randolph's best efforts. In the fall of '93 he was unable to make payments on the Varina mortgage. He wrote to ask the mortgage holder "whether it would be to my advantage to ship wheat this winter or next spring to New York." [16] Apparently unable to make these vital decisions, he often left them up to his father-in-law.

Jefferson could not have failed to observe this trait in the younger man. Nevertheless, he was careful to avoid the *appearance* of taking over. Influence, when exerted, was indirect. He no longer addressed his letters to "My dear Patsy": she had become "My Dear Martha" or "My Dear Daughter." Tom was always now "Mr. Randolph." But we still find the entries in his account book, "paid for Patsy," "gave Patsy for small expenses," etc., constantly occurring as in earlier days.[17] Little had changed really but the form of address.

Old Colonel Tom, whose health had been rapidly failing at Tuckahoe, was too ill to draw up his own will. His father-in-law, John Harvie, presided at this effort. In any case, although TMR, Jr., was named co-executor, with his brother William, of his father's estate, John Harvie was appointed guardian of the younger sisters. Tom took it as a major blow. "It carried with it," he said, "more than a suspicion of incapacity."[18] It struck, moreover, at one of his own best qualities, his family feeling and his protective attitude toward these all too vulnerable sisters.

In 1794, when Jefferson at last escaped the toils of office, his son-in-law's confidence was at a low ebb. Randolph had never been one to drive his slaves; in that sense the system was as repugnant to him as it was to Jefferson, and now there was little profit to show. It must have been with mixed feelings, and incidentally with severely depressed health, that he reacted to his father-in-law's return. For Martha, of course, there was only unmitigated joy.

Chapter 11

The Architect

Architecture is my delight, and putting up and pulling down one of my favorite amusements.

ALTHOUGH WE WOULD NOT go so far as Garry Wills, who calls Monticello "an economic blasphemy," nevertheless we must admit that, profit or no profit, Jefferson never gave up expensive plans for his house. The house that he found on his return from France was the one he had left completed, or virtually so, at the time of his wife's death. One would have thought that a widower with no idea of remarriage, and particularly a widower already engaged in demanding work elsewhere, would have been content with this house as it was. As we know, the first Monticello had been designed with a double portico and semi-octagonal end rooms. It was both Palladian in feeling and comfortable, but it came nowhere near meeting the ideal that Jefferson had acquired in Paris.

There, in the company of his great friend Maria Cosway, Jefferson had seen those domes, those rooms of oval and octagonal shape, those great skylights and the long windows open at ground level, so perfectly adapted to his own hot summers in Virginia. They were the work of architects described by Frederick Nichols as "romantic classicists."[1] There was Ledoux, architect of Mme. du Barry's pavilion at Louveciennes, and Boullée, designer of Chaville, the house of his friends the de Tessés. Clearly the principle of the best building in France demanded a single story: "That is of the height of 16 or 18 ft. generally, and the whole of it given to rooms of entertainment; but in parts where there are bedrooms they have two tiers of from 8 to 10 ft. high each, with a small private staircase. By these means great staircases are avoided, which are expensive and occupy a space."[2]

In obedience to this principle, Jefferson decided that the second story must go to make way for the new Monticello. "The space that would be lost, by abandoning the second story could be regained, and more than regained, by doubling the width of the house. . . . A mezzanine . . . might . . . be adapted to the new portion, with windows so arranged that the effect of one story should not be destroyed."[3]

The whole front had to be torn down, and the portico moved forward to make room for the new east side of the house. One now entered through the great hall, connected by double doors with the parlor beyond. On either side of these two principal rooms there was space for two floors of the smaller rooms of half their ceiling height. On the east front the windows of the second floor were simply elongations of the first-floor windows. It was through this arrangement that Jefferson attained the desired appearance of a one-story villa. As these second-story windows were necessarily nearly at floor level, one hopes that the occupants were impervious to drafts.

Lateral halls divided the two sides of the new house; they accommodated the two small staircases, surely a minimum allotment of space for these essential elements. This was to become a typical feature of Jeffersonian design. The end rooms retained their semi-octagonal shape that had given character to the first house; they were joined by arched loggias which Jefferson called piazzas. The one on the south side off his bedroom suite was enclosed and used as a greenhouse. This whole symmetrical but far from simple design was crowned by the dome originally inspired by the Hôtel de Salm. The walls of the original second-story rooms on the west front were lowered to match the ceiling height of the parlor, on which the dome rested.

All this, of course, was not accomplished in a day. In fact it took some seventeen years, but Jefferson was impatient to start. In the winter of 1792, while still actively employed as secretary of state he was taking the necessary first steps: "This winter is employed in getting framing, lime stone, and bringing up stone for the foundation of the new part."[4] He calculated with his usual precision that tearing down the old walls plus 20,000 new bricks should suffice building to the water table. For building, as on the farm, Jefferson was forced to rely heavily on Randolph, the man on the spot. Randolph found it something of a burden.

Jefferson had hoped to return home the following spring, but the trouble with Hamilton and the attacks of the Federalists in Philadelphia determined him not to quit his post under fire. In 1793 Randolph wrote the beleaguered secretary of the problems of building with slave labor. "They are more awkward and clumsy than you can conceive and are really incapable of raising the coarsest building without someone to direct them in every part of the work."[5]

Jefferson replied that he had "entertained hopes of running up one flank of my house this fall, but I now apprehend we shall have to weather another winter in it as it is." As to employing "some industrious white person to direct them," it would surely have relieved his son-in-law, but Jefferson was in no financial position to do so. It was remarkable that he was able to complete this sophisticated construction with slave labor while he himself was so often absent from the scene. One feels it a strong possibility that without the arrival of James Dinsmore in 1798, the finishing work, at least, would have had to wait upon his own retirement.

To Jefferson this building of a home had something in it larger than the personal equation. True, he wished to bring the best of the old world to the new, but his vision did not stop there. He aspired always to a formal ideal, based ultimately on mathematical proportion. In this he followed Bacon, who believed that the basis of the natural world was mathematical, and as such was accessible to human intelligence. He had been seduced by the charm of the Hôtel de Salm, but when he set to work to adapt its plan to his own needs he was governed also by the strictest adherence to what he had learned of the golden mean and other examples of mathematical proportion as applied in architecture.

He owned *The Architecture of A. Palladio* in four volumes in the Leone edition, and there he found what he sought: ideal form related to a personal philosophy. Like Palladio's ancient sage, quoted in our first chapter, Jefferson was the center, the sun around which the design "for as much happiness as can be attained here below" revolved. The design has been criticized as "inconvenient, impractical," but Jefferson was not designing a modern brick rancher where every member of a nuclear family is made equally comfortable. His own quarters were located in the south wing where he could house a library of upward of six thousand volumes, instruments for scientific observation such as his theodolite and telescope, and a greenhouse with a variety of plants. Above all his own "cabinet" or study offered privacy and space where he could read and write in that special "whirligig chair," all this protected by double doors from any distraction from the public rooms. Martha and her husband had a comfortable bedroom above this wing, or, at other times, in the ground floor north wing, but the second- and third-floor bedrooms as a whole sacrificed interior comfort to exterior design. It was necessary to house a maximum number of family and guests while maintaining the exterior appearance of a one-story villa in the style of the Hôtel de Salm.

This relative inconvenience is gloriously compensated for by the dome room placed directly above the two-story parlor below. This roughly octagonal chamber with its row of circular windows floats above the landscape. Its dimensions approximate those of a Buckminster Fuller dome designed for individual use. Corbusier used the same idea in his little pavilion at Garche; he speaks of it as representing "at the same time a temple of love and the bridge of a ship." At Monticello it was to have varied uses, principally as a playroom for the Monticello grandchildren and later indeed as a "temple of love" when the eldest grandson and his bride spent their first year of marriage there.

The first-floor "public rooms" were designed not for public receptions or display, but for the private pleasure, and even instruction, of a select group of family and friends. In the long course of his remodeling, his plan of making his home a museum, as well as the resort of "virtuous friends and relations," was not much altered. As a young man Jefferson had visited the collection of Dr. John Morgan in Philadelphia and determined to do something of the same sort himself. The Hall now served his passion for scientific collection, and was later adorned with such scarcely decorative displays as elk heads, Indian weapons, and massive prehistoric bones. If Mrs. Jefferson had lived one can imagine that some of these items, although of undoubted scientific interest, might have been retired to the basement level.

The north wing contained a dining room, a tea room, and a bedroom for most-favored guests, now called the Madison Room because James and Dolley Madison slept there on their frequent visits to Monticello. When the family were alone in winter they often sat in the dining room, around the white-manteled fireplace with its charming blue-and-white Wedgwood insets, where Jefferson could enjoy his book, a candle, and his favorite armchair. In the summertime this room opened into the parlor; a long French mirror extended the line of sight.

In the words of an English visitor, Augustus Foster, the overall impression was one of "country elegance." The moderate size of the dining room was suited to a choice company rather than to public entertainment, nor was the presence of servants ever much favored by Jefferson. The table was served by dumbwaiters from a kitchen and wine cellar at the basement level at the other end of the house. Dishes were carried by servants the length of the cellar corridor. In fact the design of the dependencies functioning as two sides of an open-ended rectangle were opened at a lower level and were turned to the outside, away from the house, a device which effectively screened the service areas from contact with the house and west lawn.

All this, of course, was not completed in these early years. By dint of putting together various records from the Garden Book, the account books, and other sources, we may arrive at a sort of construction diary with which to follow the course of building. In 1794 Jefferson wrote to George Wythe that "we are now living in a brick kiln, for my house, in its present state, is nothing better."[6] Bricks werc all made in kilns on the place, located southwest of the house in a corner of the deer park, where the clay was most suitable. In the spring of 1795 we see John Hemings and four companions "turning over the brick earth."[7] Stone too, used in the foundations, was gathered or quarried on the place, and timbers were cut on his own or his neighbors' land. It was this use of native materials that made the Virginia mansions so much a part of the landscape in which they stood. In the case of Monticello the red brick and white trim gave the French styling an *American* look. On the other hand, in 1792 he could write to England "to have a sash made, and a skilled mason engaged."[8] Glass and paint were bought in Richmond or Philadelphia.

In the summer of '96, Ellen Wayles Randolph, the granddaughter of whom we shall hear more later, was born in the south pavilion. No other room was ready. Even Peter Carr, perennial resident, had been forced to take rooms in Charlottesville. Nor was the situation to change appreciably in the next two years. Around the end of November two major events occurred to interrupt the building program. One was "a severe frost" that put an end to work on the house for that year; the other was Jefferson's coming election, apparently without any effort of his own, to the vice-presidency. In 1797 the house could not be "covered," that is to say, adequately roofed, for Maria's wedding to her cousin Jack Eppes. The bride stepped through an opening in the half-completed floor and sprained her ankle, which delayed the start of that happy married life at Eppington.

In the records for early 1798 we learn that only two rooms, the parlor and the study, were covered. By May even Jefferson had yielded to a degree of impatience. He hopes that "I shall find the house nearly covered, and that we shall not be long without a shelter to unite under. 'Oh! Welcome hour whenever!'"[9] Luckily for future progress on the house it was at this time that he engaged the "fine housejoiner" James Dinsmore.

By 1799 things were looking up. Martha and her family moved over from Belmont, where they had been staying near the Edgehill property. By this time there were three little Randolphs and a fourth, Cornelia, was well on the way. Work at Monticello, of course, was still going on. Dinsmore and Johnny Hemings, fast developing into a housejoiner himself, put up the semicircular arch between the hall and parlor. For encouragement in his work Dinsmore received nearly one-half pint of whiskey a day, without apparent ill effect. It was Dinsmore who put up the dome, crowning the new house.[10]

During this year Jefferson was able to divide his time fairly equally between Monticello and his duties in Philadelphia as vice-president. In the following year, the year of his election to the presidency, an insurance record valued the dwelling at $5,000; the "Out Chamber" at $400; a stone house at $300; a joiners shop at $400; a stable at $200.[11]

Isaac Jefferson, Monticello slave, photograph taken in 1840s—*Alderman Library*

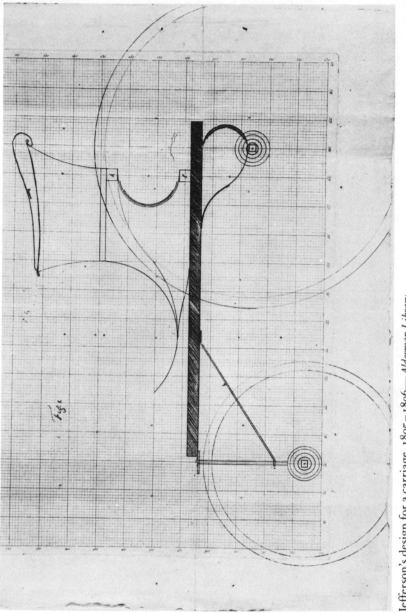

Jefferson's design for a carriage, 1805–1806—*Alderman Library*

Clothes press, 1765. An identical press was made to Jefferson's specifications by Peter Scott, Williamsburg, in 1773–1774—*Colonial Williamsburg*

Hôtel de Salm, oil on canvas, c. 1784. It was this Paris *hôtel* that influenced the rebuilding of Monticello

—*Musée Carnavalet, Paris*

Maria Cosway, self-portrait, engraving by Valentine Green
— *Thomas Jefferson Memorial Foundation*

Parlor, Monticello, two views. Of special interest in the upper picture are
the pier glass mirror, paintings, French chairs, and the beech and cherry
wood parquet floors—*Thomas Jefferson Memorial Foundation*. The lower photograph shows the door opening on the west portico and the "siesta chair"
made by John Hemings. The busts are of Alexander I and Napoleon—
Llewellyn

Jefferson's cabinet, with "whirligig" chair, polygraph or copying machine, and reading stand. His theodolite stands in the window at left, and a telescope and the Coffee bust of granddaughter Cornelia are in window at center—*William Faust*

Fig tree, southeast corner of terrace, showing Chinese trellis railing—*Lindsay Nolting*

Monticello, east front—*Thomas Jefferson Memorial Foundation*

Chapter 12

Reluctant Politician

Whenever I find myself very strongly compelled to any act, a doubt whether it be right always arises.

DURING THIS PERIOD of what Dumas Malone has referred to as that of "the flying brickbats" Randolph was for the most part absent from Monticello. With returning health he began to bethink himself of that long-deferred career in politics. He spoke from experience when he referred to "little specks of land, which so often prevent mental effort in youth."[1] From his not so little speck of land at Varina, Tom now summoned courage to declare his candidacy for the state legislature from Albemarle in the spring elections of '97. His father-in-law had already been elected vice-president of the United States, and although there is no record that Jefferson had renewed his earlier suggestions that the young man go out to win "the highest emploiments of your country and . . . its highest esteem,"[2] he did encourage his son-in-law's candidacy for the state legislature. Randolph himself had never forgotten his lofty ambitions dating from those Edinburgh days when Jefferson had first fired his political ambition.

It was one thing, however, to declare his candidacy from the relative peace and security of his own farm at Varina, but quite another to go politicking in Albemarle. The rough and tumble of polling day on the Court House Square is well described by an earlier observer:

At the place of voting the candidates would always have a barrel or two of mean whiskey for the gratuitous use of the voters. In those days faucets were scarce, so the 'sovereigns' would knock in the head of the barrel, and thus convert it into a great bucket; and as glasses were then unknown, and gourds very scarce, I have seen the people take their shoes and use them to drink the whiskey from, dipping them, without ceremony, into the barrel. Fights in those days were of course innumerable.[3]

It is not hard to imagine that Tom Randolph would not have felt at home in such a scene. He had never exposed himself in any public capacity; he had serious and, as it turned out, well-founded doubts about whether he would be able to take it. On the other hand, any occasion for scientific observation always appealed to him. Polling day, as always, was to be held in Charlottesville in the first week of April. The date happened to coincide, providentially as it may have appeared to the candidate, with an opportunity to have his children vaccinated against smallpox. Jefferson himself, of course, approved of vaccination. Randolph accompanied his children on this medical excursion, and simply failed to appear on polling day in Charlottesville. Martha was left to explain his absence, an explanation which did not arrive in time to be of any use. For the first time in their relationship Jefferson permitted himself a slight sign of disillusionment. He had asked his son-in-law to "inquire after our clover" on his way through Richmond to Charlottesville. After the fiasco at the polls (Wilson Cary Nicholas and Francis Walker were elected) Jefferson wrote the missing candidate:

Yours of March 31 did not come to hand till the 5th instant. It is a pity that it had not been received before the election, as it gave much uneasiness and embarrassment to your friends to be unable to give any account of you. It made a serious impression even on the zealous; and I have this day written a circular letter with the apologies your letter furnished, addressed to every militia captain for his company, which I hope will set the thing to rights. I am more anxious you should possess the affections of the people than that you should make any use of them. Their esteem will contribute much to your happiness: whether the offices they might confer would do so is another question. I will take care for the clover box. . . .[4]

If Tom was not chastened, he should have been.

During this year of trials the unsuccessful candidate consoled himself by writing in a commonplace book. It was always his fate to be intelligent enough to be aware of his own shortcomings, without the emotional stability to combat them. Martha, so intelligent herself and so perfect a partner for her father, seems to have been of little help in what would have been the considerable task of keeping her husband on an even keel. We have none of the letters that passed between husband and wife; following the example of Jefferson who had apparently destroyed every scrap of the letters to and from his own wife, Martha must have destroyed hers and her husband's, but there are enough comments in letters to other family members to show something, at least, of their relations. She was loyal, and there are indications of shared pleasures, particularly in regard to the girls. At times, in the words of their daughter Ellen, she "suffered greatly from [his] sullen moods and angry furies," although this aspect of Randolph's character was not to emerge fully until later years.

Martha's name does not appear in Randolph's commonplace book, where, along with practical notes on farming, he set down some intimate and revealing reflections. There was the fact, real enough but not yet overwhelming: "In the struggle between the farmer and his farm if it prove too much for him ruin ensues." And then the moment of self-knowledge: "Whenever I find myself very strongly compelled to any act, a doubt whether it be right always arises. The voice of reason is low and persuasive, that of passion is loud and imperious."[5] Of all her husband's traits Martha may have found this fatal indecision the most difficult to deal with. She had been raised by a man of absolute concentration of purpose, who never gave up a point. She herself was steady as a rock. To Martha, Tom's vacillations must have been a great trial. Others greater still were to follow.

The greatest source of worry, of course, was what were always referred to in the family as "pecuniary embarrassments." As early as 1793 Randolph had written to Jefferson that he feared "the price of Edgehill may be lost." Strapped as he was himself, such a thought was intolerable to Jefferson. He came at once to his son-in-law's aid, as indeed he was to do many times in the future. In the event of Randolph's being forced to borrow, he wrote, "I freely add my responsibility to your own."[6]

In early 1797 Jefferson, the determined foe of this culture, had been forced to "make tobacco for taxes and clothes." At this time Virginia planters were suffering from high British duties on tobacco, and from severe discrimination against American shipping. John Jay had been sent to Britain with the hope of negotiating better commercial relations with the British, or so Jefferson hoped, but the treaty that Jay brought back home with him secured even more firmly the British dominance in overseas trade. It prohibited any new or higher tonnage duties on British vessels, yet reserved to Britain the right to impose countervailing duties on the American.

Concessions such as these struck Jefferson with particular force. All his earlier work in Paris had been directed toward improving conditions of American overseas trade. Opposition to the evils of monopoly had become, for Jefferson, almost a moral principle; it was the very evil that the Jay Treaty now appeared to promote. The treaty, as we now know, was largely the work of the Anglophile Hamilton; it inevitably widened the gap between Republican and Federalist policies in the affairs of the nation.

Tobacco prices had always fluctuated, sometimes extremely. The causes for this were, of course, numerous: competition, the effect of European war on the market, and even the natural effects of good and poor growing seasons. But perhaps the Virginia planters were not far off the mark in charging most of their difficulties to the European monopolies and to the high duties on tobacco. Jefferson was also aware that monopolies catered to private interests and even led, as Hamilton himself frankly admitted, to corruption. The Jay Treaty confirmed all that he found most objectionable in the policy of his colleague at the Treasury.

In addition there was a matter that struck even nearer home to the Monticello family: the planters' debt to the British merchants. By the terms of the treaty this debt had to be paid. It was not that Jefferson wished to evade his own obligation; here again principle was involved. In October 1777 the state legislature had passed a law providing for the sequestration of the debts owed the British.[7] It could be considered an indemnity for war damage. Jefferson had paid the full amount of his own debt to be held by the state loan office. Eventually the state paid off at what amounted to about one dollar out of forty.[8] As he himself put it, the return from selling land that would have paid off his whole debt before the Revolution now left him just enough to buy an overcoat. To make matters worse, the bulk of this public debt had gone into the hands of city people, "the money men" as Jefferson called them, and the nation was being taxed to pay off at par securities that they had purchased for a few cents on the dollar.[9] It was a situation surely not calculated to endear the banking system to the Virginia planter.

Jefferson himself now had to pay a large debt a second time, under conditions much less favorable than had existed before the Revolution. However, personal hardship, real as it was, was not the crux of the matter. He saw it as an attack on government itself, at that most essential point, the division of powers. When the British merchants brought suit to recover the prewar debt, the Supreme Court of the United States decided in their favor, so that the treaty, that is, the executive branch of the government, was allowed to invalidate the Virginia law contrary to it. To Jefferson it was a major concern, clear evidence of the "monarchical" views of Hamilton and his Federalist supporters. It went a long way toward turning a country squire back into the political arena.

Jefferson, at times a reluctant politician himself, had been perfectly sincere in wishing for retirement, but as always there had been a conflict, the pull between his public and his private life. He took no part in the campaign that put his name forward in the election of 1796, but his sympathies were strongly engaged in what he saw as a fight to preserve Republican principles. In the event, he was called into service almost by public acclaim as the representative of Republicanism in the Adams administration. It was to be a sort of holding action, the beginning, perhaps, of the concept of "a loyal opposition" in a two-party system.

In the meantime the matter of the British debts fell very heavily on the Jefferson-Randolph family. Thomas Mann Randolph, Jr., and his brother lost a suit brought against them by three British firms, creditors of their father's estate. Out of a sum of almost $65,000, approximately $43,000 was levied against the defendants' own property, and the remainder was charged against the estate under their administration.[10]

The question of how and when to sell their tobacco was of course a highly-critical one to both Jefferson and his son-in-law. In February 1800 Randolph again found himself unable to meet payments on the Varina mortgage. He had held his own tobacco too long off the market and was forced to turn to Jefferson once more for help. He was of course aware of his father-in-law's own financial difficulties. A few weeks before Randolph's problem became pressing Jefferson had written, "My anxiety to get my lands rented is extreme," as he too was suffering from the rapid fall in the price of tobacco.[11] However, he had rallied what resources he could, and in March 1800 he managed to send George Jefferson, his Richmond agent, $1,000 on his son-in-law's account, with more to follow. Randolph's gratitude was almost abject. He was always as ready and unrestrained in admitting his faults as he was prone to commit them. "I cannot express the feelings your kindness excite: I was really on the point of ruin from my own neglect. I knew all along that I should not have one moment when the Varina debt *did* come on me, and should have sold my tobacco in full time to meet it if I had acted wisely: but a great price for that crop [would have] rendered me perfectly easy for life and I risked ruin with the hope of obtaining it and I fear have procured embarrassments for life."[12] In this supposition he was absolutely right.

For some reason which is not quite clear the young Randolphs' move to Edgehill was delayed. The family moved to Belmont, a house on land adjoining the Edgehill property, early in '98. The house may have been preferable to the building on Edgehill, but its comforts were not outstanding. Martha wrote her father of "the extreme dampness of the situation, and [of the] absolute want of offices of every kind to shelter the servants." There was more sickness than she had ever seen in any one family in her life. Such discomforts were not exceptional. Many of the gentry seem to have lived no better than the whites of "the meaner," or, as Martha more delicately put it, "the less considerable" sort.

This letter elicited an urgent invitation from Jefferson to his daughter to avail herself of the amenities of Monticello, but by this time Randolph was experiencing a keen desire to have his own place. Martha was willing to oblige him so long as her father remained in Philadelphia, but whenever he was at Monticello the whole family removed there. Her feelings had not changed. "I feel every day more strongly the impossibility of becoming habituated to your absence. Separated in my infancy from every other friend, and accustomed to look up to you alone, every sentiment of tenderness my nature was susceptible of was for many years centered in you, and no connexion formed since that could weaken a sentiment interwoven with my very existence."[13]

There is an almost Brontësque fervor in Martha's passion for her father. Both were happy in the knowledge that separation now could only be temporary; the move to Edgehill was imminent. From this time forward, in fact, on his return to Virginia from public business Jefferson always stopped first at Martha's home, insisting that she leave husband and children and accompany him to Monticello before he himself would set foot there.[14] In the light of the suppositions concerning Sally Hemings this is an interesting point. Would a lover rushing to the arms of his mistress wish always to be accompanied by his highly moral and shrewdly observant daughter?

The move to Edgehill, when it finally came on the first of the year 1800, brought no great improvement over Belmont. This time it was Tom, not Martha, who wrote Jefferson that "our situation from smoke, rain and wind thro badly finished windows and mud from the fresh earth taken out of the cellar still lying all around, is as uncomfortable as possible."[15] There was another baby in the house, Cornelia, Martha's fifth, but this was routine. Ellen Wayles had been born in '96; the first Ellen Wayles, the only child Martha was ever to lose, had died in infancy the year before. Tom reported his family "in good health and spirits," but the emotional climate was not perfectly tranquil.

Martha wanted to go to Eppington to be with her sister for the birth of her first child, but Tom objected. When word came that Maria had lost her baby, a tiny daughter, Martha reported her feelings in one short sentence: "I would give the world to fly to her comfort at this moment but having been disappointed before in doing what perhaps my *anxiety only* termed a moral duty I am afraid to indulge any more hopes upon that subject." [16]

Tom may have felt some remorse, for two weeks later they visited Eppington together. When it was a matter of medical treatment he was in his element. The dear old family doctor, Dr. Currie, whose cures, Jefferson declared, were more to be dreaded than the disease, had kept Maria in bed and dosed her with castor oil. Tom managed to relieve her suppurating breasts and to recruit her strength. It must have been a happy visit after all.

Chapter 13

The President's Daughters

The heart swellings with which I address you when absent and look forward to your return convince me of the folly or want of feeling of those who dare to think that any new ties can weaken the first and best of nature.—MJR to TJ, July 1, 1798

ALL DURING HIS vice-presidency Jefferson had longed for home. Nothing but the most critical conditions at the capital could have persuaded him to prolong his absence from this most desired scene. His position as vice-president in John Adams's presidency had become increasingly difficult. Honest John Adams, the staunch old patriot, was reacting more and more aggressively to the pressures of politics, until he appeared to embrace the most extreme Hamiltonian views of the executive power. The Alien and Sedition acts were indeed the last straw. Anti-French hysteria was rife at the time, and the Alien Act empowered the president to deport any alien that he thought dangerous. Equally arbitrary was the Sedition Act, aimed at suppressing all criticism of the government by the press, and hence effectively muzzling the Republican party.

Such measures struck at the very heart of Jefferson's political philosophy, and when the Republican party called upon him as their leader, personal preference faded into the background. He rose automatically to meet the public challenge. As the favored candidate of the Republican party Jefferson ran for president in the election of 1800.

Unfortunately the electoral procedure of the period had made no distinction between candidates for president and vice-president, so that a tie vote developed between Aaron Burr and Jefferson, although there had never been any doubt as to which man had been the public choice for top place. The vote was then thrown from the Electoral College into the House of Representatives, to become at once a political football. Dumas Malone put it succinctly: "Jefferson would be supported by the states with a Republican majority, Burr by those with a Federalist."[1] For six desperate days the tie persisted. On the thirty-sixth ballot James A. Bayard of Delaware changed his vote, and Jefferson became the third president of the United States—in the words of du Pont de Nemours, "the greatest man in [the] greatest place."[2]

One can imagine that tempers throughout the country had run high. There had actually been fears of a Federalist coup to keep Jefferson from the presidency. Tom Randolph had been all for raising a company of volunteers to enforce the will of the people. He designed a banner emblazoned with the words: "No repose! But *on* the lap of liberty or *in* the bosom of earth!"[3] He was not alone in this militancy, and in fact Randolph, now a major in the militia, was sent by Governor James Monroe on a special mission to make sure that the Federalist opposition should not seize arms and ammunition from the arsenal at New London. Randolph performed this mission with tact, and returned home feeling better about himself. The role of military man had an irresistible appeal to this belligerent Randolph, who had so often to confess failure in civilian affairs. With the departure of Jefferson for Washington, where the capital was now placed, Randolph again shouldered the additional responsibilities of Monticello, as well as of Varina and Edgehill.

We would not know Jefferson if we did not realize that these events in no way lessened his expectations and concern for family life. Two years earlier, when Martha had had every expectation of his returning home she had written the passionate expression of her devotion: "The heart swellings with which I address you when absent and look forward to your return convince me of the folly or want of feeling of those who dare to think that any *new* ties can weaken the first and best of nature."[4]

So much for Tom! Now, for the next eight years, she must share her father with "a concourse of strangers." Jefferson took a brighter view. He assured his younger daughter that the distance from

Washington, the site of the new capital, "is so moderate that I should hope a journey to this place would be scarcely more inconvenient than one to Monticello."[5]

The distance, however, was more than geographical. When urged to visit her father Maria replied much as she had when asked to leave Eppington for Paris: "It would make me most happy to go to Washington to see you but I have been so little accustomed to be in as much company as I should be in there to receive the civilitys and attentions which as your daughter I should meet with and return, that I am sensible it is best for me to remain where I am."[6]

Maria was speaking from a long-held conviction. She had always done her best to please her father, but somehow she had never felt her best to be good enough. Eppington was her spiritual home. Maria's childhood correspondence with her father has a certain fascination. Called upon to list the birds she has seen, in the spirit of natural philosophy, she tells him "As for the martins, swallows and whippoorwills I was so taken up with my chickens that I never attended to them and therefore cannot tell you when they came. . . ."[7] This although Jefferson had threatened to tell her aunt Eppes to make her go without her dinner until she had answered his letters.[8] As a father he was rarely punitive—this letter seems to be the only example—but it was always difficult for him to accept that his younger daughter was simply incapable of turning into a replica of himself. That feat was reserved for Martha. Maria admired her father, she loved him in an awestruck sort of way, but clearly she could not see herself in the role of the president's daughter.

Jefferson's reply is significant as it throws a somewhat different light on his usually expressed attitude toward retirement. "I am convinced our own happiness requires that we should continue to mix with the world, and to keep pace with it as it goes. . . . I can speak from experience on this subject. From 1793 to 1797 I remained closely at home, saw none but those who came there, and at length became very sensible of the ill effect it had upon my own mind, and of its direct and irresistible tendency to render me unfit for society."[9]

Maria had no illusions. She never counted herself as behind her sister in love for their father, but in this year of 1801 she wrote that she was "sensible of the distance which Nature has placed between my sister and myself, the tender affection I feel for her, makes me judge what yours must be, and I rejoice that you have in her so great a source of comfort and one who is in every way so worthy of you, satisfied if my dear Papa is only assured that in the tender love to him I yield to no one."[10]

The modest girl had turned into an exquisitely beautiful woman. Peachy Gilmer's description of Maria's beauty is particularly touching when we think how little she herself regarded it. This friend of the Monticello family had ample opportunity to know both sisters, and his descriptions, if a trifle overblown, bring both to life. Of Maria he wrote: "Her complexion was exquisite, her features all good, and so arranged as to produce an expression such as I never beheld in any other countenance: sweetness, intelligence, tenderness, beauty were exquisitely blended in her countenance. Her eye, fine blue, had an expression that cannot I think be described."[11]

Gilmer has also given us a nicely contrasting picture of Martha:

Mrs. Randolph is decidedly the most accomplished woman I have ever known: her person tall, large, loosely made, and awkward; but her actions and manner are graceful, easy, and engaging, her face not what would be esteemed beautiful, but her features are flexible and playful, and agreeable. An expression of intelligence always animates her countenance; a turn for the ludicrous, a sweet and variable voice, the contraction of the muscles about the eyes when she speaks, vast and various information, frankness and eloquence far above what I have ever met with in any other person of her sex, give a charm to her manners and conversation.[12]

Although Martha may have had some faults not noted by this admirer, his observation appears nevertheless to be accurate. Maria's beauty was always remarked, but she could be vexed by allusions to it. "People only praise me for that," she said, "because they cannot praise me for better things."[13]

Another glimpse of the sisters is given by the slave Isaac, who shows us Maria standing one day in the garden:

Billy Giles courted Miss Polly, old Master's daughter. Isaac one morning saw him talking to her in the garden, right back of the nail factory shop; she was lookin' on de ground. All at once she wheeled round and come off. *That* was the time she turned him off. Isaac never so sorry for a man in all his life—Sorry because everybody thought that she was going to marry him. Mr. Giles give several dollars to the servants, and when he went away that time he never came back no more. His servant Arthur was a big man. Isaac wanted Mr. Giles to marry Miss Polly. Arthur always said that he was a mighty fine man. He was very rich; used to come to Monticello in a monstrous gig— mighty few gigs in dem days with plated mountin's and harness.

Isaac also had his view of Martha: "a mighty peaceable woman; never holler for servant; make no fuss nor racket; pity she ever died!" [14]

Without being aware of this himself Jefferson had tended to show his preference for Martha's society, and Maria had felt it deeply. Never one to hide her feelings she told Martha that their father, however equally he might divide his attentions and his gifts between them, had made a most unequal division of his affections. Martha's daughter Ellen described the situation to Henry S. Randall at the time of his inquiries about family affairs: "My mother told her father, who had not been aware of the state of his younger daughter's feelings. . . . From this time it was almost always upon Maria that he called for the little personal attentions that he sought from his daughters. He addressed himself to her for many small offices which brought them closer together. My aunt became perfectly satisfied, at ease in the coveted share of her father's love—while my mother rejoiced that the shadow had passed from her sister's spirit." [15] Perhaps, but we may suppose that it did not entirely pass until her marriage to her kindly and cheerful young cousin, Jack Eppes. While her admiration for her father remained unbounded, Eppington was always Maria's spiritual home.

Jefferson was almost as assiduous in his efforts to bring Jack and Maria near to Monticello as he had once been to bring the young Randolphs to Edgehill. Pantops, just across the river from Monticello, was to be the Eppes part of the family enclave. In the fall of 1801 he was urging Eppes to level Pantops Mountain for a building site. "This business," he wrote (referring to a plan to divide a part of his Bedford land between his two sons-in-law), "and Pantops would give you so much to do in the upper country [i.e., Albemarle and Bedford] that I should think you and Maria had better make Monticello your headquarters for the next year." [16]

Eppes turned a deaf ear to these blandishments. There was an enormous attraction to the Monticello circle, which Maria undoubtedly felt; the difference between the Randolphs and the Eppeses was that Jack Eppes remained in the lower country. He remained his own man. Without at all separating Maria from her place in the Monticello family, he contrived to keep her an Eppes in a way that Martha never really became a Randolph.

In 1802 Eppes was elected to the House of Representatives of the Eighth Congress by his neighbors of Chesterfield, Amelia, Powhatan, and Goochland counties. The ensuing separation from her beloved husband was not easy for Maria. Her letters to Jack are natural and unstrained: "Our little one is well," she tells him, "and the most affectionate thing breathing." She is with Martha at Monticello, and she chides him for neglecting to write. "Have the pleasures of Washington made you already forget us? . . . My sister proposed by way of retaliation to direct this letter for you and raise your expectations [perhaps that Maria was on her way to join him?] . . . but I could not agree that you should feel so much disappointment from a letter of mine." [17]

Another letter, from Monticello, is like a window opening on that domestic life:

I have only time to write a line to you, my dearest husband, the incessant round of company we are in scarcely allowing time to dress to receive them. I am at this moment writing whilst waiting for a gown to be smoothed, though the drawing room is full of ladies. Your dear son . . . is now venturing across the room alone and begins to do it very boldly. How often do I wish that you could behold his dear little figure tottering along with his hands extended to balance himself. . . .

Adieu most beloved of my heart. Nothing can equal the joy with which I shall return to you after so long a separation.[18]

So we see that Maria, when inspired by uninhibited affection, could write after all.

Chapter 14

"An *Affectionate* and Loyal Servant . . ."

THESE YEARS WERE also to mark changes among the slave families, which Martha reported to her father. Sally Hemings's first child, "poor little Harriet," born in 1795, had died during the cold winter of '98.[1] Sally's next child, Beverly, was born in the same year. He was a bright boy, nearly white in color, who could, and did later, actually pass for white after he had been allowed to "run away" to the north.[2] In his memoirs, Isaac remembered him in Petersburg "when the balloon went up, the balloon that Beverly sent off."[3] As he does not elaborate further, we do not know what exactly was Beverly's role on this occasion.

The most serious loss to Jefferson had been, of course, that of his old favorite, Jupiter. Betty Hemings's grandson Burwell, then a lad of seventeen, was soon to fill this most intimate and important place in the Monticello household. In addition he was an expert house painter. As late as 1809 Bacon, Jefferson's longtime overseer, described him on the roof of Monticello painting the tin roof, and giving precise directions as to the necessary quantities of oil and white lead required.[4]

In 1800–1801, as so often before, the key role in the Jefferson-Hemings story goes to James. After his return to Monticello James spent about two years training his brother Peter in the arts of French cookery. As with everything else at Monticello the standard was high. Some of the recipes, preserved in handwriting, were bilingual, as in "Meringues: 12 blanc d'oeuf, les fouettes bien ferme, 12 cueillerres de sucre en poudre, put them by little and little into the whites of eggs, fouetter le tout ensemble, dresser les sur un papier avec un cueiller de bouche, mettez les dans un four bien doux, that is to say an oven after the bread is drawn out."[5] In any case the results were delicious.

At last the job was done; James, and presumably Jefferson, was satisfied with Peter's skill. In 1796 James received his freedom, and left for Philadelphia with Jefferson's blessing and $30 in his pocket.[6] Plainly he had not wanted to stay at Monticello, but Philadelphia, for the freedman, did not turn out to be the expected haven. The simple truth was that James belonged nowhere. James was an artist, and the Paris he had sensed, even the Philadelphia he knew, could never be wholly his. He was never content with the subsidiary role open to the freed blacks of the day.

Even in Philadelphia there was prejudice. Benjamin Franklin himself had demanded, "Why increase the sons of Africa, by Planting them in America, when we have so fair an opportunity, by excluding all Blacks and Tawneys, of increasing the lovely white and red?"[7] When James returned to Philadelphia, a free man, this attitude had not substantially changed. If any, it had hardened.

From what James's nephew Madison tells us of his own life it is clear that at least one Hemings slipped easily enough into the subordinate role, but it was not for James. His years in Paris, even—I think—his lifelong association with Jefferson, had taught him differently. It is difficult to escape the conclusion that Jefferson himself, not his roots in his black family at Monticello, was James's security blanket. The relationship, however, was ambivalent. In the last year of James's life it became one of advance and retreat, as much on Jefferson's part as that of his servant. To James, in fact, goes the distinction of showing us Jefferson in a rare moment of indecision, even of self-doubt.

It appears that James had not settled permanently. Only a little more than a year after his departure from Monticello Jefferson met him in Philadelphia, and speaks of his "return to this place. . . . He tells me his next trip will be to Spain." Obviously James is restless. In his choice of Spain he has shown considerable sophistication, for in Spain, then as now, there was less than the usual amount of prejudice against the blacks. But the state of James's finances would hardly have permitted such a trip, as Jefferson seems to have been aware. "I have endeavored to persuade him to stay where he is, and lay up money." Sage advice, but like most sage advice not apt to be taken. There had been a rumor that James was drinking, but he did not appear "given up to drink" at this meeting.[8]

The next we hear of James is some four years later. He is now in Baltimore. It is 1801, and the slave revolt in Sainte Dominique, compounded by Gabriel's rebellion nearer home in Richmond, has not made the freedman's lot any easier. Jefferson, newly elected to the presidency, needed a cook, and James wanted to come back. At least he has intimated as much, but apparently cannot quite come out with it. The following exchange is through an intermediary, William Evans, a former employer of James. On February 22, five days after his election on the thirty-sixth ballot as the third president of the United States, Jefferson's thoughts again turn to James. He writes to Evans:

You mentioned to me in conversation that you sometimes saw my former servant James and that he has made his engagements such as to keep himself always free to come to me. Could I ask the favor of you to send for him and tell him that I shall be glad to receive him as soon as he can come . . . ?

I told him if I should be able to employ him I would write to him and he returned to Baltimore on this ground. In truth I would rather he would decline it. Should he be with you, or fall with your way, I would thank you to discourage him from the idea. He was *an affectionate and loyal servant* to me which makes me unwilling to reject him—and yet the fear of his drinking . . . induces me rather to wish that [he] decline the thought. I owe you many apologies for troubling you with these small things, but the truth is that I am as confounded awkward in engaging a good household for myself, as in providing a good administration for the country.

This, from Mr. Jefferson, is a less than usually guarded letter, particularly in regard to the almost unprecedented use of the word "confounded" (spelled "conf."), and also a very untypical note of indecision. Jefferson is clearly torn, between loyalty to James and a by-now well-founded doubt that James is the man for the job.

Evans replied on February 27:

Honored sir: Your favor of the 22nd instant came duly to hand. That part of the contents of which relative to your former servant James I immediately communicated to him. He told that he was under an engagement to Mr. Peck, a tavern keeper of this place, which he said was out of his power to relinquish for a few days. I told him to be particular in mentioning the time he could be in readiness to go [to] you. He gave me for answer that he would make up his mind in the course of the evening and let me know his determination, but on finding that he did not call agreeable to promise I sent for him a second time. The answer that he returned to me was that he *would not go until you should write to him himself*.

So we see Jefferson advancing, if hesitantly, and James retreating nervously, perhaps from pride, or perhaps, as Jefferson now suggests, from "some attachment formed in Baltimore." In any case Jefferson's reply is not received until nearly a month later, on March 31:

I supposed I saw in the difficulties caused by James unwillingness to come, arising wholly from some attachment he has formed at Baltimore, for I cannot suspect an indisposition towards me. I concluded at once, therefore, not to urge him against inclination, and wrote to Philadelphia where I have been successful in getting a cook equal to my wishes. . . . I cannot bear a servant who drinks. . . . I wish James to understand that it was an acquiescence to what I supposed his own wish that I did not repeat my application, having so long rested in the expectation of having him.[9]

James may have sensed his employer's attitude, for certainly Jefferson is feeling well out of a difficult situation. Nevertheless, for Jefferson it is a self-justifying letter. The whole episode suggests the vicissitudes of an ambiguous relationship rather than the straightforward one of employer and employee. On James's side there is ambivalence and pride; in Jefferson caution and reason must struggle with a sense of responsibility: James has been "an *affectionate* and loyal servant." He is unwilling to reject him, and yet he does. Emotion is involved on both sides, and Jefferson comes as near as he ever did to admitting a sense of guilt. The condition of slavery has marked both men: it is the unseen spring motivating their responses.

The story does not end here, for James does return, not to Jefferson in Washington, but to Jefferson at Monticello. His return is even more dubious, even more hesitant. Nerves had been strained all over Virginia by the recent aborted uprising known as "Gabriel's Rebellion." James wonders about being "among strange servants," which must be his euphemism for the slave society, as the servants at Monticello obviously are not strange, but his own family. At the time of his return there was "a fracas" at Monticello, upsetting enough to cause James's sister Critta to wish to leave.[10] She had gone with Maria to spend the winter in the more tranquil surroundings of Eppington. The "fracas" is not described further, and whether or not it had to do with James is never stated, but surely James, the alienated, the freedman, and moreover already drinking heavily, would have been a source of disturbance at Monticello. Whatever the cause he stayed only a little more than six weeks. When Jefferson left for the capital James too was off again.

In November Jefferson wrote to Evans. He wished to know whether the report was true that "James Hemings, my former cook, had committed an act of suicide."

"Yes," replied Evans, "the report is true . . . [James] had been delirious for some days previous . . . drinking too freely was the cause."[11]

What had happened to the bright boy that Jefferson had known since childhood, the boy, moreover, who had been ambitious enough to study French grammar on his own? More than other Hemingses he had seen the promised land, and found the gate barred. James's story is a footnote to history, as well as a personal tragedy. Jefferson's interest in colonization of the blacks, and his increasing conviction that free black and white could not prosper together in the new world may well have taken its strongest impulse from the troubled career and tragic end of his servant James.

Trouble, indeed, was a built-in factor of the Jefferson-Hemings relationship. The confused and bitterly contested election of 1800 had exacerbated party feeling to a degree unheard of even in that day of violent political controversy. Old ladies in New England were hiding their Bibles in hollow trees in anticipation of the election of the atheist Jefferson. An edict was expected banning their use. Party feeling took to the streets: "Before the government was removed from Philadelphia [Mr. Jefferson] had repeatedly the Rogues March played after him in the streets. If he found a crowd before him he found it prudent to pass through some less frequented street. A volunteer company of clerks [?] called by their opponents silk stocking gentry became noted for their insults to the Republican members of the government. A company of 'butcher boys,' Republicans, was formed, and threatened an attack on the silk stocking gentry. . . ."[12] Perhaps Tom's fear of a coup had not been so farfetched after all.

During the campaign these attacks against Jefferson had mainly been on religious grounds, and even, in South Carolina, on his liberal views on slavery. The sex-oriented slanders came later, shortly after his inauguration. Their disgruntled author and virtually sole originator was the hack journalist Jack Thomson Callender.[13] It was this man, disappointed in his bid for the position of postmaster in Richmond, who started the story that has reverberated to this day, that Sally Hemings was Jefferson's mistress. Without mentioning any source of information Callender claimed that Jefferson had a son called Tom by Sally. The boy as described by Callender was at this time ten or twelve years old. The only other source of this story of Jefferson's amour with Sally as told today by Fawn Brodie and others is an interview with Sally's second son, Madison, who incidentally failed to mention the existence of Tom. In fact there is *no* contemporary evidence to the Sally Hemings story, and it was more than once explicitly stated by those familiar with the scene that Peter Carr, Jefferson's nephew, was the father of Sally's children.[14]

It is not my purpose here to go over these somewhat tired charges. They have been answered, so far as such undocumented charges are capable of being answered, by virtually every Jefferson scholar in the field. The legitimate point of interest, I think, is in the quality of the slanders, and the family reaction to them. It is true that Sally was almost white, and we do know that she was beautiful; she was remembered by a Monticello slave as having long straight hair down her back. Perhaps naturally she became the subject of scurrilous verses hurled at Jefferson by political enemies during his presidency. John Quincy Adams, who should have known better, produced the following:

> Let dusky Sal henceforth bear
> The name of Isabella;
> And let the mountains, all of salt,
> Be christened Monticella—[15]

This was intended as a lampoon upon the journey to the west by Meriwether Lewis, which was, of course, one of the great achievements of the Jefferson administration. It is mild indeed compared to the effusions of Federalist hacks. The following appeared in *The Philadelphia Portfolio*, a "genteel" publication:

> *"A Song supposed to have been written by*
> *the sage of Monticello."*
>
> Of all the damsels on the green
> On mountain or in valley
> A lass so luscious ne'er was seen
> As Monticellian Sally.
>
> CHORUS
> Yankee Doodle, whose the noodle?
> What wife were half so handy
> To breed a flock of slaves to stock,
> A blackamoors the dandy.[16]

"Every decent man," exclaimed Jefferson, "revolts at such filth." It was a private response. Publicly he remained silent. But the relatively more polished verses of the Irish poet Thomas Moore finally drove his daughter to revolt. Moore had felt himself snubbed by Jefferson, and retaliated in this fashion:

> The patriot fresh from freedom's councils comes,
> Now pleased retires to lash his slaves at home,
> Or woo perhaps some black Aspasia's charms,
> And dream of freedom in his bondsmaid's arms.[17]

Hot with indignation Martha confronted her father with this latest outrage. Jefferson only smiled.[18] Long ago he had decided that abuse of this kind "must be submitted to like the physical scourges of tempest, fire, etc." His considered opinion was written to his friend James Logan in Philadelphia: "As to political slanders I never wished them to be answered but by the tenor of my life." And to another friend he wrote in a rather more practical vein: "It has been so impossible to contradict all of their lies that I have determined to contradict none, for while I should be engaged with one, they would publish twenty new ones."

During all this *sturm und drang* most Hemingses, in fact, were remaining quietly and busily at home. John Hemings was working with Dinsmore on the details of the interior woodwork. As soon as the new rooms were plastered, boxes of composition ornaments began to arrive from the shop of George Andrews in Washington.[19] As he was to do later at the University of Virginia, Jefferson was planning to use specimens of different classical motifs at Monticello. Models for the friezes were taken from Antoine Desgodetz's *Edifices Antiques de Rome*. In antique times these models had been charged with symbolic meaning; ox skulls, for example, referred to religious sacrifice and were symbols of fecundity. The sacrificial instruments portrayed in the parlor frieze belonged to this idea.[20] While Dinsmore or James Oldham, another white craftsman, were installing these ornaments, John Hemings was also doing fine work. In 1803 a memo in Jefferson's own hand shows that he was doing "all the Chinese railing, folds of window shutters, Venetian blinds," and other work on virtually a cabinetmaker's level. He himself was later to have complete charge of the ornamental friezes at Poplar Forest.[21]

On the domestic scene it was John's task to cut up the meat. Ursula (we have heard of her as pastry cook and will hear of her later as the children's mammy) was to take care of the salting. These instructions too came in Jefferson's hand. Nothing was too small, or too detailed, for his personal attention. But one cannot please everyone, nor could everyone appreciate what was so painstakingly taking place at Monticello. There was, for example,

Mrs. William Thornton. She visited on a dreary day of autumn, while Jefferson was still obviously in the throes of architectural creation. An extract from her diary of 1802 follows:

Tho I had been prepared to see an unfinished house, still I could not help being much struck with the uncommon appearance and which the general gloom which prevailed contributed much to increase— We went through a large unfinished hall, loose plank forming the floor, lighted by one dull lantern, into a large room with a small bow and separated by an arch, where the company were seated at tea—no light being in the large part of the room and part of the family being seated there, the appearance was irregular and unpleasant. When we went to bed we had to mount a little ladder of a staircase about two feet wide and very steep, into rooms with the beds fixed up in recesses in the walls—the windows square and small and turning on pivots. Everything had a whimsical and droll appearance.

Clearly she had not been given the best room.

When outdoors Mrs. Thornton was no less critical:

There is something grand and awful in the situation but far from convenient or in my opinion agreeable—it is a place you would rather look at now and then than live at. . . .

The President was very much engaged and interested in a phaeton which he has had constructed after eight years preparation—The mind of the P. of the U.S. ought to have more important occupation.

Four years later on a second visit Mrs. Thornton allows that there has been considerable improvement: "It is now quite a handsome place. The floor of the drawing room is laid with beech and cherry tree woods in a very neat manner. It cost 200D the workman said. He would not do another like it for 400D."[22] Mrs. Thornton knew something that had cost money when she saw it, but she probably was not aware that the wood from the floor had come from Albemarle trees, from Col. Coles's cherry trees,[23] to be exact, or of the careful work of the black and white hands that had transformed plank into parquet floor. Nor had the president of the United States told her of some other concerns that had occupied his attention at the time of her first visit. Along with the design of the phaeton there had been the little matter of the cession of the

Louisiana Territory to France with all the enormous threat that this posed to the western states. As usual Jefferson was performing his incredible balancing act: the world and Monticello were equally on his mind, and at the same time.

Not everything, of course, was as successful as the parquet floor, or even as the Louisiana Purchase. While sitting for his portrait the president asked Gilbert Stuart for advice: What color should he paint the hall floor of Monticello?

"Grass green," replied the Master, without batting an eye, and no doubt this was the color that Burwell used.[24]

In regard to one slave in particular it has been asked why the special target of so much abuse was not simply removed from Monticello. Later references to Sally, which we will come to in due time, show that she was a valued member of the Monticello "family." It is worth noting that no Hemings, with the possible exception of Jamey Hubbard, was ever sold from that house unless at his own request. The Hemingses' position was secure. They played, in fact, an important role; they were an essential part of the character of the house.

Chapter 15

A Silly Bird Among the Swans

IN THE PUBLIC ARENA the problem of Louisiana was looming large. So long as a nearly powerless Spain controlled this territory there was virtually no threat to American trade using the Mississippi. It was the outlet to the sea essential to the new states forming east of the river. In 1802 the position dramatically changed, when Spain ceded Louisiana to France. Jefferson had now to deal with Napoleon, an alarming change indeed. Fortunately for America the emperor (he was still at this time called first consul) was to suffer a reverse in the West Indies. Napoleon decided that perhaps one hemisphere was sufficient to occupy his depredations.

Jefferson proceeded cautiously. By means of negotiations too complicated to detail here he achieved the greatest single success of his administration: the Louisiana Purchase. A territory, of which the actual extent could not be determined at the time, passed to the United States without the shedding of one drop of blood. For a while the outcome had hung in the balance. The European situation was notoriously unstable; there was the very real danger that Napoleon might change his mind. For a man committed to a strict interpretation of the Constitution, Jefferson took a great deal upon himself in consummating such a deal, but in such a case he was prepared to act. Later on he described the situation succinctly: "A strict observance of the written laws is doubtless *one* of the high duties of a good citizen, but it is not the *highest*. The laws of necessity, of self-preservation, of saving our country when in danger, are of higher obligation." [1]

The news of the signing of the treaty with France reached Washington on July 3, 1803, and thus was published to the nation by the *National Intelligencer* on July 4. [2] It was indeed the physical consummation of the moral statement of the Declaration. A whole continent was opening up, preparing to embrace those principles of freedom.

During this summer so charged with public events Jefferson was at home at Monticello.[3] He could give his attention to improvements there as well as to world events (the official correspondence concerning Louisiana was conducted by Secretary of State Madison), but the plantation was rapidly becoming too heavy a burden. Neither Jefferson nor his son-in-law was out of debt at this time. With Jefferson there was always the matter of not driving his slaves on the land, and of using many of them for improvements unrelated to profit. It was this, and not only his long absences from home, which caused him to say: "I am not fit to be a farmer with the kind of labor we have."[4]

He was not alone in this predicament, although admittedly it affected him to a greater extent than it did his less scrupulous or less imaginative neighbors. Slavery was the burden on the back of every Virginia planter, and so long as wheat and tobacco remained the money crops, it hung about their necks like an albatross. There was no getting away from slave labor. In 1800 one of Jefferson's slave rolls showed that, out of ninety-six slaves, twenty-seven were children ten years and under; of the remaining sixty-nine some were too old to work. In 1810 a similar list showed that ninety-five out of two hundred slaves were under the age of fourteen, and that twenty were more than fifty years old.[5] In the prevailing economy there would have been no way of supporting this crowd of dependents in conditions of freedom. Even independent white landowners were heading for better conditions out west. The black freedmen who did subsist in the neighborhood were a recognized menace, known to support themselves by thievery for lack of other means. Jefferson had put this situation fairly enough: "A man's moral sense must be unusually strong, if slavery does not make him a thief; he who is permitted by law to have no property of his own, can with difficulty perceive that property is founded on anything but force."[6]

It was force, black force, that was now widely feared. Gabriel's

Revolt, even aborted, had left its mark on all the surrounding counties. Even at Monticello the threat had been felt. In a letter to Monroe, Jefferson said that he thought the hangings had gone far enough, but he did not question the mood that had inspired them.

Randolph had never been really happy in that society. He had always had misgivings about conditions at Edgehill; he had not originally welcomed the responsibility of so large and so hilly a tract, necessarily cultivated by slaves. According to the later judgment of his super-realist son Jeff, his father was too easy on his slaves. He did not, said Jeff, give sufficient authority to his overseers, an important point as his farming operations were so scattered as to make his own constant presence impossible. Randolph could lose his never very secure temper at bungled work, but never carried severity very far. One day, riding through a field of badly shocked corn, he had spurred up his horse and overturned a whole row of the offending stacks. Arriving at the barn he had only exclaimed "in his big grum voice," "the old bull must have got loose in the field."[7]

The greatest difficulty, and the greatest physical strain, were due to the distance he was required to cover in overseeing his farms. This of course was particularly true when he stayed with his family at Monticello. If he wished to see his family this was the only course open to him. He had been known to insist on his wife's presence when it had been a matter of her going to her sister's confinement, but to delay her going to her father by as much as twenty-four hours was quite beyond his capacity. "If my grandfather," said Jeff, "visited home for a week he came to my father to breakfast and would not leave until every member of the family accompanied him."[8] Martha, in fact, was quite willing to leave her oldest son alone at Edgehill, save for the Negroes, so that he could attend day school nearby, while she herself stayed with her father at Monticello.

To attend to his own farms Randolph moved at a desperate pace. In the winter months he might breakfast by candlelight, and not return until after dark. Rain or snow he was on horseback, traveling from farm to farm, often on business to Richmond eighty miles away. If dark caught him miles from home he would still push on, fording or swimming in the night the treacherous rivers. Even the Secretary's Ford, at the foot of Monticello Mountain, was bridge-less, so that his late homecomings were rarely free of effort and danger. His reputation for this breakneck activity was well known. In the recollections of a certain Dr. Massie, Thomas Mann is erroneously referred to as Jeff Mann Randolph, but the anecdote recorded there has the ring of truth:

Jeff Mann Randolph was a very eccentric man, if not deranged. His most striking eccentricity was an invariable habit of traveling to any point he might desire to reach by the most direct line even if his course should be across fields, rivers, mountains, or any other impediments of man or nature. This habit was so inveterate that he would prefer to encounter the forests and cliffs of mountains if they lay in his way, rather than go a mile further around by an excellent road. And he would swim the most dangerous streams, in times of freshets, rather than cross a bridge. I remember that he once bought an excellent horse, from a gentleman in the western part of Virginia. This man did not see Randolph until four years afterwards, when happening to meet with [him] he asked him how he liked his horse. Randolph's reply was that the horse was an admirable one, and had but one fault, which was that of dodging floating trees when swimming swollen rivers.[9]

Randolph himself never followed the example of the horse!

His second daughter, Ellen, was to understand her father very well. In a later description she declared that nothing would have pleased him more than "the ability to surround his wife and children with all that wealth could give." It was at this time that a dream of this sort lifted the spirits of the besieged planter. His plan was to buy land and to plant cotton in Mississippi. He gave Jefferson a detailed account of his reasons.

You know the risk of loss from large slave establishments after the West Indies manner at this day in Virginia, and the little hope of profit from the culture of tobacco now; with the certainty of immense gain from that of cotton. You know that the oeconomic husbandry now necessarily introducing here from the multiplicity of objects it em-braces; animals of various kinds, grapes, grains, roots, manures, various and complicated instruments, geometric methods; cannot be suc-cessfully pursued by means of slaves (who tho admirable for labor are little worth for care and judgement), unless upon a very small scale and when the person feeling the first interest joins in the daily business of the farm. You know that a climate without winter suits the constitu-tion of Negroes and have heard that the culture of cotton is the least laborious of any ever practised, never occasioning great fatigue and leaving abundant time for the raising provisions of every kind. It all works for the comfort of the laborers.

Mere calculation, however alluring the result, would never have influenced me against my feelings: instead of suffering those to be blunted by dreams of wealth I have encouraged my fancy to imitate and quicken them, yet they join with cool reason to determine me on this step: they urge me strongly to remove these persons, whose hap-piness fortune has thrown upon my will, to a mild climate and gentle labor . . . rather than to keep them at extreme hard labor and great exposure here or to trust them to the mercy of strangers. . . . The same feelings will induce me to accompany them on this journey and impel me to visit them often enough to ensure their ease and comfort.

The first affections of my heart will be tortured by the disposal of my person this plan for a time commands but the greatness of the end will give me patience: the prospect it affords of putting within my power the means of executing the first wish I have; to endow two sisters and to be prepared to give my son the most complete education by attending institutions of learning and traveling abroad.[10]

The picture was a glowing one. It might have won for Randolph the self-respect that he was always to lack. Even so it was only half a plan. He did not intend to move the family; he had not brought himself to put this final question to Martha. He assured Jefferson that "the children all declared at once they could not leave Grand-papa, when asked if they would go to Mississippi." These were Martha's feelings exactly. One wonders if anyone, even the slaves, believed the fiction that the family would go.

How feasible Martha thought the plan is not known. To Jeffer-son must go the credit of realizing that it was not feasible at all; that, to all practical purposes, Martha must lose a husband, or, in the more likely event, that he himself would lose Martha and her family. His response is a model of diplomacy: cotton is indeed profitable, "a laborer will make $200 worth a year," but the territory is so isolated, so exposed to Indian attack, altogether such a "little helpless speck" of a settlement, that he advocates taking "a comparative view of other places . . . with a view to the same rich culture." Georgia, for example, has every advantage. "You could visit your possessions in Georgia spring and fall with greater ease and much less danger to your health than you could the Mississippi Territory once in half a dozen years." The president, with his superior view of the European situation, also warned that "if the French get possession of New Orleans . . . I shall consider the commerce of the Mississippi as held by a most precarious tenure." That Jefferson was already busily at work behind the scenes to prevent this very eventuality he perhaps naturally enough did not confide to his son-in-law.[11] On the other hand his enthusiasm for Georgia knew no bounds, he even spoke of sending Negroes of his own to the same locality.

Randolph had already considered Georgia, and rejected it, because he feared that "the best pine land of Georgia would not yield more corn than our old fields," and corn, after all, was the slaves' staple diet. By contrast, on the Mississippi the rich loam assured abundance almost without labor. Again he was right; the great fortunes were made not in Georgia, but on the Mississippi low grounds. If he had acted boldly, pulled up stakes, he might have become master of a seigniorial estate, but the seed of indecision had been planted. ("Whenever I feel myself very strongly compelled to any act, a doubt whether it be right always arises.")

Whether or not Jefferson was conscious of playing on his son-in-law's weakness, the result was the same. Randolph now wrote of looking for a place in Georgia. As the summer progressed, difficulties mounted, chiefly in connection with moving a party of slaves through a highly nervous South Carolina, and at last even the Georgia plan expired. Jefferson, as was his custom, had offered any financial help within his power, and Randolph responded with gratitude, but with a certain degree of independence. And then it all came out:

The last passage of your letter [offering help] which seems to embrace me within the narrow circle of your family affects my heart deeply, but there is a mixture of pain with the emotion; something like shame accompanying it and checking the swell of tenderness, from consciousness that I am so essentially and widely different from all within it, as to look like something extraneous, fallen as by accident and destroying the homogeneity. I cannot like the proverbially silly bird feel at my ease in the company of swans. Yet I can, alone, or surrounded with any number nearly on the same social and intellectual level with myself, be as happy and as benevolent as any being alive.[12]

Randolph's feelings then carried him beyond himself to express his truly worshipful feelings toward his father-in-law.

The sentiments of my mind when it contemplates yourself alone is one of the most lofty elevation and most unmixed delight. The rapture of my fancy when it takes in view your extraordinary powers and considers the manner in which they have been, with unceasing and unvarying force for so many years employed and directed, is too strong for a man of less enthusiasm to feel. The feelings of my heart, the gratitude and affection it overflows with when I attempt to estimate the value to the whole human race, as an example; the precious worth, to all who live under it, as the benignant sky which covers them; of the incredibly, inconceivably excellent political system which you have with much more hindrance [and] opposition than aid, created, developed, [and] matured, and at last I think permanently established....[13]

Both feelings, that of personal shame and worshipful adoration, are present at the same time. Nevertheless, it had plainly occurred to Randolph that he would be better off worshipping from afar—"alone, or surrounded with any number nearly on the same social or intellectual level with myself, etc."—but he was easily overborne. Once again, and this time for good, he missed the boat. From now on he was to remain a prisoner of debt, and as he himself so aptly put it, a silly bird among the swans of Monticello.

To what degree was Martha aware of her husband's problems? He was not the only inhabitant of Monticello to suffer feelings of inferiority. Maria had felt them keenly, and Martha had been aware of it,[14] but with her mercurial husband, day-to-day life must have been problem enough. Nor could she have admitted any consideration that involved leaving her father. Sticks and stones may not a prison make, but indeed the emotions may.

Chapter 16

Martha and Maria in Washington

Two wigs, the color of the hair enclosed.

DEFEATED IN HIS PLAN to remove to Mississippi, or even to Georgia, Randolph now took to investing all his effort and skill in his own upland farm. It often required mind-boggling exertions; even so he seemed never able to free himself from debt. If it had only been a question of making good crops, he would have been in a fair way toward succeeding. Jefferson referred to his son-in-law as one "of our best farmers,"[1] and actually he was a good deal better at practical farming than Jefferson himself. Even in the field of scientific agriculture Randolph excelled. His principle of plowing on the contour, a complete innovation at the time, was of no less benefit to agriculture than was Jefferson's own invention of the moldboard plow. Much of the cultivated land in Albemarle lay on ridges, necessarily involving steep slopes. The locally heavy rains, appropriately called gully washers, would pour down an inclined furrow, taking all the precious topsoil with it.

By the time Randolph started serious farming at Edgehill this brutal erosion had taken over most of the land in Albemarle, the owners having sold at low rates and moved to new land in the west. Fields previously green with tobacco or corn were now abandoned to broom straw or field pine. Randolph, perforce, had set to work to fight this decline. His system was to contour his furrows to the slope so as to keep them always level, no matter how curving a course the plow must take. His neighbors thought this a mere Randolph oddity, until the first good rain showed them that the curved furrows were holding water and topsoil, while theirs were, as usual, washing away. The master farmer at Edgehill was making good crops, but something far more subtle stood in his way.

These skills, in fact, scarcely ever prevailed over bad management and endemic insolvency. Always, at the very brink of success, something got in his way. Perhaps, so long as he could not afford to take his family from Monticello, he need never put Martha to that final test.

As it was Martha soon learned to get on without him at home. She explained to her father that Mr. Randolph's movements were so rapid that in one crisis of the children's illnesses it was easier to cope by herself than to attempt to reach him. Indeed, his absence may have been a relief, for in the autumn of 1801, when whooping cough was running through the family, their father seems to have been of little more use than another child in the small house. There were now five children; Cornelia had been born in 1799, and Virginia, the baby, in August of 1801. Martha wrote her father:

It was a terrible moment. Ellen and Cornelia were particularly ill both delerious one singing and laughing the other (Ellen) gloomy and terrified equally unconscious of the objects around them. My God what a moment for a parent. The agonies of Mr. Randolph's mind seemed to call forth every energy of mine. I had to act in the double capacity of nurse to my children and comforter to their father. It is of service perhaps to be obliged to exert oneself upon these occasions. Certainly the mind acquires strength by it to bear up against evils that in other circumstances would totally overcome it. I am recovering from the fatigue which attended the illness of my children and I am at this moment in more perfect health than I have been for years.[2]

There were preoccupations other than illness. Although Randolph was hardly the blockhead that Jefferson had feared would be his daughter's fate in matrimony, nevertheless the children's education did rest mainly on her shoulders. She worried that "they increase in age without making those acquirements which other children do." Anne and Jefferson even "excite serious anxiety with regard to their intellect." Martha admits that some of these fears are unreasonable: "Surely if they turn out well with regard to morals I *ought* to be satisfied, though I *feel* that I never can sit down quietly under the idea of their being blockheads."[3]

In this she is only echoing the concern her father had once so feelingly expressed in regard to herself. Now Jefferson hastened to reassure her in regard to young Jeff:

It is not every heavy-seeming boy which makes a man of judgment, but I never yet saw a man of judgment who had not been a heavy-seeming boy, nor knew a boy of what are called sprightly parts become a man of judgment. But I set much less store by talents than good dispositions: and shall be perfectly happy to see Jefferson a good man, industrious farmer, and kind and beloved among all his neighbors. By cultivating those dispositions in him, and they may be immensely strengthened by culture, we may ensure his and our happiness: and genius itself can propose no other object.[4]

Jefferson may have felt that there were already enough geniuses in the family. Whether or not young Jeff Randolph may wish it he is to be the solid citizen, in whom steady virtues are to be sedulously cultivated, for the benefit of all. Nor was Jefferson ever to be disappointed in his "heavy-seeming boy."

In the following summer of 1802 the measles, although rampant, passed the Randolphs by. Jefferson's letters continued to urge them to visit him in Washington. "Captain Lewis [Meriwether Lewis was at this time Jefferson's secretary] and myself are like two mice in a church," he wrote Martha. He sorely needed a hostess, and although Dolley Madison was ever helpful and not averse to the role, he naturally preferred his own daughters. But hostess or no, and Martha was never really to assume this role, Jefferson's need for family went deeper than this. Randolph's admiration, fulsome as it was, was not too far off the mark in describing the magnitude of his father-in-law's task and the counterpressures with which he had to cope. Even if he were unwilling to pay the price of marriage, he did always need the solace of women close to him, and the . company of children where alone he could totally unbend. At this crucial point in his career, the beginning of the period in which he was to dominate the affairs of his country, Jefferson felt that the principles for which the Revolution had been fought were hanging in the balance. Martha's contribution could be a very real one. She now determined to make the break from the all too demanding cares of home, and to yield to her father's urging. He had long wanted both girls to visit him at the capital.

In 1802 Jack Eppes was already in Washington as a member of the House of Representatives. In spite of missing him sorely Maria was loath to leave the quiet of her home. Even Martha admitted doubt of her fitness to reenter what she called "the world," but it was not a doubt to which she was prepared to yield. In October she took the precaution of ordering two wigs through their friend Mrs. Madison, "the color of the hair enclosed, and of the most fashionable shapes that they may be at Washington when we arrive."[5] Maria had to yield, because, as she said, "my sister will not agree to put off [the visit] any longer."[6] Perhaps too the idea of the wig had had its effect. Thus fortified the sisters set off to brave the Washington scene.

The city that they saw was a sort of trial run, or preliminary sketch of a city. The site was entirely new, chosen by Washington, on the "Potowmac" between the villages of Alexandria and Georgetown. When the girls arrived they found the necessary buildings only begun. The new city had a sort of raw, made-up look, the made-up part of it it retains to this day, principally, I think, because it became a capital before it became a city. Today it still bears its Jeffersonian stamp, for Jefferson presided over its physical, as carefully as he had over its political, structure. Both were new, and both, somehow, *American*.

Martha and Maria, on their arrival in the capital in December, must have been more aware of the deep mud on the mile-long avenue between the capitol building and the President's House than they could have been of any burgeoning architectural style. Abigail Adams, complaining bitterly, had hung her washing up to dry in the unfinished East Room, but this at least Martha and Maria were spared. They were in the enviable position of guests. Without the responsibilities of housekeeping they could thoroughly enjoy their visit. Society was pleasantly masculine, for most congressmen left their wives at home. There was, in fact, no place for them to stay. It was also, to a degree, cosmopolitan. Following Jefferson's example the general style was informal, resembling the relaxed hospitality of a Virginia plantation rather than that of a formal court. There were to be no more of the large levees at which the Adamses had entertained, admittedly more from a sense of duty than of pleasure. The president himself entertained a small company at dinner, never less than three times a week. As he had assured Maria, there was every reason for the girls to feel at home, and it appears that they were an immediate success.

Mrs. Samuel Harrison Smith, that tolerant but surely observant chronicler of the Washington scene, wrote to her sister-in-law:

I ought to tell you a great deal about Mrs. Randolph and Mrs. Eppes. Mrs. Eppes is beautiful, simplicity and timidity personified when in company, but when alone with you of communicative and winning manners. Mrs. R. is rather homely, a delicate likeness of her father, but still more interesting than Mrs. Eppes. She is really one of the most lovely women I have ever met with, her countenance beaming with intelligence, benevolence and sensibility, and her conversation fulfils all her countenance promises. Her manners, so frank and affectionate, that you know her at once, and feel perfectly at your ease with her.[7]

It appeared that Martha spoke freely of family affairs to this sympathetic audience, giving "an account of all her children, of the character of her husband, and many family anecdotes."

Martha had brought two of her children with her. She would hardly have chattered on in this fashion if, combined with a certain amount of disillusionment, she had not been basically in sympathy with her impulsive husband. Her disillusionment at this time was confined to what she described to her father as "the Randolph temper," and no one, surely, could have lived with Tom Randolph without observing *that*. The other side to their marriage was a real warmth and affection, and this it takes two to create. In Washington it was the largest part of the charm which Martha and her father radiated; this sense of family was the inestimable boon which she brought to her father. The intimacy of the girls with their father was all the more marked as Congress was not sitting. Their husbands were at home taking care of the children!

After such pleasures the girls were not sorry to return home to Edgehill. Maria was the first to write her father announcing their return. Martha had been preoccupied with the affairs of her large and ever-demanding family. Although their absence had been a short one, less than two months, the baby Virginia had not recognized her mother until she had changed her dress to a familiar calico. Maria's confident letter appears to show that her father had been right when he had assured her that a little society would do her good. In a few months more she would be pregnant again; but a few months after that would see the end of this gentle and affectionate life.

Chapter 17

Death of a Daughter

This morning between eight and nine o'clock my dear daughter Maria Eppes died.

EARLY IN 1803 "after going to a vast amount of trouble,"[1] Jefferson reported to his son-in-law that the ordinance preventing the passage of slaves through South Carolina had been lifted. Randolph had already lost momentum. He wrote his father-in-law that he was now "unsure," and thought that he would stay where he was and improve his present lands. Jefferson then had the last word, commending Randolph on his decision, which was, of course, to remain at Edgehill. Although apparently Jefferson had only confirmed Randolph's own decision, the young man felt vaguely depressed by this commendation. It was at times such as this that the image of the silly bird among the swans may have recurred to his mind.

Even moving about freely as he did that summer failed to assuage Randolph's endemic restlessness, and the fact that his brother-in-law, Jack Eppes, had appeared so effortlessly to establish himself in the U.S. Congress did not soothe his ever-competitive feelings. The incumbent from the Albermarle-Amherst-Fluvanna district was Samuel Jordan Cabell, a loyal supporter of the president, who had lain "two nights on a blanket" during the hectic balloting of 1800 in order to elect his chief. Without consulting Jefferson, Randolph threw his hat in the ring against the incumbent. It was not an easy position for the president. In any event Randolph won, by the narrowest possible margin, and that autumn he arrived in Washington, to try his hand at "the highest profession in the gift of my country." He was to go alone, for Martha, expecting her sixth child, Mary Jefferson, in November, stayed at home.

That winter, with both husbands in Washington, the sisters remained together at Edgehill. If Maria had not been ill it would have been a happy time, but she was increasingly unwell and depressed. Jefferson attempted to cheer her with what seem now in hindsight some rather inept remarks about childbirth. "Some female friend of your mother's (I forget whom) used to say that it was no more than a jog of the elbow." "Courage," he told her, "is as essential in your case as in that of a soldier."[2] Jack could not be with her as Congress was still in session, although Jefferson must have remembered a time twenty-two years before when he himself had abandoned the field of battle in a similar case. After the birth, when he knew that she had been seriously ill, he was touching in his anxiety. He recommended sherry: "The sherry at Monticello is old and genuine, and the Pedro Ximenes much older still, and stomachic." But sherry could not cure what ailed Maria.

She continued, mysteriously, to decline. Jefferson had seen it all happen before, at Monticello in 1782, but to Jack Eppes it was new, and not at first too alarming. He could not bring himself to believe that Maria was slipping away from him. Freed from Congress at last he had wished to hurry home, but everything conspired against him. The roads were a mass of snow and ice: "I had a terrible journey," he wrote Jefferson. Often his horse had been slowed down to a walk, and in many places he had had to get down from his horse to break the ice before they could go forward. He reported at once to Jefferson.

"I found Maria at my arrival here [March 9, '04] free from fever, and sitting up. She has no complaints at present but weakness. . . . I have no fear but that in a short time she will be restored to health. Her child is well also from the kindness of Patsy who has nursed it with her own. Maria . . . has lost her milk entirely, and although she expects its return, I fear we shall be obliged to rely principally on feeding the child."[3] The bulletins continue, almost from day to day.

March 11: "Maria continues in the same situation as when I wrote last. . . . I shall endeavor to prevail on her . . . to lay aside her phials, and to depend on gentle exercise and fresh air. . . ."

Jefferson replied on March 15, offering, as he always did, all the amenities of Monticello. "I hope you will take up your residence there . . . I hope you will consider it your home until we can get you fixed at Pantops. I do not think that Maria should be ventured below after this date." Besides his anxiety to have them near, he genuinely feared the effect of the "low country" on Maria's health.

Jack Eppes to Jefferson, March 19: "[Maria] has been threatened within the last two days with a rising of her breast. She took before this scarcely any nourishment and now takes still less. This has thrown her back. I feel dreadfully apprehensive that the great debility under which she labors may terminate in some serious complaint." He agrees with Jefferson in his fears of the low country, that is to say, of their home in Chesterfield County. "For the offer you make us I return my thanks, and shall consider any little benefit to my affairs in the lower country from my presence as not to be considered while Maria's health can be restored by remaining here."

March 23: "Maria has had a return of her puking. She is again recovering. Her breast is still somewhat inflamed, but not I hope, in much danger of going further. . . . We have prevailed upon her to ride out twice and she will ride again today. . . . She is extremely thin, a mere shadow, but as debility is now her only complaint, I have the pleasure of feeling that the recovery of her health, although slow is absolutely certain."

March 26: "Maria is not worse. I am sorry I cannot say she is better."

On a day between that bulletin and April 4, when Jefferson was at last able to leave Washington for Monticello, Maria had been carried in a litter borne by hand to Monticello. From Edgehill one went down to the Secretary's Ford. Did Maria look about her at the leaves just burgeoning on the willows and the purple Judas trees, or did she shut her eyes and pray on that arduous journey? We do not know, only that her father's presence braced her, or, as he put it, "Her spirits and confidence are favorably affected by my being with her." In the presence of so much vigorous life it was difficult even to die. But when he looked out on the morning of the 13th this inveterate optimist could find no cheer in the peach blossoms and the poplar beginning to leaf, although he noted them as usual.

To Madison, his closest friend, he wrote on that morning: "My daughter exhibits little change. No new abscess has come on, but she rather weakens. Her fever is small and constant. Affectionate salutations."

April 17: "This morning between eight and nine o'clock my dear daughter Maria Eppes died." [4]

What are the uses of grief? Jefferson could never quite decide. Only perhaps that it may bring closer together those left behind. For a few hours Martha and her father grieved alone, until word came for her to go to him. Praying for control she went into his room, and found him there with his Bible in his hands. At the sight of this daughter remaining to him Jefferson wept. "Oh, my daughter, I did not send for you to witness my weakness, for I thought I could control myself, but to comfort me with your presence." [5] Father and daughter wept together. Then as always happened with Martha, she felt that surge of strength that was his to call upon. As had happened at her mother's death, their dependence was now on each other alone, and that dependence was absolute.

Chapter 18

The Washington Scene

Fit to grace any court in Europe . . .

FOUR YEARS LATER, after Maria's death, Martha managed one more visit to Washington. The diary of Isaac Coles, at that time the president's secretary, and Jeff Randolph's memoir give us a fuller picture than was possible for the first visit. Mrs. Harrison Smith had this to say:

On Sunday morning Mrs. Randolph and Mrs. Madison called and I promised to take tea with Mrs. Randolph in the evening. We found no company, and all the family were out, but Mr. J. and Mrs. R. She was seated by him on a sopha and all her lovely children playing around them. With what delight did I contemplate this good parent, and while I sat looking at Him playing with these infants, one standing on the sopha with its arms round his neck, the other two youngest on his knees, playing with him, I could scarcely realise that he was one of the most celebrated men now living, both as a Politician and Philosopher. He was in one of his most communicative and social moods, and after tea, when the children went to bed, the conversation turned on agriculture, gardening, the difference of both in different countries and of the produce of different climates. This is one of the most favorite pursuits and indeed the conversation the whole evening turned on his favorite subjects.[1]

The children, of course, made their own observations. Jefferson Randolph recalled years later what he had observed at age ten, seated at the president's table. The dinner hour, he wrote, was about four o'clock. The president sat at one end of the table and his secretary at the other.

When my mother was with her father and there were ladies she presided at the head of the table. The Maitre d'Hotel announced dinner, remained in the room seeing that the servants attended to every gentleman, but not waiting himself, placing on the first dish of the second course. The fashion was to sit long at table after the cloth was removed, sip their wine and converse. Mr. Jefferson often remarked that the easy flow of after dinner conversation around the wine table was . . . most agreeable, amusing and instructive and he was very fond of it: [he] himself drank nothing stronger than claret. These dinners were more costly than those of the present day—more wine of a costly character was drunk. The dinner altogether more full . . .[2]

It was Jeff's proud privilege to pass this expensive wine, which he did with gusto, and sometimes with disastrous effect. On one occasion the Dutch minister, stooping to retrieve his napkin, tipped a plate of rice pudding with hot sauce over his bald head. Snatching the plate from his head and wiping furiously at his face he exclaimed, "I vish I was in hell!" It was Jeff's finest moment.

The menus of two of these dinners have survived in the diary of Isaac Coles, the secretary who served Jefferson during his second administration. With Dolley Madison, Isaac has been called one of the two "Washington charmers."[3] His charm is a quality we may readily recognize in the portrait bust of this young man taken by William Coffee. Even in terra cotta his eyes twinkle. He was one of that large and lively family from Enniscorthy, Jefferson's neighbors in Albemarle, and actually he was Dolley's cousin. Unfortunately for all the four years that he sat at Jefferson's table, the diary informs us regularly of the weather, the names of dinner guests, and the state of Jefferson's health, but never of the conversation, a loss we can only assume to be great if we may judge the liveliness of the conversation from the amount of wine consumed. In one period of twelve days during December of 1802 Jefferson's account book shows that 125 gentlemen consumed fifty bottles of champagne, two bottles to five persons.

On a brisk spring day in 1804 the diary tells us that four guests—Messrs. Madison, Gallatin, Smith, and Dearborn, in other words, the principal members of Jefferson's cabinet—sat down to "Soup, bouille, bear, a quarter, partridges with sausages and cabbage (a French way of cooking them) Turkey, potatoes, rice, spinnage, beans, salad, pickles. A ham of bacon in the center of the table. 2nd course: a kind of custard with a floating cream on it, and at the bottom of the table apples in cloves in a thin toast. A French dish on each side, four dishes and three in the middle. 3rd course: Olives, apples, oranges, and 12 other plates of nuts, etc." The wines were imported.[4]

No wonder that Jefferson left the President's House $10,000 poorer than when he entered it! The president's salary was nowhere near adequate to such hospitality, but Jefferson refused to stint. His country's credit was upheld out of his own pocket. Martha was skeptical. ("He could have used a judicious wife to look after his domestic concerns.")[5]

If Republican simplicity obviously did not extend to the table, it did create a good deal of havoc in the sensitive realm of protocol, which Jefferson stubbornly ignored. His Britannic Majesty had perhaps deliberately sent to Washington a mediocre little man with the inappropriate name of Merry. He was accompanied, however, by a formidable, social-climbing wife. As American commissioner Jefferson had received cavalier treatment at the British court, and he saw no reason to give the Merrys the precedence to which they thought themselves entitled. Indeed he seems to have taken pains in the opposite direction. At their first state dinner he had given his arm to Dolley Madison.[6] The Marchésa Yrujo (wife of the Spanish minister) took the seat at the president's left. Madison would have inaugurated some sort of protocol, but the president was adamant: the system should remain "pell mell" and Republican.

Somehow the Merrys were always odd man out: at the next dinner, at the Madisons, Mrs. Merry was left partnerless, and forced to fall back on the arm of her husband. Mrs. Smith's description of Mrs. Merry's costume is formidable:

White satin with a long train, dark blue crape of the same length over it and white crape drapery down to her knees and open at one side, so thickly covered with silver spandles that it appeared to be a brilliant silver tissue; a breadth of blue crape, about four yards long, and in other words a long shawl put over her head, instead of over her shoulders and hanging down to the floor, her hair bound tight to her head with a band like her drapery, with a diamond crescent before and a diamond comb behind, diamond ear-rings and necklace, displayed on a bare bosom. She is a large, tall well made woman, rather masculine. . . . He is plain in appearance and called rather inferior in understanding.[7]

Mrs. Merry rather resembled the Statue of Liberty. For such a figure to be forced to enter on such an arm! Merry was not slow to complain to his own foreign office, where he went by the nickname of "*toujours gai*." His complaints apparently fell on deaf ears.

Mrs. Merry was still proceeding on her stormy way. Still the cause of innocent *Merriment*, as Isaac Coles put it in his diary. On Martha's arrival, Mrs. Merry had sent to inquire: as the president's daughter would she expect the first call, or, had she come as the wife of a congressman, in which case Mrs. Merry would expect Mrs. Randolph to pay the first call. Martha consulted her father on this formidable question, and on his advice replied that Mrs. Randolph took pleasure in informing Mrs. Merry that she had come to Washington as the wife of a plain Virginia gentleman and as such would look forward to the first call customarily paid to strangers in the city. Needless to say, no calls were exchanged.

There was, however, a good deal of gaiety. From the Coles diary there appears to have been a party every night, most frequently at Mrs. Madison's or Mrs. Duval's. How often Martha went out we do not know, but we know that she enjoyed herself, for a granddaughter, Sarah Nicholas Randolph, remembered her relating "many a good story with which that winter furnished her."[8]

She attended at least one ball; Anne Cary, then fifteen and not yet "out," was permitted to go with the daughter of a friend. Martha, who we now learn was nearsighted, arrived late. She exclaimed to her friend Mrs. Cutts, "Who is that beautiful girl?" Mrs. Cutts's reply: "Why, woman, are you so unnatural a mother as not to recognize your own daughter?" It was Anne's first appearance on the public scene.[9]

There was also the Yankee member of Congress who repeatedly asked the president's daughter to join him at cards. Martha finally told him "that there was not a game of cards that she could play."

"Is it possible, Madam?" exclaimed the gentleman. "Why with us it is the universal impression that you are the greatest gambler in the country, and that if a person wants office nothing would favor him so much as having lost money with the President's daughter."[10]

Sad evidence indeed, Miss Randolph infers, of the state of morals in Washington compared to "the pure and simple life" of Edgehill and Monticello! We may remark, however, that Martha was in fact well suited for a larger social life than the plantation afforded. The Marqués Yrujo, the Spanish minister, pronounced her fit "to grace any court in Europe."[11] One cannot escape the conclusion that she would have been the ideal consort for her father if consanguinity, and her own husband, and eleven children, had not prevented it.

Chapter 19

Randolph Meets Randolph

Clever we may be, eccentric we often are, but no one ever said that the Randolphs were amiable.

—George Wythe Randolph[1]

THE PRIZE FOR THE MOST eccentric and least amiable of Randolphs clearly goes to John Randolph of Roanoke. This Randolph was more Republican than the Republicans. Formerly an able supporter of the president in Congress he turned against him in the second term, fomenting, and then leading, an opposition group within the party. Early in 1806 when Jefferson would have negotiated with Spain and her French ally for the purchase of Florida, Randolph would have no part of, as he claimed, "greas[ing] the fists of Napoleon with American gold." This was hardly a favorable description. Instead, this doughty warrior expressed indignation at the hostile spirit of the Spanish, asserting that this in itself constituted ample cause for a declaration of war.[2]

In the end Jefferson carried his point in Congress, receiving a grant of $2,000,000 for an unspecified diplomatic object. Even the Federalist William Plumer had complained of the insufferable language used by Randolph in debate on the floor of the House. In his high, effeminate, but ever-eloquent voice he had missed no opportunity to castigate the administration. "His speeches were too personal—his allusions to brothels and pig sties too coarse and vulgar. . . ."[3]

It was Thomas Mann Randolph's ill luck—and when, we may ask, had he ever been lucky?—to sit in his new place in Congress listening to the tirades of his cousin, the ancient enemy of Bizarre. He sat in a rage of frustration, for he knew that he was no match for this Randolph's eloquence. He feared, as he later admitted, to trust himself "to the rude sea of debate, with the tempest he [John Randolph] had raised on it." On the last night of the last session of the Eighth Congress he had broken this notable silence. The members had returned to their seats after dinner, where both solid and liquid refreshment had been offered. A member from Pennsylvania, Mr. Findley, who was rather obviously affected by the latter part of his refreshment, challenged John Randolph, accusing him of attempting to embarrass the administration. A second member rose to defend Randolph, and was called to order by offended members, in which call Thomas Mann Randolph joined. It was then that John Randolph took the floor, asking, with elaborate innuendo: "What has thrown us into this heat? Is it the dinner we have just eaten? I hope no honorable gentleman who has heretofore kept the noiseless tenor of his way, because we have adjourned for half an hour, has permitted his passions to indulge in an asperity not shown on any former occasion." He also deplored the "contumely and hostility" demonstrated during debate.

When it was a point of honor Tom knew how to respond, and now, at last, eloquence did not fail him. He rose to his feet.

The gentleman [John Randolph] made use of the word "contumely." To this and other offensive terms, with an allusion, which, as to me, is as unjust as it is insulting, I am sorry to think myself obliged to reply. . . . I know the extreme irritability of the gentleman's temper; I know as well the principles which govern him on occasions of this kind. I know the point to which his is disposed to carry disputes [he was of course referring to a duel]. . . . I inform him that I have the same principles and sentiments myself. . . . I have always thought, and always shall think, that lead and even steel make very proper ingredients in serious quarrels. . . .

If the Edgehill Randolph had stopped here, one might have admired his resolution, but as usual he went on to indulge his instinct for self-abasement: "The tenor of my course has been, I confess, little noisy. . . . My diffidence, and, no doubt, incapacity for such exertions, have been the main reasons, and I am not ashamed to confess it, for I have no hope to make myself other than nature intended I should be, and no shame to appear as I am. I acknowledged that the gentleman's example influenced my conduct. . . ."[4] With a final thrust in which he declared his opponent bankrupt forever as a popular statesman, Tom left the chamber.

To no one's surprise John Randolph responded with equal celerity. He sent James Mercer Garnett to demand immediate satisfaction, in other words, the lead that his cousin had suggested. Thomas Mann Randolph in his turn got hold of Isaac Coles, who may have already been in the building, as the whole maneuver took place during the evening, while the House was still in session. Garnett and Coles repaired to the Senate gallery, where they agreed that the wise course lay in defusing this quarrel. Certainly it was not at all sure to whom John Randolph was referring in his sneering remarks about the effects of "the dinner we have just eaten." It could well have been that he meant Findley, the member from Pennsylvania, who obviously had been the worse for liquor, or—and it seems to me quite likely—that Tom was correct in taking the "honourable gentleman who has hitherto kept the noiseless tenor of his way" to refer to himself.

Tom met the two seconds at the head of the stairs leading to the gallery, and here Mercer Garnett took it upon himself to say that his principal, John Randolph, had not meant to direct the offensive remarks at his cousin. Other members had been assuring him of the same thing. The member from Albemarle suffered his usual reversal of feeling. "I never will, unprovoked," he said, "seek a quarrel with anyone." He told Garnett that if he could once be convinced that the offensive observations had not been intended for him, "that then there was no apology that a man of honor could or ought to make, which he was not ready to offer; observing to Mr. Garnett at the same time that Mr. John Randolph had always the other alternative, and that he would meet him at any time." Garnett repeated his assurance in a positive fashion, so Randolph returned to his seat to wait, as he later said, for the disclaimer to come in a more positive form from John Randolph himself.

It was at this point that Garnett confided to Coles that "John Randolph would not say to Mr. Thomas Mann Randolph that observations either were, or were not, intended for him, and that he would expect Mr. Thomas Mann Randolph to meet him, either that night or in the morning."[5] John Randolph was in fact more than ready. He had expressed himself "happy that this occurrence had given him a chance to answer every scoundrel who had attacked him in the House, and that he was happy that an opponent so respectable [i.e., another Randolph] should have now offered." Although Bizarre and Nancy were not mentioned, no doubt the old rancor was not forgotten.

Coles and Garnett retired to the empty gallery, where they continued to confer. Faced with this new picture of John Randolph thirsting for blood, Coles thought it best to ask for time, to which Garnett readily agreed. They left Tom Randolph in an agony of suspense, for indeed there was no time. As he later explained, the House was within an hour of the last adjournment of the session; gentlemen would be scattering to every corner of the Union with, as he phrased it, his disgrace upon their lips. Better to make it clear, then, that the insult had not been directed at himself, as he now sincerely believed. Never one for half measures, or for "wait and see," Randolph got to his feet. Speaking in a low tone, so low as to be hardly audible, he addressed the Speaker:

A little while since I made use of some very harsh and severe language towards a gentleman of this House, such as I acknowledge altogether improper to be used in it. . . . I believed that certain expressions of a disrespectful nature which dropped from him were directed to me. . . . By a rapid movement of my mind I came to a resolution not to go home with such a load on my feelings as was imposed by the recollection that the treatment I had received was in the face of a company of one hundred men, who were to disperse tomorrow, and spread my disgrace through all quarters of the Union. . . . Since then I have been told by six or seven different gentlemen, that I was mistaken, that the words were not addressed to me. . . . I have even had the mortification to be asked if it was not a studied attack on my part on the gentleman, for the course he has taken this session. . . . I could not have done so with honor, unprovoked, for private reasons. . . . I am conscious of the disrespect I have shown the House. . . . My mistake was honest and natural—I regret it, and the expressions I used in consequence of it.[6]

John Randolph expressed himself as satisfied. The whole affair might have ended there, if an anonymous letter to the *Aurora* had not reopened the sorry affair. In effect, it was a question of which gentleman had backed down first. By June the prospect of a duel had again been revived. It was at this interesting point that Jefferson entered the lists, of course with but one object, that of getting his son-in-law to see the light.

"Even the striplings of fashion," he adjured him, "are sensible that the laws of duelling are made for them alone." He hoped that Randolph will "suppress all passion," and that "such a course will be pursued as will leave us in possession of that domestic happiness we now enjoy. . . . I see all this depending on your prudence and self command. . . ." Tom Randolph may not have recognized himself under this description. No one had ever accused him of "prudence and self command" before, nor was it at all the self-image that he liked to project. An appeal to dignified silence, a noble indifference, might have worked, although even this is doubtful. The truth was that Jefferson was never able to cope with sensibilities so different from his own. Randolph of Edgehill repaired to Richmond, quite ready to meet the Randolph of Roanoke, but time was on Jefferson's side, and the duel was allowed to die of inanition, rather by default than by prudence.

It is Jefferson's description of Martha, admittedly framed to touch the heart of her husband, that seems furthest off the mark. In describing the possible (and they were very possible) results of a duel, he let himself go. "Seven children, all under the age of discretion and down to infancy, would then be left without guide or guardian but a poor broken-hearted woman, doomed herself to misery the rest of her life. And should her frail frame sink under it, what is then to become of them?"[7]

The phrasing is exaggerated, but the sentiment is genuine. It can hardly have escaped him that Martha was superior in judgment and strength of mind to her husband. It was simply that to Jefferson public matters of business and politics, and perhaps above all the social relations between men, were not women's affairs. Their "trade," as he forthrightly put it, was childbearing and, happily, soothing the brow of a husband troubled by masculine cares. Such had been the case with his own wife, and perhaps even more to the point, with his own mother, for Peter Jefferson had depended on masculine companionship rather than on the company of his wife, Jane.

We have only to read the letters of Abigail Adams and, nearer to Monticello, of Hetty Carr, Peter's widow, to know that not all women of the time played such a subordinate role. But up to this point, at least, it does not seem to have occurred to Jefferson that Martha might have taken a more active part in the management of family affairs, or even that she would have been the logical person to soothe and check her fiery husband. This role, as with so many others, Jefferson took upon himself.

Chapter 20

Incidents of Stress

IN JUNE 1806 JEFFERSON was suffering what must have been a profoundly upsetting experience. Early that month he had been informed of the murder of his old and beloved friend and mentor, George Wythe, under circumstances that could only have aroused his deepest, if ordinarily suppressed, forebodings.[1]

The venerable and greatly revered Chancellor Wythe, professor of law at William and Mary, had lived in a modest home on Grace Street in Richmond, with his faithful servants Lydia Broadnax and Benjamin Brown and the mulatto boy Michael Brown. The black couple had been freed long before by the chancellor and lived with him on terms of devoted and voluntary service. It was widely supposed that Michael was Wythe's son by Lydia, a supposition borne out by Michael's position in the household. Wythe himself had been taught Latin and Greek at an early age by his mother, and he was pursuing this same course with Michael, to discover, as he said, the aptitude of the other race. Even more conclusively he had drawn up a will naming Michael as a joint beneficiary with his great-nephew and namesake, George Wythe Sweeney. This wild young teenager, given to drink and gambling, was also a member of the household on Grace Street. There is no record that the chancellor was giving *him* lessons in the classics.

Sweeney, in fact, was badly in debt, and had been putting his revered uncle's name on forged checks. There is also every reason to suppose that he felt outraged at the favor shown Michael as he sat with the chancellor over their books. When Sweeney discovered the terms of the will placing this member of an "inferior" race on an equal footing with himself, whatever sense the boy had seems to have left him. There was even a clause in the will stating that in the event of Michael's prior death Sweeney would inherit the whole. His creditors were pressing, and the checks were an ever-present danger. There seems to have been no question in anyone's mind that on the morning of May 25, 1806, Sweeney helped himself to an early cup of coffee and then poured a liberal dose of arsenic into what was left in the pot.

Chancellor Wythe partook of his usually frugal breakfast that morning, including a cup of Aunt Lydy's coffee. After the pot had returned to the kitchen Lydia and her family helped themselves out of the same pot. With the exception of Lydia all of these coffee-drinkers, after varying lengths of time, died agonizing deaths. George Wythe had the strength at one point to cry out, "I am murdered." He had time besides to change his will. This loss of an inheritance appears to have been the only consequence suffered by the multiple murderer.

Lydia Broadnax who could have been the state's star witness, was not allowed to testify. The Virginia penal code, revised by Jefferson and Wythe himself in 1779, had perpetuated the provision of Colonial law which made it impossible for Negroes to testify against whites in a court of law.

Jefferson's own thoughts on racial violence had long been known: "I tremble for my country," he had written. The Wythe murder was as surely an act of racial violence as had been Gabriel's Revolt. It was one, moreover, in which Jefferson's own guilt of compromise, his sins of omission, were reflected in the law that he himself had considered and allowed to remain on the books. Because Lydia Broadnax was not admitted in court the execrable Sweeney went free. Jefferson commented with his usual sincere feeling and measured eloquence on the loss of his dear friend and old master:

He was my antient [sic] master, my earliest and best friend; and to him I am indebted for first impressions which have had the most salutary influence on the course of my life. I had reserved with fondness for the day of my retirement, the hope of inducing him to spend much of his time with me. It would have been a great pleasure to recollect with him first opinions on the new state of things which arose soon after my acquaintance with him [that is, the struggle for and winning of American independence]; to pass in review the long period which has elapsed since that time, and to see how far those opinions had been affected by experience and reflection, or confirmed and acted upon with approbation.[2]

Would the law prohibiting the witness of slaves have been considered in this review? Perhaps, but Jefferson was clearly able to keep it unexpressed in this year of his presidency, 1806. Nowhere does he reflect on the irony of the law forbidding Negro testimony, of *that law* as applied to the Wythe case. Nor was Jefferson alone in this omission. It had been mentioned by editor Ritchie in the *Richmond Enquirer* of contemporary date, then resolutely ignored, with the exception of but one fictional version of the case, for the next one hundred and fifty years. It seems that when the giants are silent smaller men will not be heard.

Randolph, less stoic than Jefferson, had complained to his sister about his life in Washington. Suffering from very real frustration in connection with his aborted duel, he was finding the capital less appealing than ever, and the President's House the center of his discontent. Once more he was reduced to the status of that silly bird extraneous in another's house, while his brother-in-law, like his wife, seemed to thrive in that extended society. In February 1807, during the second session of the Ninth Congress, he upset everybody by leaving the President's House.

Without a word to anyone he removed himself to the boarding house of Frost and Quinn, a Federalist stronghold. We may well ask why an ardent Republican, such as Thomas Mann Randolph undoubtedly was, would repair to a Federalist house. Such houses offered considerable sociability to their boarders, and Frost and Quinn was no exception. "We all eat at one table," William Plumer reported in his diary, but Thomas Mann Randolph "always eats in his own room. He has never once dined in company since he has boarded with us." It may have been easier for this unsociable congressman to dine alone among political foes, than among his political friends. In any case the rumor at once spread that he and the president had quarreled. Not so, said Plumer, "for he speaks of the President with great cordiality."[3]

Three days after his departure he returned to dine with the president, no doubt attracted by the presence at dinner of Shawnee chiefs, among them Logan, the Black Wolf, and Blackbeard. For Randolph the opportunity of indulging his taste for the extraordinary, and for scientific observation, could not be missed, even at the cost of facing his brother-in-law once again at that interesting table. Meriwether Lewis, returned at last from his great expedition from Washington to the Pacific, had brought the chiefs with him, along with many scientific treasures discovered in that great continental crossing.[4] Later in the spring Randolph was happy to be able to present his father-in-law with a "mamaluke bit" needed for the Philadelphia Museum of Charles Willson Peale, where Isaac Coles was "engaged with Peale in stuffing the animals."

Randolph, of course, was not unaware of developments in the western country of even greater moment than the appearance of Lewis's chiefs. By the spring of 1806 there was no doubt in anyone's mind that Aaron Burr was fomenting rebellion in that newly acquired territory. There was considerable doubt, however, concerning the loyalty of General Wilkinson, Thomas Jefferson's military commander in the Missouri Territory. This slippery and flamboyant character had indeed flirted with Burr, and had once been in the pay of Spain, but lately he had come over to the side of the government, and to Jefferson as his commander-in-chief. In 1807 the general was perhaps dealing a little too strenuously; he was taking things into his own hands, making arrests and holding suspects without regard for *habeas corpus*. The issue was taken to Congress, where Jefferson chose to support his general, probably because Wilkinson had made himself almost indispensable as his witness against Burr. The president made no bones about his own feeling that "On great occasions every good officer must be ready to risk himself in going beyond the strict line of law, when the public preservation requires it."[5]

During all this Randolph remained isolated in his room at Frost and Quinn. Nothing, not even treason, could have been more alarming to Jefferson than this threat of family alienation. For years he had walked this delicate emotional tightrope with his daughter's husband. Now, without restraint, he poured out his true feelings: "I have not one glimmering of hope left, if the last ties of nature which hold to the human heart are to be torn from mine. [In that case] I sincerely wish that the hour which closes the career of my public duties, may close that of my life also."[6]

The pressure was enormous, all the greater as Randolph could not doubt his father-in-law's real affection. The self-exiled member at Frost and Quinn took what was perhaps the only course open to him. He fell ill. So, according to Isaac Coles, did Jefferson. "Although ill," wrote Coles, "the President signed 27 bills on March 3." Isaac had been dispatched to care for Randolph. "I sat up the whole night, viz, from 8 o'clock to 7 the next morning, with Mr. Randolph." On the fourth John Eppes, the man whom Randolph believed had supplanted him in Jefferson's affections, left for Virginia, and on Saturday the seventh the invalid returned to the President's House. As Randolph gained strength Jefferson gave in to his periodical headache, "with which he had been afflicted for some days." On the twenty-third, Jefferson, who must have been desperate to resort to medicine, sent Coles to Georgetown to get something for his head.[7] By Thursday, the twenty-sixth, the party at the President's House had recovered sufficiently to go out with Captain Lewis to spend an hour at Mr. Madison's. Aaron Burr's trial for conspiracy began in the U.S. Circuit Court in Richmond on March 30. Jefferson and his son-in-law arrived home at Monticello early in April, and so, to the distress of neither, Randolph's career in Washington came to a close. Affairs at Monticello may have remained in rather precarious balance, maintained perhaps only by Jefferson's unrivaled ability to rise above such stress and strain.

Chapter 21

The *Chesapeake* Affair and Its Consequences

NATIONAL AFFAIRS WERE hardly calculated to ease personal stress. Freedom of the seas, that is to say, the safe conduct of American trade, had always been an essential part of Jefferson's program. The United States was still predominantly an agricultural country, dependent on Europe for the products of industry. Great Britain, locked in conflict with France, now issued Orders in Council, closing continental ports to neutral vessels, i.e., to American shipping.[1] In November 1807 Jefferson told his son-in-law that Congress would now have to decide on one of three courses: "War, Embargo, or Nothing."[2]

These affairs at the capital were to have their impact at home, but in the meantime there were already problems enough. A quiet family wedding took place at Monticello in August when Virginia (Jenny) Randolph married Wilson Jefferson Cary of Carysbrook. Martha informed her father at this time "of the dismantled state of our tea equipage, being reduced to *four tea cups*."[3] No doubt Jefferson hastened to supply this lack. He was also busy sending seeds and plants, for he was now spending money freely on the landscaping at Monticello. This spending seems to have been only very partially modified by the fact that, far from being able to retire the old debts, he was actually leaving the presidency with a deficit of about $10,000, incurred during his years of office. There were also, of course, unexpected expenses on the farm, as in January 1807 when word came from his builder, James Walker, "I am sorry to inform you that the walls of the new addition to the toal [*sic*] mill has fallen down. . . ."[4] He was a long way from the happy conclusion of his affairs that he had outlined in his letter to Randolph in 1803. It certainly had not helped the family finances that her brother had made this youngest sister, Jenny, a wedding present of $5,000. His sister, he may have thought, may have been married *from* Monticello, but she was still *his* responsibility.

Unfortunately the affairs of the whole Tuckahoe Randolph family were going from bad to worse. Tom's brother William was bankrupt in 1807 and Thomas Mann, already harassed, was forced to assume the whole of the debt on his father's estate. Martha, who was worrying at the time about her father's toothache, sent Jefferson a full account of what seems to have moved from the usual condition of "pecuniary embarrassment" to the more advanced state of pecuniary disaster.

"Mr. Randolph has been a fortnight in Richmond setling [*sic*] David Randolph's affairs." (This was David Meade Randolph, who had married the oldest Randolph sister, Mary.)

Sister Randolph has opened a boarding house in Richmond, but she has not a single boarder yet. Her husband has gone to England upon some mercantile scheme with barely money to defray his expenses. The ruin of the family is still extending itself daily. William is ruined. His negroes during his absence remained three days in the dwelling house to save themselves from the sherif. Archy is without a shelter for his family but her Father's, and Will. Fleming goes constantly armed to keep the sherif off. I ought rather to say *went* for in consequence of the pistol going off in his pocket he is rendered a cripple for life. He has never moved but as he has been lifted and probably will not for many months. Mr. Randolph's trials have been great but thank heaven he has resisted their solicitations and has had the prudence not to hamper himself by security ships. His contributing to his Sister's necessities as far as he is able is a sacred duty. But a recent occurence under which he is still smarting, with my *urgent entreaties* have kept him clear of all *new* engagements.[5]

This letter elicited from Jefferson his first suggestion that Martha might become so unwomanly as to mix with her husband's affairs. "I always apprehended," he wrote, "that Mr. Randolph would be in great embarrassment between the imprudence of some members of his father's family, and the necessity of taking care of a large one of his own, and knowing his liberal dispositions I thought it possible that present pressure might sometimes prevail over a prudent foresight of the future." But Jefferson took care to offer his daring advice only as a suggestion for "moralising conversations with your children." However, the message is clear: "There is an evil against which we cannot guard," he informs his daughter, "unthrifty marriages. . . . But even here, a wife imbued with principles of prudence, may go far toward arresting or lessening the evils of an improvident management."

Martha tried, but her *urgent entreaties* could hardly prevail in the volatile mind of her husband, exposed to one sister running a boardinghouse without any boarders, and another, Nancy, now without a roof of her own and living, perhaps by choice, in other boardinghouses of doubtful repute. At least this was the word spread by her implacable enemy, John Randolph. Tom was making her, at this time, an annual allowance. Thus pressed, he had tried to sell Varina. Although he prized his low grounds there as "the most valuable spot for a farm in the state," he could find no buyer. Nor would he avail himself of the common resource of the impoverished planter, that of selling slaves. He had raised many of the Negroes himself, he said, and knew them all well.

In the meantime national affairs had taken a turn more interesting to Randolph than the lengthy debates which had bored him in Congress. Sometime around the end of June or the first of July he opened a copy of the *National Intelligencer* of June 26, 1807, and there he read a spirited account of the attack on the unfortunate *Chesapeake*. On June 22 the American frigate had sailed out of Lynhaven Bay, into the Atlantic, headed for the Mediterranean. A British squadron was lying at anchor in the bay, a not unusual sight, for in the days of sail, ships were accustomed to put in for water and fresh provisions, a necessity on any long voyage. The United States and Great Britain were at peace, and Captain Barron of the *Chesapeake* had no reason to suspect hostile action, even when he was followed out of the bay by the frigate *Leopard*. Some three leagues off Cape Henry, that is, in territorial waters, the *Leopard* hailed the

Chesapeake, which accordingly hove to in order to receive a messenger from the British ship. The messenger carried a demand that he be permitted to search the ship for British deserters. Captain Barron replied that he knew of no such men aboard his ship, and declined to permit his men to be mustered on deck for the proposed search.

There were in fact three men who had been serving on board the British vessel HMS *Malampus*, but they were American citizens, and if Barron was aware of them at all he looked upon them as just three more examples of the many American seamen impressed—that is to say, kidnapped and forced—to serve on the British ships. What then occurred on the waters off Cape Henry stirred an entire nation, not to speak of Thomas Mann Randolph, into a frenzy of patriotic feeling. In the words of the *National Intelligencer*, the Washington paper edited by Jefferson's good friend, Samuel Harrison Smith:

BRITISH OUTRAGE: We give the public the particulars of the following outrage on the American flag under the influence of feelings which we are certain are in unison with those of our fellow citizens, feelings which can not, which ought not, be suppressed. We know not indeed, if this savage outrage has a precedent in Naval annals.

Barron's message [refusing permission to search] was no sooner received than a broadside was discharged from the *Leopard*. The crew of the *Chesapeake* were at this time not at quarters, considering the *Leopard* a friend. . . . No other attempt was made to fight her than the discharge of a few straggling guns; while the *Leopard* repeated three or four more broadsides; when the *Chesapeake* struck her colors, after having three men killed and eighteen wounded.

When a British officer boarded the *Chesapeake* and demanded the four men [the fourth was in fact an English deserter], Commodore Barron said that he considered the *Chesapeake* a prize of the *Leopard*. . . . She received in her hull twenty-two round shot, her foremast and main mast were destroyed, her mizzen mast greatly injured, and her standing rigging and sails very much cut. Of the wounded men eight are considered dangerous, and two have lost an arm.

Nothing evinces in more striking colors the insolence of Captain Humphreys [of the *Leopard*] than his immediate return, after this outrage, to the Capes, where he now lies with the other ships of the squadron.[6]

Jefferson himself had recommended this account to his son-in-law as an accurate picture of what had taken place in the waters off Cape Henry. Wars have been fought for less, but Jefferson felt that his first responsibility was to play it cool. He sent a strongly worded protest to London, demanding the return of the seamen, the recall of the British admiral in command of the American station, and a disavowal of the right to search a neutral armed vessel. It was clear to Jefferson, and to the British ambassador Erskine, that this gratuitous attack on the American flag in American waters had aroused the country as nothing else could have done, but Jefferson had not advanced to our current practice of undeclared wars. He would go no further until Congress had met, and Congress could hardly deal intelligently with the situation until a reply from London had been received.

Randolph, of course, labored under no such restraint. His immediate reaction was to seize the offensive. Gunboats, he wrote to the governor of Virginia, armed with Marines "might drive the enemy from our waters. . . . Light corps armed with rifles must be the most efficient troops." He saw himself in command of such a corps, and assured Governor William H. Cabell that he would have no difficulty in enlisting locally "one hundred chosen young men." The governor, as cautious in his own way as Jefferson, was waiting anxiously for instructions from Washington. On July 8 Jefferson had given the order to call out the militia, but naval maneuvers of the kind suggested by Randolph seemed to the governor to go rather beyond his instructions. He politely refused Randolph's offer on the grounds that "a Colonel of Cavalry [Randolph's rank in the militia] could not hold the rank of Captain of a rifle company."[7]

Colonel Randolph was not the only man eager for strong measures. Jefferson himself instructed Cabell to prevent British shore parties "from taking or receiving supplies,"[8] and editor Ritchie of the *Richmond Enquirer* suggested that some men from these English foraging parties should be held hostage until the fate of the four seamen taken off the *Chesapeake* should be determined. That one of the captured seamen was later executed could not have soothed the international tension, although the fact that the victim

was the fourth man, actually an English national, somewhat softened the blow. That England herself was in serious trouble due to
the defection of her Russian ally in the war with Napoleon, when
the tsar Alexander had come to terms with the emperor at Tilsit,
could not be expected to have much effect on American opinion.
The *Chesapeake* affair was in fact a godsend to the American
government, as it gave a concrete and readily recognizable form to
the British threat to American commerce.

Unfortunately for Randolph other less exciting but more de-
pressing concerns weighed upon him at this time. In the same
month that editor Ritchie was discussing the taking of hostages his
paper carried an advertisement of land for sale: "a tract of land
lying on the east side of the Rivanna near Charlottesville containing about six hundred acres. . . . DWELLING HOUSE. . . .
The sale proceeds from a deed of trust . . . which was executed
in December 1802 by William Barber. (Signed) Thomas M. Randolph."

From the description this tract sounds as though it were Jefferson's. In any case, as he told his son-in-law, he considered "our
property as a common stock for our joint family. . . ."⁹

Less helpful to financial difficulties was the public measure
which Jefferson now recommended to the Congress. This was the
embargo on all trade with Great Britain, passed in response to the
British Orders in Council which declared that all neutral vessels
dealing with Britain's enemies were subject to confiscation. The
embargo, of course, was a two-edged sword; it was fully as hard on
the Americans as on the British. Jefferson and his son-in-law both
suffered. The president, in fact, was retiring from office a far poorer
man than when he had entered public service.

Chapter 22

A Mountain Landscape

Gardening as a 7th Fine Art, not horticulture, but the art of embellishing grounds by fancy.

WITH RETIREMENT NEAR Jefferson was turning with delight to his family, and to the care of his gardens and landscaping. His house, after fifteen years of labor, was at last complete. Never again would family and friends have to cope with roofless wings and open flooring. All this was a labor of the past. Now Jefferson could devote himself to the realization of some very old dreams, dating from his first plans for his house on the mountain. Now he could devote himself to what he described to his young granddaughter, Ellen Wayles Randolph, as the seventh fine art: gardening, not horticulture, but the art of embellishing grounds by fancy.[1]

Typically Jefferson had kept notes of all those plans which he had made years ago, when he and his bride, the first Martha, had walked on the top of their little mountain. There had been grottoes, temples, cascades in that young man's imagination. It resulted in some rather inferior verse. The magnificent prose which was later to affect the course of human events did not readily meet the case of the nymph in the grot:

> Nymph of the grot, these sacred springs I keep,
> And to the murmur of these waters sleep;
> Ah! spare my slumbers! gently tread the cave!
> And drink in silence, or in silence lave!

The nymph so addressed was to be the presiding genius of the spring, now nymphless, on the north side of the mountain. There was to be a man-made cave hollowed out of the hillside. "Cover with moss," Jefferson's notes to himself instructed the builder.

"Spangle it with translucent pebbles . . . and beautiful shells. . . . Pave the floor with pebbles. Let the spring enter at the corner of the grotto, pretty high up the side, and trickle down, or fall by a spout into a basin, from which it may pass off through the grotto."

For the grounds in general there were to be deer, rabbits, peacocks, in fact every sort of animal. The notes continue: "Procure a buck-elk, to be, as it were, monarch of the wood; but keep him shy, that his appearance may not lose its effect by too much familiarity. A buffalo might be confined also. Inscriptions in various places, on the bark of trees or metal plates, suited to the character or expression of the particular spot. Benches or seats of rock or turf."[2] Like the landscape parks he had read about, there were to be paths from which these beauties could be seen.

Such plans, precisely recorded in Jefferson's own hand, were the fruit of this young man's extensive reading: in Thomas Whately's *Observations on Modern Gardening*, Lord Kames's *Elements of Criticism*, and in many other books of the period. When at last, he was actually standing in these storied gardens, Jefferson studied them with a critical eye. He toured the ground with a copy of Whately in his hand, and at night he would sit down in lodgings and make notes of what he had seen. The object, of course, was to apply to his own use whatever might be appropriate to Monticello.

His friend Adams kept a diary. New England to the core, this tourist observed that "A national debt of 274 millions sterling accumulated by Jobs, Contracts, Salaries and Pensions in the Course of a Century might easily produce all this Magnificence. . . . The Temples to Bachus and Venus, are quite unnecessary as Mankind have no need of artificial incitements, to such Amuzements."[3]

Jefferson's notes contain no moral comments; he was primarily interested in design. Gardening he called the "7th fine art, not horticulture, but the art of embellishing grounds by fancy," and this art he was determined to bring to his own mountain. Design that was "modern" in the 1780s in England was still quite new in America in 1806. It was not until that date that Jefferson the public man found leisure to set about serious landscaping of his own.

There was, indeed, one model, "the only rival which I have known in America to what may be seen in England."[4] This was the garden at Woodlands, the home of his friend William Hamilton outside Philadelphia. By the word "garden" we must realize that Jefferson was not referring to an arrangement of flower beds, but to those gardens he had seen in England, which were in fact landscaped parks.

To Hamilton he took pains to describe his own site: "The grounds which I destine to improve in the style of the English gardens are in a form very difficult to be managed. The hill is generally too steep for direct ascent, but we make level walks successively along its side, which in its upper part encircle the hill and intersect these again by others of easy ascent."[5] Jefferson was describing his "roundabouts," a complicated system of some twenty miles of roads which offered the same sort of pleasant and easy access to the park that he was developing at Monticello as he had seen employed in the English landscapes.

The whole system of roads had to be accomplished by slave labor using conventional tools; we can hardly be surprised that the ideal could not be achieved in a day. When Mrs. Harrison Smith visited Jefferson in the first year of his retirement from the presidency, she wrote a wonderful description of a tour of the roundabouts, as they were at this date. One early morning Jefferson invited Mrs. Smith and his granddaughter Ellen into a small carriage of his own design (Mrs. Smith called it "a kind of chair") with the object of taking them for a drive around the mountain:

It was with difficulty [Mrs. Smith wrote] that he, Ellen and I found room in [this carriage], and it might well be called the sociable. The first circuit the road was good, and I enjoyed the views it afforded and the familiar and easy conversation, which our sociable gave rise to, but when we descended to the second and third circuit, fear took from me the power of listening to him, or observing the scene, nor could I forbear expressing my alarm . . . on driving over fallen trees, and great rocks which threatened an overset to our sociable, and a roll down the mountain to us. "My dear Madam," said Mr. Jefferson, "you are not to be afraid, or if you are you are not to show it. Trust yourself implicitly to me, I will answer for your safety. I came every foot of this road yesterday, on purpose to see if a carriage could come safely; I know every step I take, so banish all fear." This I tried to do, but in vain.[6]

Mrs. Smith jumped out and walked around the worst places. The road in Jefferson's mind did not quite match the one on the ground.

For the embellishment of his park, dreamed of if not yet wholly achieved, Jefferson turned to Whately, and to the gardens he had seen in 1786. In England, he wrote to Hamilton, beauty in gardening depends "on the variety of hill and dale. . . . Their canvas is of open ground, variegated with clumps of trees distributed with taste." Whately's pages show what Jefferson often observed: how closely landscape design is related to the art of landscape painting. Whately's treatment of the use of groves at Claremont and Esher Place, both places seen by Jefferson, was surely of interest to the landscape architect at Monticello. Whately had written:

Each . . . clump [of trees] is composed of several others still more intimately united; each is full of groupes, sometimes of no more than two trees, sometimes of four or five; and now and then in larger clusters: an irregular waving line, issuing from some little croud, loses itself in the next; or a few scattered trees drop in a more distant succession from the one to the other. The intervals winding here like a glade, and widening there into a dale. . . .[7]

Whately's spelling is hardly modern, but his sense of design is as useful now as it ever was. Jefferson expressed his own enthusiasm in his notes on Esher Place: "The clumps on each hand balance finely. A most lovely mixture of concave and convex."[8]

The trees on Jefferson's mountain presented the landscape architect with quite a different problem. "Under the beaming, constant and almost vertical sun of Virginia," he wrote his friend Hamilton, "shade is our Elysium." Under these conditions open ground must be avoided; the walks, to afford any kind of enjoyment, must be beneath the shade of forest trees. Jefferson suggested what amounts to a compromise:

Let your ground be covered with trees of the loftiest stature. Trim up their bodies as high as the constitution and form of the trees will bear, but so as that their tops shall still unite and yield dense shade. . . . Then, when in open ground you would plant a clump of trees, place a thicket of shrubs presenting a hemisphere the crown of which shall distinctly show itself under the branches of the trees. [With this object in view he would plant] red cedar made to grow in a bush, evergreen privet, pyrocanthus, Kalmia, Scotch broom. . . .

Looking at Monticello today, heavily wooded up the north slope, we may indeed question this idea of "thickets of shrubs" serving in the place of clumps of trees. Jefferson's plans for landscaping the mountain show far more cleared land than exists at present, and no doubt views would have been far easier to manage in the greater areas of cleared land which did, in fact, exist in his day. James Bear tells us that "As early as 1769 [he] had cleared on the north side of Monticello mountain a park of 1850 yards circumference in the vicinity of the north spring near the future location of the Fourth Roundabout. When the Marquis de Chastellux visited TJ in 1782 he reported a score of deer in the park."[9]

For the embellishment of this cleared space Jefferson instructed his overseer at Monticello, Edmund Bacon, "in all the open grounds on both sides of the third and fourth Roundabouts, lay off lots for the minor articles of husbandry, and for experimental culture, disposing them into a ferme ornée by interspersing occasionally the attributes of a garden."[10] Thus he was attempting to create on his mountain a *ferme ornée* on the English model, as he had seen it done at William Shenstone's Leasowes.

The idea of a *ferme ornée*, that is to say the combination of a farm with the attributes of a park, had been in Jefferson's mind ever since his early reading in William Shenstone's description of the Leasowes,[11] the Shenstone place in the west of England. On his visit there in 1786 Jefferson had been well aware of the superior possibilities of his own mountain site. His notes on this visit are almost patronizing. "This is not even an ornamental farm. It is only a grazing farm with a path round it. . . . Architecture has contributed nothing. The obelisk is of brick. . . ."[12]

Time passed, but the president of the United States had not forgotten his plans for landscape gardening. Notes dated 1804[13] show plans no less extensive than those of 1771, often dismissed as mere flights of a young man's fancy. They appear under the heading of "General ideas for the Improvement of Monticello" partially quoted below:

The ground between the upper and lower roundabouts to be laid out in lawns and clumps of trees, the lawns opening so as to give advantageous catches of prospect to the upper roundabout. Vistas from the lower roundabout to good portions of prospect. Walks in this style [a small sketch of diagonal lines linking the horizontal], winding up the mountain. The spring on Montalto either to be brought to Monticello by pipes or to fall over steps of stairs in cascade, made visible at Monticello through a vista.

A fish pond to be visible from the house. . . .

The North side of Monticello below the Thoroughfare roundabout quite down to the river, and all Montalto above the thoroughfare to be converted into park and riding grounds. . . .

(The Thoroughfare was a public road running through the south side of Monticello.)

In addition there are plans for temples in various styles: "A Tuscan Temple . . . proportions of Pantheon; Chinese pavilions copied from the pavilion in Kew gardens; another in the Gothic style, and one to be a model of cubic architecture," such as the Maison Carrée admired by Jefferson in the south of France.

As Jefferson pursued these plans he could recall his visit to Woburn in 1786. With Whately in hand he had observed, "On the top of the hill is a large, octagon structure, and not far from it the ruin of a chapel. . . . The lawn is further embellished by a Gothic building . . . little seats, alcoves and bridges continually occur." [14] Jefferson had returned a second time, more closely to observe these elements of a romantic landscape.

The question is, of course, how much of such landscaping—let alone temple-building—was actually accomplished at Monticello. We know that a considerable quantity of plants were sent down to Monticello from Main's Nursery in Washington. A cart would come up laden with good things for the president's table; it would return with plant material accompanied by detailed instructions as to where and how it should be planted. Such plans, chiefly recorded in Jefferson's Garden Book for 1804, 1806, and 1808, are not hard to find. The difficulty today is to discover which were executed, and which were successfully established. Jefferson, the absentee gardener, had his failures, like the thorn hedge on the north hill side, which turned out "very foul." [15]

By 1806 he was able to describe to his friend Hamilton the various views from his mountain: "Of prospects I have a rich profusion and offering itself at every point of the compass. Mountains distant and near, smooth and shaggy, single and in ridges, a little river hiding itself among the hills so as to show in lagoons only, cultivated grounds under the eye and two small villages. To prevent a satiety of this is the principal difficulty."

It was this satiety which he planned to prevent by "advantageous catches of prospect," in other words, openings through which later guests, following the path of Mrs. Smith, might catch occasional views, judiciously varied, as they rode or walked on the roundabouts.

All this reflects the eye of the landscape painter, traditionally allied with the landscape gardening of the period. Whately carried the art of landscaping one step nearer to the art of painting when he considered the effect of light at different seasons of the year, and at different times of day. At the great park at Stowe he described the light of the setting sun as it shone on one of the many temples that adorn the grounds. Jefferson's siting of his own house shows a similar regard to the effects that only nature may produce. The east-west axis of Monticello was sited toward the point where the Blue Ridge rises behind Carter's Mountain, which he called Montalto. Jefferson had acquired this steep mountain slope with no other apparent object than its relation to the view from his west portico. In a letter to Mrs. Smith he observed the effect of a storm seen approaching over the mountains: "To see it in all its grandeur you should stand at my back door: there we see its progress—rising over the distant Allegany, come sweeping and roaring on, mountain after mountain, till it reaches us, and then when its blast is felt, to turn to our fireside, and while we hear it pelting against the window to enjoy the cheering blaze, and the comforts of a beloved family." [16]

Nothing was permitted to interfere with the view from Jefferson's "back door," that is, from the west or garden front of Monticello. The dependency wings, running from east to west, were roofed at floor level in relation to the house. Unlike the Palladian model for similar wings, they opened outward down the slope, rather than onto the west lawn. Those standing on the steps had a perfectly open line of sight to the summit of Carter's Mountain and beyond to the great mountains. It was what Jefferson was later to plan for his rotunda at the University of Virginia, now unfortunately blocked by Stanford White's Cabell Hall, where only mountains should have met the eye.

After the storm Jefferson typically turned from the grandeur of nature to the simplicity of the fireside and of family joys, and of these the grandchildren were to have a large share. On his return home to enjoy that long-sought retirement, his mind seems to have turned to flower beds rather than temples. For a man leaving the presidency $10,000 poorer than when he had taken office, flowers had one great advantage over temples. They were cheaper. From the President's House he had sent his eldest granddaughter, Anne Cary Randolph, a plan of the beds that he intended to lay out on the west lawn. It showed a "winding walk surrounding the lawn before the house, with a narrow border of flowers on each side of the walk. The hollows of the walk would give room for oval beds of flowering shrubs." [17]

On his retirement the young gardeners, of whom Jefferson now declared himself one, entered on this new hobby with zest. One of the youngest of that team, Ellen Wayles Randolph, described the scene in a letter written many years later to Jefferson's first major biographer, Henry S. Randall:

I remember the planting of the first hyacinths and tulips. . . . The roots arrived, labelled each one with a fancy name. There was Marcus Aurelius, and the King of the Gold Mine, the Roman Empress and the Queen of the Amazons, Psyche, The God of Love, etc., etc. Eagerly and with childish delight I studied this brilliant nomenclature, and wondered what strange and surprisingly beautiful creatures I should see rising from the ground when spring returned. . . .

What joy it was for one of us to discover the tender green breaking through the mold, and run to Grandpapa to announce that we really believed Marcus Aurelius was coming up, or the Queen of the Amazons was above ground! With how much pleasure, compounded of our pleasure and his own, . . . he would immediately go out to verify the fact, and praise us for our diligent watchfulness.[18]

The beds had been laid out with Jefferson's usual precision. Even a flower bed required the same care for true mathematical proportion as would any other design. He took an axis from the center of the west portico, and on this line laid a horizontal grid. The effect, far from being mechanical, is both spacious and interesting, leading the eye to the mountains beyond.

Up until recently authorities were agreed: no temples were built. Now Monticello's resident archaeologist, William Kelso, has laid bare the foundations of an actual temple, at the very spot where one would have wished to find it. At the midpoint on the south border of the long terraced vegetable garden south of the house, overlooking the slope planted in vines and fruit trees, there had stood a garden temple, a viewing place, adapted from the Tuscan style. A 12′6″ square foundation (a workman's error, for Jefferson had specified a 13′6″ square) was uncovered three feet below the present ground level. The bricks for the walls, ordered in 1807, had lain unused until 1812, when Jefferson had paid Hugh Chisholm $28 for laying 7,000 bricks "in the temple." In order to preserve the desired dimension of a cube, the reduced size of the foundation forced Jefferson to omit the architrave which would ordinarily have been used below the roof line. The result is a rather foreshortened effect in what otherwise appears as a pavilion in the correct Palladian style, a deviation from the norm which has been faithfully reproduced.[19]

Placed at this point, parallel to the south edge of the garden and opposite the south pavilion, the temple served to link the house with the garden, and the garden with the park below. To sit there in the spring of the year, above an orchard in full bloom, must have been like sitting on a cloud. From here one can watch the sunset behind the long southern slope of Carter's Mountain, which acts as a frame to the wider view. Close at one's feet the sun gilds the fields of Tufton Farm; in the far distance there is no break in the horizon, no accent point in the wide expanse, other than Willis's Mountain. Tiny in the distance, it appeared like the pyramid of Cheops to those seated in the temple.

There it was, fields and orchards, distant prospect, all laid out before the viewer; views and beauties on a scale that the Leasowes could not touch. If the whole is ever restored, then the whole extent of Jefferson's art as a landscape gardener will again appear. At the present moment Monticello still has something of the character of a busy workshop, as architectural historians, archaeologists, and horticulturists all bend to their work to restore what once was there. It was such a scene, after all, that Jefferson himself met on his return from the presidency to take up life at his beloved Monticello. The house was complete; the landscape was in the process of creation. There was nothing like it, surely, in the whole of that new world.

Tea room, looking
into dining room,
cut glass epergne
in foreground.
Dining room man-
tel shows Wedg-
wood inserts; open
panel on right is
door to dumb-
waiter to wine cel-
lar—*Frank Lucas*

Tea service, Monticello—*Llewellyn*

Northeast bedroom, sometimes called Madison Room because James and Dolley Madison often stayed there. Note the alcove bed, trellis wallpaper bought by Jefferson in Paris, and the folding shutters made by John Hemings—*William Faust*

Hall frieze: composition ornamental design from Desgodetz, *Les Edifices Antiques de Rome,* made in Alexandria, Virginia, by George Andrews, who did ornamental work for Jefferson in 1801–1807—*Thomas Jefferson Memorial Foundation*

Thomas Jefferson: St. Mémin engraving, 1804. This likeness was a family favorite—*Pauline Page: Elizabeth C. Langhorne*

Isaac Coles: St. Mémin engraving, 1807. Coles was Jefferson's secretary during the second administration—*Pauline Page: Elizabeth C. Langhorne*

Meriwether Lewis: an unusual watercolor by St. Mémin showing him in
frontiersman costume, 1807—*New-York Historical Society*

Garden pavilion and view over vegetable garden to Carter's Mountain—
Llewellyn

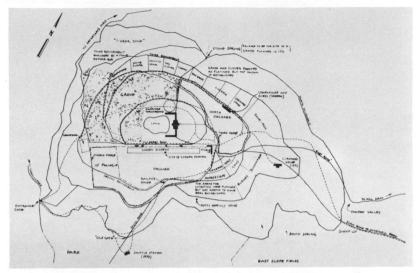

Jefferson's concept for *ferme ornée,* with the articles of husbandry inter-
spersed with the attributes of a garden—*William Beiswanger, Thomas Jefferson
Memorial Foundation*

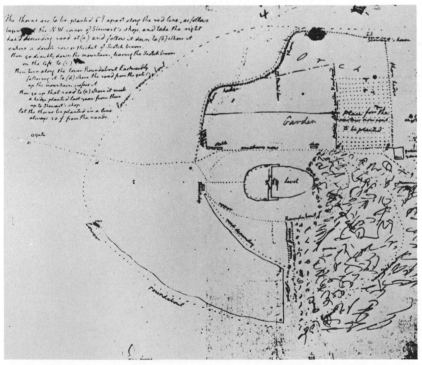

Detail of site plan above, with Jefferson's directions for planting, 1806—
Massachusetts Historical Society

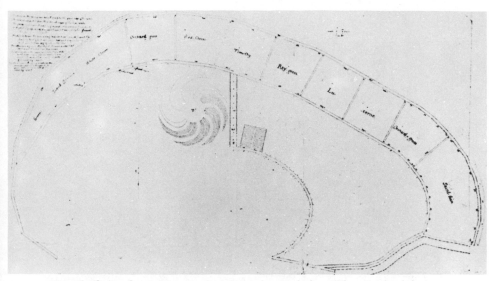

Detail of plan for *ferme ornée*, showing cultivated plots. The pinwheel design
is for a labyrinth of broom—*Huntington Library*

General ideas for the improvement of Monticello, 1804: Jefferson holograph—*Massachusetts Historical Society*

West Lawn, Monticello, watercolor by Jane Bradick Petticoles, commissioned by Ellen Wayles Coolidge. George (age seven), Mary, and Cornelia are shown in middle ground—*Thomas J. Coolidge, Jr.*

Chapter 23

Monticello's Children

As much happiness as can be attained here below . . .

THE PICTURE OF THAT romantic park would have been splendid indeed if ever fully realized. First lack of time and now lack of money hindered the man, who at age sixty-eight explained to his old friend Mme. de Tessé that he preferred flowers to trees, for he should live to see them flourish. If there were to be temples, if there were to be domes, they would appear later, in the public domain, in that last perfect design, his University in Charlottesville.

In the meantime there were the "comforts of a beloved family." Foremost among them, of course, was the presence of Martha, who was her father's housekeeper, his hostess, and his intimate companion. Next in importance were the grandchildren. An elderly scholar in a house with eleven children, give or take a few, of all ages, may not sound like an infallible receipt for family comfort, but this scholar had his own quarters and enjoyed inviolable privacy. Moreover, Jefferson never became "elderly." Keen intellectual curiosity, invincible optimism, and directness remained with him to the end of his life, and his rapport with the children around him was extraordinary. In the complicated arena of politics he had sometimes relied on his friend Madison to steer a course between the ideal and the politically possible. He could be patient, but he had no love of political maneuver. "Political party hatreds," he had told Martha, "destroy the happiness of every being here."[1] This was from Philadelphia as secretary of state. Always the company of children had come as a blessed relief.

The children, too, looked forward to every moment with Grandpapa; they had perfect confidence and could absorb all that he had to offer without the slightest sense of constraint. Where sometimes he had been too demanding a father he could now point out childish error without a hint of rebuke. He could, for example, thank Ellen for her letter, while pointing out that the letter had no date. In her first letter to her dear Grandpapa, Ellen, aged five, asks for books and adds a postscript: "Make haste to come home and see us and all our books in the press." Her letter not only asks for something, she is sure that he will enjoy seeing what they already have. The president answered promptly: "When I left Monticello you could not read, and now I find you can not only read, but write also. I enclose you two little books as a mark of my satisfaction, and if you continue to learn as fast, you will become a learned lady and publish books yourself." [2]

Ellen certainly became a learned lady, but to have published books herself would have shocked her tremendously. Nineteenth-century inhibitions caught up with the lady who could write such charming and perceptive letters to her grandfather's biographer, but who could also close the finest and best account with claiming a woman's privilege: her name must never, never appear in print!

With apologies to Ellen, later to become Mrs. Joseph Coolidge of Boston, we will quote one of her letters to Henry Randall:

I was fond of riding, and was rising above that childish simplicity when, provided I was mounted on a horse, I cared nothing for my equipments. . . . I was beginning to be fastidious, but I had never told my wishes. I was standing one bright day in the portico, when a man rode up with a beautiful lady's saddle and bridle before him. My heart bounded. These coveted articles were deposited at my feet. My grandfather came out of his room to tell me they were mine. . . . My Bible came from him, my Shakespeare, my first writing table, my first Leghorn hat, my first silk dress. . . . Our Grandfather seemed to read our hearts, to see our invisible wishes. . . . [3]

He also played games with the children. Virginia recalled that "cross questions" and "I love my love with an A" were two that she learned from him; they, in turn, would teach him some of theirs. "He would gather fruit for us, seek out the ripest figs, or bring down the cherries from on high above our heads with a long stick, at the end of which there was a hook and a little net bag. . . ."[4] Never had the famous Jefferson ingenuity been put to better use.

When they were all together Jefferson would take out his violin, and Jeff remembered "my grandfather playing . . . and his grand-children dancing around him."

In fact there was no way of growing up at Monticello without being aware of music. Jefferson himself had once practiced the violin for three hours a day; his skill at this later period, as described by Ellen, was that of a "gentlemanly amateur." Walking the floor of his study he would hum to himself, "between writing and reading chores, old Psalm tunes or Scotch melodies." He had an extensive music library and continued his interest in acquiring the finest and latest instruments into nearly the last year of his life. It was in 1825, against Jeff Randolph's strong financial objections, that he bought the fine Currier and Gilbert piano for Virginia. This purchase, a major undertaking, was arranged by the Coolidges in Boston.[5] Jefferson's letter reporting its arrival is warm and even funny: "The piano forte is in place, and Mrs. Carey *happening* to be here has exhibited to us it's full powers, which are indeed great. Nobody slept the first night, nor is the tumult yet over on this the third day of its emplacement."[6]

The young people had their own music for singing and dancing. It could be formal, with a dancing master, or often just as the notion struck them. It was the most fun with a black fiddler. As the girls were growing up, there were usually young men around, Maria's son Francis and then the Trist brothers, Nicholas and Browse. Several of the girls and boys played flageolets. Cornelia Randolph had one, and so did the Trist boys.[7]

There were more formal occasions in Richmond, where Martha Randolph and her daughters had taken part in the local balls. The musicians on these occasions would be black; the most celebrated was Sy Gilliat, a fiddler, and his companion, London Briggs, who played flute or clarinet. The spring and fall race meetings in Richmond and Petersburg would bring these two to perform at the *Race Ball*, vividly described in the book *Richmond in Bygone Days*.

Etiquette required shorts and silks, and pumps with buckles, and powdered hair. The ball was opened by one of the managers and the lady he thought proper to distinguish, with a *minuet de la cour*, putting the grace and elegance of the couples to a severe ordeal.

Such bowing and curtseying, tip toeing and tip fingering, advancing and retreating, attracting and repelling, all in the figures of Z or X, to a tune which would have served for a dead march! A long silken train following the lady, like a sunset shadow; and the gentleman holding a cocked hat under his arm, or in his hand, until at last the lady permitted the gentleman, at full arms-length, to hand her by the very tips of her fingers to a seat, when, with a most profound bow, he retreated backward to seek one for himself.

Then commenced the reel, like a storm after a calm—all life and animation. No solemn walking of the figure to a measured step—but pigeon wings fluttered, and all sorts of capers were cut to the music of Sy Gilliat's fiddle, and the flute or clarinet of his blacker companion, London Briggs.

Contra dances [these were country dances imported from England] followed, and sometimes a congo, or a hornpipe; and when the music grew fast and furious, and the most stately of the company had retired, a jig would wind up the evening.[8]

The order of this entertainment is important, as it illustrates both the aspirations toward European elegance and the natural, home-grown tastes of the participants. This ball was held in the large ballroom of the Eagle Tavern in Richmond, as were all the regular assemblies of the winter season.

Anne Cary, married at seventeen, had not perhaps much opportunity, but Ellen danced her way through many hearts and most of the eastern cities. Later on, the younger girls also went to dances in Richmond, and there were even local balls in Charlottesville, rather patronizingly described by Virginia. Everywhere was the black fiddler, for music was his domain.

Another pleasure shared by black and white was a love of horses. Wormley was the chief Monticello gardener, but originally it had not been so. His first and true love had been the stable. Wormley was a third-generation Hemings, old Betty's grandson, not a Wayles-Hemings but the son of Betty Brown, one of Betty's daughters before her connection with John Wayles. He could describe every one of Jefferson's horses, and how they were used. In this he resembled his master, who prized his daily ride, even into old age. There were three carriage horses, Wormley told the biographer Randall, and besides Jefferson's personal riding horse there were the beautiful matched bays driven to that phaeton which Mrs. Thornton claimed Jefferson had been eight years in building.

The libelous account of Jefferson's abuse of his horses in Gore Vidal's novel *Burr* had its origin, no doubt, in Wormley's description of Arcturus, a riding horse which shied regularly at a very dangerous spot on the mountain. Jefferson "punished him with whip and spur,"[9] as indeed he would have had to do to get by the place at all. Clearly he was not a timid rider, but the wanton abuse attributed to him by Vidal is utterly false.

It is generally believed that Jefferson, for all his love of thoroughbred horses, did not race his own. Actually his roan colt Tarquin, by the famous Eclipse, is described as winning a race from President Washington's Magnolio in Alexandria, while Jefferson was secretary of state.[10] It was this animal, sent back to Monticello, that ran away with the young Patsy, who had rashly mounted him in her father's absence. Jefferson was known to believe that "a lady should never ride a horse which she might not safely ride without a bridle."[11] It is interesting to note that Patsy simply let the horse run himself out up the mountain. She could not have handled the crisis better had she been of the male sex.

Chapter 24

Br'er Rabbit and Br'er Fox

MUSIC, TO THE WHITE FAMILY, was a cherished recreation, one of the amenities of life and of social intercourse. To the plantation blacks it was an essential, all-embracing part of life. In the open land or jungle setting of Africa, the land and its creatures spoke to the people; their response was musical rather than verbal. The form was one of call and response to a leader; in their songs the single line and repeated chorus naturally took shape. In their mutual activities of work and worship their music became a sort of social cement, joining one fellow to another. It offered the slaves a code in which to assert their own egos vis-à-vis the master. A spiritual such as "Steal Away to Jesus" often meant literally steal away to a secret camp meeting in the woods. In their tales of Br'er Fox and Br'er Rabbit, the buckra must have been dull indeed who did not see the intention to put down the white Br'er Fox by the black Br'er Rabbit.

Force alone could not have sustained plantation slavery. The system required accommodation on both sides, even, we may say, on a cultural exchange. We can see it today in the way Western music has been affected by African rhythms. Nothing of this sort occurred with the Indian slaves in the Spanish colonies: the result was simply death under forced labor. The blacks in the American South achieved an extraordinary rate of survival, psychic as well as physical.

Some music, of course, was for the blacks alone, and this was as true for Monticello as for any other plantation. One Christmas, Cornelia Randolph, on her way to the smokehouse, happened upon a black fiddler. Pausing to look she saw "the fiddler as he stood with half closed eyes and head thrown back, with one foot keeping time to his own scraping in the midst of a circle of attentive and admiring auditors."[1] If Cornelia had not appeared, one may be sure that there would have been foot-tapping too among that spellbound audience. So at least it always happened in those clandestine meetings in the woods. "Patterollers" (patrols) were the bane of the slave gatherings, but slaves whose masters were known to permit such gatherings could be exempt. "Up dere 'rounst Monticello ole patterollers would keep away."[2] Or the blacks themselves, stopped on the road, would explain, "We so and so's niggers," and would be allowed to pass on.[3]

There is the wonderful story of how on one occasion, apparently between Monticello and the Coles plantation on the Hardware Creek, the slaves got their own back:

Down at de foot of de mountain was a creek, "Hardware Creek" was its name, an' dere was log laid 'cross it so's you could git to de other side widdout gittin' wet. My brother got down dere 'fore all de res' an' stuck a slice-bar under one end of de log, an' den dere come de patterollers. Henry was hid 'hindst de bushes, an' when de fus' two three patterollers git to walkin' careful-like in de middle of de creek, Henry took an' pried up dat log an' thowed 'em all in de water. Patterollers yelled an' cussed de slaves somep'n terrible, but time dey got dey clothes rung out de slaves was home in bed.[4]

An ex-slave called Sally Ashton described a dance in the quarters (also in Albemarle County) where the fiddler crossed between two worlds: "Ole fiddler was a man named Louis Cane. Chile, he sho' could strung dat fiddle. Never did so much work but Marsa use to keep him, 'cause he use to have him play fo' de balls in de big house. Marse use to pay him too. We never did pay him, 'cause we ain't never had nothin'. But he use to play an' call de figgers 'long as dere was anyone on de floor. Chile, when I was a girl guess I'd ruther dance than eat."[5]

Among their own people some of the black fiddlers clutched the fiddle to their stomachs and played like mad. At the white balls they assumed a more conventional stance. Madison Hemings, we know, played the fiddle, probably at both sorts of dances.

Jefferson himself showed but faint interest in black music, and so far as we know none of the family but his brother Randolph was ever present on such occasions. It was "Old Master's brother, Mass Randall used to come out among black people; play the fiddle and dance half the night."[6] For a description of a religious meeting we can turn to Mary Boykin Chestnut's superb diary:

Jim Nelson, the driver, the stateliest darky I ever saw, tall and straight as a pine tree, with a fine face, and not so very black but a full-blooded African, was asked to lead a prayer. . . . It was the devotional passion of voice and manner which was so magnetic. The Negroes sobbed and shouted and swayed backward and forward, some with aprons to their eyes, most of them clapping their hands and responding in shrill tones: "Yes, God!" "Jesus!" "Savior!" "Bless de Lord, amen," etc. It was a little too exciting for me. I would very much have liked to shout too. . . .[7]

There was one form of black music that the family at Monticello did know well: the songs and stories that Mammy Ursula told the children. Martha was asked by a young friend of the family to set down the words, so that he might use them in a book that he was planning. Eugene Vail had lived in France, and in 1841 he published a book in Paris: *De la Littérature et des hommes de lettres des Etats Unis d'Amérique*. Martha's songs and tales were included in a literal French translation, without, happily, any attempt at dialect. Retranslated into English they still retain, I think, the original folk sound.[8]

Most of them came directly from Monticello, although "The Dairy Key" Martha had probably heard in Richmond. That song was a composition by an old Negro man called Titus, who also sang the song about Old Colonel Tom, Martha's father-in-law. Titus played the mandolin and sang for people of his own race. He was shown in a picture that has now disappeared, but which was known to Vail at the time that he wrote. Unfortunately Vail did not set down the music that should have accompanied the words.

Old Colonel Tom
While Old Colonel Tom lived and prospered,
There was nothing but joy at Tuckahoe.

Now that Old Colonel Tom is dead and gone,
No more joy for us at Tuckahoe.

Vail says that he has omitted the chorus as "being guttural sounds impossible to imitate on paper," although one senses that this chorus may have been an important part of the whole.

The Dairy Key

Young Mary was the dairy maid,
But Nancy lost the dairy key.
Oh! For forty days and forty nights,
We looked in vain for the dairy key!

We were so far beyond the sun,
Searching for the dairy key,
That we could see there blacks that we couldn't understand,
All that, alas, without finding the dairy key.

This was Titus's song, but Martha herself, and perhaps all the world, might have gone looking for the dairy key.

The rest of these songs came from Monticello directly. Captain Shields was a police officer in Richmond noted for harassing the Negroes. Next we have one called by Professor Perdue a corn-shelling song; it is in the traditional call and response form. Nancy reappears here in a better light, but traditionally she is one of the less respectable members in the black cast of folk characters.

After the songs we have two tales. The last one has been published elsewhere, but to the best of our knowledge Mammy Dinah and her dogs could have been lost to posterity if Martha had not set them down. The devil is a familiar character in such tales, not always of too bad repute, but here he is certainly no friend to Mammy Dinah. Her story is told as half-song, half-tale.

Captain Shields

I was an old hare, I was born in the snow,
I was pursued by the black horse of shields.
Grass grows green, tears roll down my cheeks,
Still Shields is mayor of the town.
Oh! Mr. Koon, you come too soon,
Just let us rest until tomorrow.

A Corn-Shelling Song

I bought me a fine horse in Baltimore County,
   Oh! Nancy, Oh!
And then a house with seven chimneys,
   Oh! Nancy, Oh!

I bought me a chair to sit next to my Nancy,
   Oh! Nancy, Oh!
And boots of leather to walk with my Nancy,
   Oh! Nancy, Oh!

Oh Miss Nancy is proud and haughty,
   Oh! Nancy, Oh!
Oh Nancy dear, Nancy my dear, why don't you marry me?
   Oh! Nancy, Oh!

(One voice will start these songs, then all together will join in the chorus.)

A Rowing Song

My old mistus don't love me,
Cause I won't eat her black-eyed peas,
   Oh yo! Oh yo! Oh yo!

Up there on the mountain, I whipped up my horse,
Then I galloped further than Diffiki,
   Oh yo! Oh yo! Oh yo!

I tied my horse to the doctor's post,
The poor beast caught the whooping cough,
   Oh yo! Oh yo! Oh yo!

The Turkey Barn

I went behind the turkey barn,
There I fell upon my knees;
I almost died of laughin',
Listening to those turkeys sneeze.

I went behind the turkey barn,
I didn't want to stay;
But how could I keep from laughin',
When I saw those gluttons pray?

Mammy Dinah and Her Three Dogs

There was once a woman they called Mammy Dinah. [In the French she is called "Diah."] She had three dogs, George, Ring, and Duncan, who were so mean and so strong that she could hardly hold them behind nine doors locked with nine keys. These dogs obeyed her always, and were so devoted to her that wherever she might be, even out of sight and hearing, Mammy Dinah had only to sing a certain air which she used to call them, for them to surmount all obstacles and make their way to her side. This woman, with her dogs, enjoyed supernatural power; but as she was good-natured she never used it to do harm to anyone. For the very reason of this power and her virtue there was an evil spirit who, jealous of her and hating her bitterly, never ceased his efforts to destroy her.

One day Mammy Dinah locked up her dogs as usual, and went early to the woods. There she met the evil genie, who ran toward her at full speed, in order to slay and devour her. As it was impossible to run as fast as he, she did her best to escape by climbing a tree. The devil could not climb, but he was an experienced wood cutter, and never went out without carrying two hatchets. In order the quicker to reach his prey he took a hatchet in each hand, and began to chop the tree with terrifying speed. Mammy Dinah's heart trembled. However, she did not lose her nerve. Perched in her tree she began to sing the tune which possessed the magic charm for her dogs. It went something like this:

> Oh help Mammy Dinah, George! and you, my Duncan!
> And you also, Ring! Come then, Oh my Ring!
> How slow you all are in coming to me!

To which the Devil replied:

> Death to you! I'll kill you. Death to you, Caby.
> Soon I'll have you. Oh! I'll get you at last.
> Go on! Soon I'll have you! You will be mine!

And all this time the hatchet was going at a great rate:

> pan, pan, pan, ducka, ducka, ducka, . . .

(Dinah's part is taken in a voice slow and plaintive; the Devil is abrupt and rapid.)

At the first call from Mammy Dinah her dogs forced three of the doors closed against them, at the second they broke down three others, and finally at the third the last three fell. Before she could sing for the fourth time they were at her side. They fell upon the evil genie and tore him to pieces, thus delivering Mammy Dinah forever from her mortal enemy.

Mr. Fox Tricks Mr. Rabbit and Is Tricked in Return

One day a fox, pursued by hounds, fled to a rabbit hole, begging the rabbit to let him in, so that he might hide. "None of that," replied the rabbit, "I am afraid that you will eat me if I let you in." "Oh no," said the fox, "I wouldn't do that for the world." But knowing that the rabbit had little faith in his words, he added, "Let me just put my nose in your home; you know that with all the rest of my body outside I could not hurt you." The rabbit was good-natured, and although he hardly understood what good it would do the fox to have only his nose in the hole, nevertheless he opened his door just a crack, enough to let in the nose. But hardly had he done this when the fox begged him to let in one of his ears; this being granted, he made the same request for the other. Soon it was a matter of one paw, then another, then for the body, and then, one after another, for the two hind paws, and when the whole was in except for the tail which the rabbit held pinched in the door, thus still holding the fox in his power, the latter said in the most submissive tone in the world: "I am sure, my dear sir, that you will not be so cruel as to allow the dogs to tear me to pieces in your very house, which they will certainly do if they see my tail sticking out, as it is at present."

The rabbit, not being cruel by nature, yielded out of pity, and decided to take the risk he would run in shutting himself up with the fox, who moreover never ceased his promises to do no harm. So he let the tail enter. Once in, the fox, claiming that he did it for security, locked the door from the inside.

The two pretended friends sat down opposite one another in front of the fire, where a large pot of water was boiling in preparation for the rabbit's supper. The latter, feeling uneasy so close to the fox, spoke little; the other, for his part, was equally silent, and seemed to be thinking of something very pleasant, for he was smiling and looking pleased with himself. Meanwhile, he was staring so hard at his companion that the rabbit became more than ever uneasy, but, hiding his agitation as best he could, he said: "Neighbor fox, what pleases you so much, why do your teeth shine so brightly?" "That," said the fox with a grimace that made the other tremble, "is because I am in a hurry to feast on some of your tender bones." Still the rabbit did not entirely lose his presence of mind, and, seeming to pay little attention to the fox's remark, he walked in a casual manner toward the window, and stood there looking out for several minutes. At last the fox in his turn asked: "What are you looking at out there, Mr. Rabbit, with so much attention?" "I am only watching the hunter and his hounds," replied the rabbit, "who are coming nearer and nearer." "The hunter and the hounds!" cried the fox. "For the love of God, dear Rabbit, hide me somewhere. I am afraid that if they come near they will break down your door and take me." "If you wish you may hide in that box," the rabbit said, showing him the box and lifting the lid. The fox jumped in at once; the rabbit closed the lid and turned the key. He took a gimlet, and pierced a number of holes in the lid. "Why do you do that?" asked the fox. "So that you may have more air," and the rabbit continued to drill more holes until the lid was completely perforated.

Taking boiling water in a gourd he poured it over the fox, who cried: "Rabbit, your house is full of fleas, I feel them biting over my whole body." The rabbit replied by pouring a second gourd of boiling water over the fox, who saw soon enough that it wasn't fleas that were bothering him. He opened his mouth to cry out, and received the whole contents of the pot down his throat, which ended his days.

So much for Br'er Fox! "I tremble," Jefferson once said, "indeed I tremble for my country when I reflect that God is just." Perhaps the fate of Br'er Fox was satisfying, in an obscure way, to both black and white, for both knew in their hearts: "His justice cannot sleep forever."[9]

Chapter 25

The Colonel Goes to War

Where stood the foremost rank, how fair they lie,
The brave and good who for their country die.

BY THE TIME OF Jefferson's retirement both the Hemingses and the Randolphs at Monticello had reached the third generation. Of the grandchildren Anne Cary had been the first to marry, in September 1808. The bride was seventeen, and the groom, Charles Lewis Bankhead, was twenty. No one at the time could have foreseen what an utter disaster this marriage was to be. Jefferson wrote happily to the bride, "What is to become of our flowers? . . . You must really make out a book of instructions for Ellen. . . ." [1]

It is not clear when Bankhead first began to drink heavily. He tried the law, he tried farming. Nothing succeeded. By 1815 he had become an incurable drunkard, and a physical menace to his wife. In the words of her sister Ellen, later Mrs. Coolidge, Anne's marriage was "the only thing . . . in our family history to which the word tragic might well be applied." [2] While the qualifying word "only" may be in doubt, there is no doubt as to the tragedy of this marriage.

Before this trouble came to a head, Randolph suffered another financial disaster, although this time, due to the hazards of war, it was not entirely of his own doing. The Embargo Act had been repealed in March 1809, and a less effective nonintercourse measure took its place. British depredations on American shipping continued, and in June 1812 President Madison asked the Congress to declare war against Great Britain. Congress readily complied, at the very time that, unknown as yet to the men on the American side of the Atlantic, the Orders in Council to which the Americans objected, were being revoked in London. As it turned out, both the beginning and even the last battle of this war might never have taken place if there had been a modern wire service in operation at that date.

While still in Washington Congressman Randolph had astonished Senator Plumer by keeping pistols and a sword over his mantel at Frost and Quinn's boardinghouse. Now, of course, he was eager to go to war. As a lieutenant colonel of the Virginia militia he spent the first year of the war at home, while others, among them his erstwhile second, Isaac Coles, went to attack the enemy on the Canadian border. Understandably restless, he embarked on a speculation in flour, lining up 23,300 bushels of wheat at the beginning of the war. In 1813, when the British had blockaded the mouth of the Chesapeake, Randolph, with his usual ill luck, was left holding 3,650 barrels of flour, cut off from the New England market and impossible to dispose of in Virginia. It was a hard plight indeed for the dedicated but inactive warrior. He would have found financial profit, not to say salvation, with peace, while with every instinct he longed for war.[3]

Peace had never treated Randolph kindly. He seems to have been conscious of his political failure when he wrote to his friend Francis Gilmer of the great exercise he was forced to take on his farm which, he said, unfitted him for mental exertion: "I find myself sometimes from the same cause neglecting the most urgent business. . . . My moral [i.e., conclusion] is treat the mind as a material existence. . . . To strengthen it give it regular exercise, but be cautious not to put it suddenly to any new exertion which you are not convinced beforehand it can perform readily and completely."[4]

If Randolph had consciously desired failure, he could not have devised a better receipt.

On March 3, 1813, the longed-for commission as a colonel in the regular army of the United States came through. He sat down to write his will. He discussed with Martha the possibility of death. Would she marry again? he asked her. He pressed the question more than once, and she repeatedly assured him, no, she would not. That he could even have suspected such a thing while her father lived, shows how inaccessible were the reaches of his own mind to Randolph. However, there was no doubt of his confidence in Martha's abilities:

I, Thomas Mann Randolph the elder of the County of Albemarle of the State of Virginia upon mature reflection and in the most deliberate manner do publish and declare this writing to be my last Will and Testament. Having from the experience of twenty-three years full confidence in the understanding, judgment, honour and impartial maternal feeling of my beloved wife Martha and considering that her time of life precludes all reasonable apprehension of her contracting another marriage which I might nevertheless have felt if I had not received from her frequently very solemn assurances to the contrary I give and bequeath to my said wife my whole estate real and personal to distribute among her children and retain for her own use as she may think fit after paying all my just debts according to such principles of settlement as I may have agreed to in my life time with the different parties as they will shew. I recommend to her to sell the Varina estate to pay the debts but I advise her at the same time to reclaim all the tide land [detailed directions for doing this follow] . . . the estate by that operation will be made worth $80 or $100,000. . . .

Again I recommend her to divide Edgehill as I have done into three separate farms after giving Jefferson the part allotted to him. . . . [More detailed directions as to this division follow.] Signed, sealed, published and declared before, etc.[5]

The document makes no mention of cash or slaves; in effect he leaves everything not specifically to do with land up to Martha.

More inspiriting than the drawing of a will were the verses he copied and sent to his young friend Francis Gilmer:

> Where stood the foremost rank, how fair they lie,
> The brave and good who for their country die.
> How wretched he who leaves his native fields
> To beg the bread a foreign harvest yields!
>
> The land and those we love let *us* defend,
> Regardless when this anxious life may end.
> Young men! in firm array prepare to fight;
> Unfelt be fear, disdained be shameful flight;

Let mighty hearts beat high in bosoms strong;
Think not of life while in the hostile throng.[6]

Such a death would have wiped the slate clean. What actually took place was a lackluster campaign on the Canadian border with, of all people, General Wilkinson in command. (Wilkinson had been cleared of the charge of conspiracy at the trial of Aaron Burr. It later appeared that he had been guilty, as Randolph had always believed.)

It was up to the colonel himself to recruit his regiment, the Twentieth Infantry. Although far from full strength, indeed with fewer than 600 men out of an authorized 1,094, the regiment proceeded on its march north in the fall of 1813, destined to join the forces of Gen. James Wilkinson. This was to be the Americans' second attempt. The campaign of 1812 had resulted in four abortive efforts to cross the St. Lawrence River. Ill provisioned and ill prepared (the troops under the command of Lt. Colonel Isaac Coles, for example, had never handled oars), these attempts at attacking across the Canadian border never got off the ground. The campaign of the following year in which Randolph took part fared little better.

The colonel shared with his men the hardships of that march north in the fall of the year, often sleeping on the ground with no more protection than a single blanket. Hardy as he was, at forty-five he feared the onset of "a permanent rheumatism." By the time Randolph joined the army on Grenadier Island, his command had dwindled to 230 men. On the morning of November 7 he received orders to join an assault on Fort Matilda, held by the British on the Canadian side of the river. Waiting for orders to embark, they could hear the Indians and the Canadian militiamen "firing, whooping and hollering" on the opposite bank. Randolph was to command the left wing of forces under Col. Alexander Macomb. As darkness fell he drew up his men in orderly fashion and loaded them into the waiting barges. When they drew near to the Canadian side, the enemy opened fire with rifles and muskets, several shots striking the water around the boats. As they approached the fortified blockhouse, several more rounds were fired, and then the enemy fled. It was Randolph's baptism of fire, and his one and only experience of that lead to which he had so enthusiastically referred.

Farther up the river other American troops were repulsed by a numerically inferior but better-led British force. Wilkinson gave the order to withdraw, and the Canadian campaign of 1813, never more than a halfhearted effort, came to an end. The troops went into winter quarters on the American side of the river. Few American lives had been lost to British fire, but many succumbed to bad food, exposure, and disease. "My men are still dying every day," Coles had written home the previous winter, and Randolph's men were no better off. Log huts were being built, but many of the sick had been exposed to wind and weather. Their colonel, in spite of his commission, was no professional soldier. After the fashion of the day, he obtained leave, and returned to his own fields at Edgehill.[7]

There were problems enough at home to engage any man's attention. Through Martha's efforts he had been appointed collector of the revenue for the Albemarle District. It no doubt felt like a comedown to the colonel, but it commanded a salary of $4,000 a year, which the Randolphs were in no position to forgo.[8] At this time his flour was still under blockade, and Varina was still unsold. Both Martha and Jefferson thought that one campaign had been enough, but when Randolph was considered for a command at Norfolk, he vacillated. In 1814 the British fleet was in the Chesapeake, threatening Washington and Baltimore, and the government was anticipating a possible move on Richmond. Although still "impatient to risk honor, fortune, life," in defense of his country, his hesitation cost him the Norfolk command. Still unable to make a definite choice by resigning his commission, he remained available for service if called. In August he solved some of his financial problems by mortgaging Edgehill; in the following month he received orders to assume command of militia forces in defense of Richmond.

Now again he could harbor hope of military glory. Unfortunately for the colonel the British were turned back by the Americans under Gen. Samuel Smith and Gen. John Stricker at Baltimore. They never got to Richmond. Randolph's command languished in camp, suffering the usual losses through illness, boredom, and desertion. Once more Randolph returned home, this time for good. He had sought every risk, courted every danger, but somehow had failed to become a hero. Without doubt he had sometimes dreamed of lying dead in that foremost rank. Randolph's military service did however have one long-term result, unanticipated, unplanned, but nevertheless decisive. During the colonel's absence his eldest son, Jeff, had taken over some of the responsibilities of management at Monticello. So it began, the takeover by the "heavy-seeming boy" of whom Martha had once despaired, and whose capabilities Jefferson had very early seen as a possible alternative to his own and Randolph's unskillful management of affairs.[9]

In 1809 we catch sight of this most important member of the Monticello family as a boy of sixteen, intensely ambitious to prove himself as a student. He was in Philadelphia taking courses recommended by his grandfather. Significantly, they did not include law, but were rather weighted toward the physical sciences, and even included surgery, which Jefferson considered a useful art for the master of a plantation. Jefferson wrote to the boy's father from Washington, "[he] is become so incessantly studious that Dr. Logan, who is here, advises me to caution him on the subject. He had got into the habit of reading until one, two, or three o'clock in the night, and then not sleeping. Mr. Peale [with whom Jeff was lodging] finds it necessary to carry him to bed when he goes himself. . . ." Jefferson also wrote of the need of a good farm overseer, and added, "It will not be long before Jefferson [as he always called his grandson] can aid us both." All this appears sensible enough, but Jeff was not unaware of his grandfather's true opinion of his abilities.

During his stay with the Peales in Philadelphia, young Jeff had become a favorite of this family of painters, and the elder Peale, Charles Willson, painted his likeness. When Jeff returned to Monticello, his grandfather hung the portrait on the parlor wall, but in the second rank of his portrait gallery, where indeed it hangs today. Jefferson pointed out this position to the young man and in words that Jeff never forgot, for he quoted them years later, observed "had you been educated you would have been entitled to a place in the first [row]. You will always occupy the second."

We have only Jeff's word for this exchange, but that Jeff, like some other members of his family, was aware of his own position is shown by the comment which follows in his memoir: "In after life when I would lament to my mother the disadvantage I suffered from neglected education, she would reply, my son if you had been in professional or in public life what would have become of us? I assented, regretting the necessity of the sacrifice, but never the sacrifice." [10]

During this period after his return to private life, Jefferson tried very hard to make Monticello self-supporting. Wine and books (at least to Jefferson's mind) were necessary purchases from abroad, as were seeds and plants, although these were often traded among his fellow gardeners, but almost everything else, with the exception of a silk dress now and then, or a guitar for a granddaughter, could be made at home. For this purpose the highly trained Hemings family were indispensable. John Hemings, Betty Hemings's son by a white carpenter at Monticello named Nielson, had been apprenticed to Jefferson's principal builder, James Dinsmore, and soon himself became a master builder and cabinetmaker. The Monticello black- smith was Joe Fosset, son of Mary Hemings and a white father. According to Edmund Bacon, long the overseer at Monticello, Joe "was a very fine workman; could do anything with steel or iron." He had learned his trade from William Stewart, a white smith who was accustomed to indulge in what Jefferson referred to as "idle frolics," in other words, much time off for drink. [11]

Apart from the regular construction work the most ambitious project in which these two Hemings craftsmen were employed (for we may consider Joe Fosset a Hemings) was Mr. Jefferson's "fine carriage," after a design made by himself. John did the cabinet work on the body and Joe the iron work. Granddaughter Ellen had been commissioned to buy fifteen yards of scarlet rattinett for the upholstery, which proved to be two yards short. Jefferson sent to Richmond for the additional yardage by mail. This carriage was perhaps the most sophisticated of the much fine work done by the Hemingses of Monticello.

Although at this time Jefferson had already freed two Hemingses, James and Robert, and would in his lifetime allow two more, Sally's two oldest, to "walk away," Joe Fosset was not freed until Jefferson's death. In July 1806, while the master was at Monticello, Joe had run away "without the least word of difference with anybody, and indeed having never in his life received a blow from anyone." Writing to a livery stable keeper to enlist his aid in apprehending the runaway, Jefferson seems genuinely indignant that Joe could have done such a thing: "I must beg you to use all possible diligence in searching for him in Washington and Georgetown and if you can find him have aid with you to take him as he is strong and resolute. . . ." [12]

His agent replied: "I met with him in the President's yard going from the President's House" (where it was thought he would have gone to see Edy, a girl to whom "he was formerly connected"). The lover, as no doubt he was, was taken and returned to Monticello.

As Joe had been "about twelve years working at the blacksmith's trade" it would seem that he might have made it on his own in freedom, and that therefore, according to his custom, Jefferson might have let him "walk away." Perhaps significantly he was not a Wayles-Hemings, nor was he nearly as white as those members of the clan. More likely Jefferson's reason for going in pursuit of Joe was a practical one. Whether or not Joe could have survived on his own in the white world, a blacksmith was needed at Monticello, one who was not given to "idle frolics."

Chapter 26

The Bankheads

The only thing in our family history to which the word tragic might be applied.

ELLEN, THE PURCHASER of the red rattinett for her grandfather's carriage, had been visiting in Richmond. She was the third eldest, and by all odds the brightest, of the grandchildren. It was to this shrewd and frank analyst of character to whom Henry Randall, the first biographer, turned, when he wanted a first-hand picture of family life. He could not have been better served if Jane Austen herself had been resident at Monticello. "Ellen," Martha had reported to her father, "is very apt."

In 1814 Ellen was visiting her father's oldest sister in Richmond, who had bought her, as she wrote her mother, "a white lustring dress trimmed with a broad silk lace and cost only $20." Ellen was seventeen, and already aware of the family need for economy. She was, however, well prepared for the social pleasures of the city, especially those of music and dancing. In this, as in most other things, she had before her the example of her mother, and of the many opportunities of listening to music at Monticello. There were also the many times she had danced at home to the music of a black fiddler. Monticello had certainly not been a bad school for the formal dances to which Ellen was now introduced.

Ellen adored her mother. Visits in those days of difficult traveling over roads deep in mud and spring rains were lengthy affairs. Ellen, not yet eighteen and out in the world for the first time wrote, "I never knew the extent of my feeling toward you until I have been separated from you some days."[1] Four weeks later she wrote again: "I have never time to say all that I wish to say, or to tell you how sincerely I love you, in fact how completely my affection for you is the passion of my life, and how trifling every other feeling is in comparison with that. No human being ever loved a mother as much as I do you, but then no one ever had such a mother. . . ."[2]

These outpourings were not in any way due to boredom or to lack of success on the social scene. "I have frequently been attended by the *elegant Barksdale*, and as that is an honor which he has never yet paid to any other lady, the town has decided that my charms have thawed his heart." She has been entertained, it would seem, by the whole town, and has looked over all its eligible young men. All are coxcombs but Francis Gilmer and Able Parker Upshur, a member of the Virginia House of Delegates from Accomac County. Barksdale, once so attentive, has now cooled. Perhaps an earlier suggestion by Ellen that "he is easily offended at a mere hint of his faults" may have had something to do with that.

"I am beginning to get weary of Richmond," she wrote at last, "or rather of the dissipated life I lead at present." Several years later in another letter this highly intelligent and sensitive young woman compares the life of the town with the life that Monticello offers: "At Monticello I live in the almost constant exercise of my heart and understanding, having constantly before me objects of warmest affection and highest admiration—the conversation I hear there is completely the feast of reason and I would not *permanently* change my situation with anyone living."[3]

A young visitor from Boston, George Ticknor, accurately described the scene at Monticello which so charmed Ellen, as it appeared to him in February 1815. Although more tolerant than Mrs. Thornton, Ticknor too is aware of certain eccentricities. He is struck by the strange furniture of the hall:

On one side hang the head and horns of an elk, a deer, and a buffalo; another is covered with curiosities which Lewis and Clark found in their wild and perilous expedition. On the third was the head of a mammoth . . . containing the only *os frontes*, Mr. Jefferson tells me, that has yet been found. On the fourth side, in odd union with a fine painting . . . is an Indian map on leather, of the southern waters of the Missouri, and an Indian representation of a bloody battle, handed down in their traditions.
    . . . Mr. Jefferson [is] more than six feet high, with dignity in his

appearance, and ease and graciousness in his manner. . . . As dinner approached he took us into the drawing room. . . . Here are the best pictures. . . . These include portraits of Columbus, Americus Vespucceus, Magellan, etc., copied, Mr. Jefferson said, from originals in the Florence gallery. Farther around, Mr. Madison in the plain, Quaker like garb of his youth, Lafayette in his Revolutionary uniform, and Franklin in the dress in which we always see him. There were other pictures, and a copy of Raphael's Transfiguration. This drawing room opened on west portico—high ceilings, parquet floors [observed by Mrs. Thornton] highly polished. Long French windows, French mirrors, and Louis XVI chairs. At dinner—Mrs. Randolph and Col. Randolph, Thomas Jefferson Randolph and Ellen—Mr. Jefferson's conversation: Discursive manner and love of paradox, with the appearance of sobriety and cool reason. He seems equally fond of American antiquities and especially the antiquities of his native state, and talks of them with freedom. . . . He has too the appearance of fairness and simplicity—love of old books and young society.

[His] library—arranged according to the divisions of human learning made by Lord Bacon. Jefferson particularly relished a collection which he called the Book of Kings, documents of royal scandal.
Daily Schedule:

At eight o'clock the first bell is rung in the great hall, and at nine the second summons you to the breakfast room, where you find everything ready. . . . After breakfast the children retire to their schoolroom with their mother, Mr. Jefferson rides to his mills on the Rivanna, and returns at about twelve. At half past three the great bell rings, and those who are disposed resort to the drawing room, and the rest go to the dining room at the second call of the bell, which is at four o'clock. The dinner was always choice, and served in the French style; but no wine was set on the table till the cloth was removed. The ladies sat until about six, then retired, but returned with the tea tray a little before seven, and spent the evening with the gentlemen; which was always pleasant, for they are obviously accustomed to join in the conversation, however high the topic may be. [An education in itself, of which Ellen took every advantage.] At about half past ten, which seemed to be their usual hour of retiring, I went to my chamber, found there a fire, candle, and a servant in waiting to receive my orders for the morning, and in the morning was waked by his return to build the fire.

. . . The night before we left young Randolph came up late from Charlottesville, and brought the astounding news that the English had been defeated before New Orleans by General Jackson. . . . His grandson went to [Jefferson's] chamber with the paper containing the news. But the old philosopher refused to open his door, saying he could wait till the morning. . . .

One morning, when he came back from his ride, he told Mr. Randolph, very quietly, that the [mill] dam had been carried away the night before. From his manner I supposed it an affair of small consequence, but I found the country ringing with it. Mr. Jefferson's great dam was gone, and it would cost $30,000 to rebuild it.[4]

Ticknor was impressed by this household—as who would not have been? Nevertheless, he found the philosopher "notional," both in matters of dress and of ideas. For the former, "sharp toed shoes, corduroy small clothes, and red plush waistcoat . . . have been laughed at till he might perhaps wisely have dismissed them." Most upsetting of all to this son of New England, he talked of "the natural impossibility that one generation should bind another to pay a public debt, one of the curious *indicia* of an extraordinary character, but a perfect gentleman in his own house."

The above passages might have been called "Jefferson at Home," a picture, not perhaps of the flawless sage generally presented to us, but one nevertheless of a unique and durable charm.

Some years later it was this young friend who sent Joseph Coolidge to visit Monticello. Coolidge was the man who at last succeeded where so many others had failed. It was as Mrs. Joseph Coolidge that Ellen Randolph was finally persuaded to leave Olympus for that other intellectual mecca, Boston, Massachusetts.

Young Jeff Randolph, bearer of the news of the battle below New Orleans, had matured since his days as a student in Philadelphia. In his post as collector of the county revenue, he had had some experience of business, and he had spent the summer of 1814 on active duty with the militia east of Richmond. This Randolph was not so much a Randolph as a Jefferson of an earlier day. He had inherited the physical strength and practical ability of his grandfather Peter, and felt little sympathy for the type represented by his paternal grandfather, the lordly but improvident Colonel Tom of Tuckahoe.

As a boy of ten, Jeff had been given a gun, and had roamed the woods alone. He had spent much time with the Negroes while his father was absent on the road to his various farms, and his mother had left him at Edgehill. He was allowed, he said, to wander as he pleased, usually with his boyhood companion, little Phil (John Jupiter Ammon Philip Evans). Phil was to become the faithful body servant of later years. "The old slaves," Jeff said, "lorded it over the children of the family, and we got reprimands or punishments on their complaints." If there was any switching to be done, Ursula, who had been in the family since Martha's childhood, was the one to do it.[5] Jeff, not extraordinary in his time and place, grew up to have conventional ideas about slavery. He believed, as long as he lived, in an "inferior race."

As a plantation manager of the period, Jeff far surpassed both his father and his grandfather; Jefferson, indeed, could not have made a wiser choice. The change occurred gradually. Jeff had taken over the mill in his father's absence at the wars; and in 1815, a climactic year, the entire operation was put into his hands. Financial pressures were still acute. Early in February Jefferson had sold his magnificent library to Congress for $23,950, a sum fixed by an appraiser who had valued the books by so much per volume, depending on their size. It was, perhaps, a rather inadequate method. Sarah Nicholas Randolph believed that this price was probably little more than half their original cost.[6] It helped, but the financial relief was not as great as Jefferson had a right to expect. Randolph's efforts to sell Varina remained unavailing, nor was he happy to see his son taking over responsibilities, however irksome, that had once been his.

A happy event of this year was Jeff's marriage to Jane Hollins Nicholas, daughter of Jefferson's old friend Wilson Cary Nicholas of Mt. Warren. To her old friend from her days in Philadelphia, now Mrs. Elizabeth Trist, Martha wrote: "Jefferson has married a lovely little woman, one whom it is not possible to see without interest."[7] Others of the family were not, at first, of this opinion. Jeff's sisters thought Jane's mother mercenary, and Mrs. Nicholas

herself, never easily pleased, told Mrs. Coles of nearby Enniscorthy
that Mrs. Randolph was "a very vulgar looking woman." Once
these slight disturbances had passed, Jane herself won all hearts at
Monticello. Martha gave the young couple the dome room, that
chamber that floats so romantically above the house, now for this
young couple in reality a "temple of love." Eight circular windows
look out on the mountains beyond. Jeff and Jane were its occupants
for their first two years of comparative holiday in what later became a fruitful and laborious life together.

Life below stairs was not always so idyllic. The Bankhead marriage, which had promised so well, by 1816 had developed into a
nightmare. Jefferson's letter to Dr. Bankhead, Charles's father, describes an alcoholic beyond control, although clearly he has made
every effort to control Bankhead's drinking, even describing the
problem as a medical one. But then, as now, there was no simple
medical cure.

There had been some hope: An early visit to Charlottesville however
damped these hopes, and this repeated and repeated till it became
daily, put an end to them; he returned usually in the evening, and in a
state approaching insanity. Among other acts indicating it he committed an assault on his wife of great violence, ordered her out of the
room, forbidding her to enter it again, and she was obliged to take
refuge for the night in her mother's room. Nor was this a new thing. In
the morning when cooled he would become repentant and sincerely
distressed, but recur again to the same excesses. . . . When sober he
spoke of selling his farm and moving elsewhere. Said he had lost all
consideration in this neighborhood. . . .

Jefferson suggested that Dr. Bankhead alone might be able to
control his son. "His habits would follow him wherever he went,
except under your roof," but this too was an idle hope. As for
Randolph, the only course was to keep that fiery gentleman as
much as possible in ignorance. "These details," Jefferson told Dr.
Bankhead, "are very much unknown to Mr. Randolph."[8]

There was, of course, absolutely nothing to be done if Anne
herself would not leave her husband, and this she would not do. At

Monticello the serenity of its master, the fixed meal hours, and the system of bells had always made for an ordered existence. Now Bankhead, when not comatose in bed, lounged about the house. From time to time he could be persuaded to go to his father, where for brief periods he might sober up, only to turn up again at Monticello. Martha wrote her father, then at Poplar Forest: "We are all well but poor Anne. Mr. Bankhead has returned, and recommenced his habits of drunkenness. . . . Sending him to the madhouse is but a temporary remedy, for after a few weeks he would be returned with renewed health to torment his family the longer." With the sight of Anne's suffering before her eyes Martha cannot be blamed for suggesting her own solution: "I really think the best way would be to hire a keeper for him . . . and let him finish himself at once." [9]

Another member of the household directly, as it were, in the line of fire was Burwell Hemings. As Jefferson's butler he was entrusted with the keys to the wine cellar. When Bankhead, in a frenzy, had struck this faithful servant, it was a blow to Jefferson at his most vulnerable point. It was bad enough to have Bankhead beat his wife, that was a family sorrow, but to have him strike an utterly dependent slave, that was to violate a point of honor.

Ignorant as Randolph may have been, the house was too small to contain both Bankhead and his father-in-law. One day Bankhead, standing in the dining room and demanding the keys to the wine cellar, was cursing the unlucky Burwell, when Randolph walked in. Taking the oaths as aimed at himself, the incensed Randolph seized a poker and laid Bankhead out on the floor, with a gash in his head. Bad enough, but there was constant fear of a more serious confrontation. [10] When it finally came, it was not the father-in-law, but brother Jeff, who took up the cudgels on Anne's behalf.

Bankhead, in some drunken aberration, wrote an abusive letter to Jane, which triggered the meeting that must have been long brewing in Jeff's mind. The family attributed the initiative entirely to Bankhead, but it is true that on the February Court Day of 1819 Jeff went to town armed with a horsewhip. Bankhead, certainly not unprepared, arrived with two knives. The best account[11] has Bankhead springing upon Jeff from behind a wagon on Court Square, with knife already drawn. Jeff, to keep him from closing, kept the whip in play over his head, backing away from his assailant. Unfortunately he tripped and fell. Before Bankhead could leap upon him he took the butt end and laid open the attacker's head. They closed on the ground, Bankhead stabbing Jeff twice—a little above the hip, and cutting his arm across. A great quantity of blood flowed in the square. Jeff was carried into Leitch's store, a building on the corner just off the square, on a street now occupied by lawyer's offices and the headquarters of the Albemarle Historical Society. He was attended by four physicians and a concourse of people. When Bankhead demanded attention for his head he was told to wait until Jeff's wounds had been dressed. A messenger was dispatched posthaste up the mountain to Monticello.

Jefferson, seventy-six years old and no longer active, had already been to town once that day, but had left before the fight. By the time the messenger arrived, night was settling in and the weather was dark and lowering, but the old man, now nursing two injured wrists, ordered his horse at once. The family listened anxiously to the clatter of his hoofbeats descending the mountain. Would he at least check at the "notch" where the rocky road took a steeper turn? But the rider continued without a check. Entering the store where Jeff lay, he knelt by his grandson's side, and burst into tears. "I had borne myself with proper fortitude," Jeff said, "but when he entered and knelt at my head and wept, I was unmanned."[12]

Jane joined her convalescent husband at a home in Charlottesville. Anne too kept by her husband's side. Jefferson wrote to Jane's father, Wilson Cary Nicholas: "With respect to Bankhead (who was threatening vengeance) there is room for fear, and mostly for his wife. I have for some time taken it for granted that she would fall by his hands, and yet she is so attached to him that no persuasion has ever availed to induce her to separate and come to live with us with her children."[13]

Mrs. Nicholas, Jane's mother, wrote her daughter that she could not understand how a delicately nurtured woman could go to bed with a drunkard. If this was Anne's problem she seems to have handled it, for once she got her drunkard to herself she appears to have kept him in tolerable order, at least when at home with her. In the meantime the whole Carr and Nicholas connection, and possibly the Randolphs too, buzzed with the affairs of poor Anne and her delinquent husband.

Chapter 27

The Young Ladies

You may possibly have perceived that an attachment has existed . . .

DURING THESE YEARS Jefferson, with his usual foresight, was preparing a retreat for himself at Poplar Forest on his Bedford County land. With each passing year such a retreat was becoming more desirable for a person with a taste for privacy. Martha's latest additions to the family were for the most part small boys. Martha herself was to deplore the fact of so many "rowdies" in the house, for her responsibilities as a mother seemingly were to have no end. There was Benjamin Franklin Randolph, born 1808; Meriwether Lewis Randolph, born 1810; Septimia Ann, 1814, called Timmie, given this odd name because she was the seventh girl; and George Wythe, 1818. Cornelia, Virginia, and Mary, who was born in 1803, were all becoming young ladies. In addition to this full house, there were innumerable visitors. To many of his fellow citizens the presence of the ex-president seems to have become a sort of tourist attraction. Unwilling to turn any of these uninvited guests from his door, Jefferson would escape to the new house then being built at Poplar Forest, usually leaving Martha to cope at Monticello.

In 1816 Ellen was taking her mother's place, while Martha escaped to one of her rare retreats at Poplar Forest. Monticello was, as usual, swamped with visitors. "A coach and four no uncommon sight at the door," wrote Ellen to her mother. "Dashing but not genteel" described some visitors from Carolina. None, by the canons of plantation hospitality, could be turned away. "Papa," Ellen wrote, "has assisted me in doing the honors of the house."[1] Randolph, if not fond of visitors, was very fond of his daughters, and may have enjoyed acting as the master of the house, with Ellen as its temporary mistress.

In addition to these invasions by strangers, there was the inevitable stream of relatives. Every Albemarle home expected visits from cousins from the lower country in the spring and fall, during the migration to and from the Virginia Springs. The popular hotels at these watering places in the Virginia mountains were always full during the summer months. Some of Randolph's sisters seem to have carried visiting to an extreme. Ellen, a great visitor herself, did not always welcome these visits with cousinly joy—for example, those of her aunt Cary, and her aunt Hackley:

Regularly every year Aunt Cary (Virginia Randolph that was) with her whole family, children and nurses, paid us a six weeks or two months visit. At first there was one child, then 2, 3, 4, 5, 6—babies, small children, school boys, young ladies—the annual and sometimes bi-annual visits continued up to the time of my grandfather's death. My aunt, Mrs. Hackley, who had married a widower with children, on her return from Spain, where she had left Mr. Hackley, then Consul at Cadiz, came to Monticello with two of her own and two step children and two Spanish nurses, and stayed on her first visit about ten, and on her second six months. This was in the years 1810 and 1811. During the first visit she was confined with a third child, had a long illness, and the time of half a dozen servants was taken up in waiting on her, her children, and her foreign servants.[2]

Ellen herself was continuing her round of visits, and her social successes. As her mother described it, "Ellen has outdone all her outdoings," a nice description of her daughter's progress. From Washington, where the widower Martin Van Buren had been paying her attention, she wrote affectionate letters to her parents, aware as always, of her father's depleted finances: "In obedience to your orders I will fill no more letters with details of bills, etc. I have always subjects to write on much more interesting to myself."[3] She had collected some banknotes due her father, and perhaps he had sent her one of his self-doubting letters. At any rate Ellen answered: "I bid you adieu my dear Papa with the hope that you will never for a moment hold in doubt the entire love and confidence of your daughter. Eleanor W. Randolph."

She told her mother of a plan to visit Philadelphia: "Now dear mother, what do you think of all this, and now what will Papa think of it? I feel secure of Grandpapa's approbation. But for him I could never have thought of it, for I would have *no means* to execute the plan. He wrote to me to say that the sale of his tobacco afforded him an opportunity for increasing my 'moyen de jouissance' and God knows how much they are increased. My stock was reduced very low."

Her father had suggested that she keep some of the notes she had collected for him, and she wrote her dear papa in this regard: "I thank you very much for your kindness in giving me leave to retain part of the money, but I am not at all in want of it. I would much rather you should receive the sum entire, dearest Papa that you may soon extricate yourself from the difficulties you speak of."[4]

How much happier he would have been if she had kept his notes, to increase her "moyens de jouissance!" Apparently neither Martha nor she recognized this at the time, although a mature Ellen came to understand her father in the portrait she later drew for the benefit of Henry Randall. Nothing, she said then, would have pleased him more than the ability to give freely to his family. Martha's careful economies only led her husband to make more extravagant gifts outside his own family.

In Philadelphia Ellen had her profile taken at the museum, a memento which has unhappily disappeared. She lamented that she could not afford her portrait by Vanderlyn. How we regret now that lost opportunity! She preferred Philadelphia to Baltimore, where she had been staying with Mrs. Harrison Smith, the old friend of her childhood visit to Washington. "Philadelphia," she wrote her mother, "is a charming residence for those who have large fortunes, in the winter the advantage of a refined society, and in summer a paradise on the banks of the Schuylkill, for the country seats deserve the name, but after all one may live comfortably any where with a plenty of money."

After her stay in Philadelphia she not surprisingly impressed her Fluvanna County cousins as a very worldly figure. There is a lighter touch now to her descriptions of the people she sees—for example, General John Hartwell Cocke: "We Cocke, by the Grace of God, of Fluvanna Prince, Lord of Cumberland, defender of the faith, do hereby make known to all my good subjects, etc." Such irreverence is now matched by some detachment even in the expression of that abiding passion, her love for her mother. She could close one of her Washington letters with "A great deal of love to all and for yourself the assurance which you do not require of my idolatrous devotion."[5]

Ellen was soon to feel that it was time for the younger girls to take her place upon the social scene. Virginia, five years younger, might have been the next in line, but Virginia's heart had very early been bestowed. Nicholas Philip Trist and his brother Hore Browse had been staying at Monticello. This was one family that never seems to have worn out their welcome. Elizabeth Trist, daughter of Jefferson's former landlady, Mrs. House of Philadelphia, had become Martha's early friend and counselor. She had later had a son, Hore Browse, whom Jefferson befriended. He had obtained a position for Trist as port collector in New Orleans, a lucrative post which, however, ended in Trist's early death of yellow fever. In 1817 Jefferson invited the Trist boys to Monticello, where a romance between Nicholas and Virginia soon developed.

Jefferson had obtained for the older boy, Nicholas, an appointment to West Point, so that when Nicholas, at eighteen, fell in love with Virginia he felt it urgent to declare his love. His admirable letter to her mother follows:

The probability of an absence of some length from Albemarle, has induced me, Dear Mrs. Randolph, to take a step which I had, a short time since, resolved to defer until I should have attained my twenty-first year: a step which if it does not entirely meet your approbation I pray you at least not to be offended at. You may possibly have perceived that an attachment has existed, for some time, in my bosom to your daughter Virginia; that the attachment is strong, and *must* be lasting, I am fully convinced.

Hoping that my sentiments may be agreeable to yourself and Mr. Randolph, I address you these lines [to] request the permission of making them known to Miss Virginia.

Accept, dear Mrs. Randolph, for yourself, the Colonel and family, assurances of the perpetual gratitude and devoted friendship of

Nicholas P. Trist[6]

On behalf of a daughter not yet seventeen, Martha made an equally admirable reply:

As the mother of Virginia, my dear Mr. Trist, and your very sincere friend, I entreat your silence upon the subject of your letter. You are both too young to be entangled by an engagement which will decide the happiness or wretchedness of your lives. Retain your freedom, with the thorough conviction that no change of sentiment, and even so probable at your age, can for a moment affect the esteem and affection which we all cherish for you. . . . Absence and a better knowledge of the world, will make you more competent to judge whether your happiness would be promoted by the connection should you persist in that opinion, I promise you that there shall be no opposition from her *friends*. Of her own sentiments, *now* as *then* I am equally ignorant.

I believe my decision is precisely what your mother would approve; and certainly with regard to myself what it would have been in the case of one of my own sons.

Believe me with every sentiment of affection, your very sincere friend,

20 September, 1818

We can hardly believe that Martha could have been totally ignorant of her daughter's feelings, but surely reserve has its own uses. The advantage of courtesy and a formal style can rarely have been better illustrated. Whether Martha discussed the matter with her husband is not clear, but certainly his name does not appear in her letter.

Nicholas's reply was as carefully framed as Martha's:

Any request from my dear Mrs. Randolph, could not possibly fail being obeyed by me, who is more proud of her friendship and esteem, than any other mark of distinction which it is in the power of the world to bestow. I shall therefore remain silent, and part from you, cherishing the hope that on my return, I may find the heart of Miss Virginia as free, as mine shall be elevated; that I may one day be entitled to the appelation of your son. Adieu: believe me most devotedly, your affectionate,

NichO P. Trist[7]

That Virginia was not entirely ignorant of his feelings may be assumed from a letter of a friend to the absent lover. The friend had found Virginia in tears, "which she confided had been shed for you. If you could have heard what she said your heart would get into your mouth, but Keep Cool."[8] One can only assume that Nicholas took this good advice, for he and Virginia were not married until six years later. It may not have escaped Martha that at the time of her own marriage she had been scarcely a year older than Virginia at the time of Nicholas's proposal.

Cornelia, two years older than Virginia, had not, one imagines, yet received any such proposal. Certainly a pretty girl by present standards, she was, like Ellen, intelligent, but unlike Ellen she lacked extraordinary social gifts. Like her aunt Maria she could be disingenuous and forthright. When Ellen attempted to show her the ropes in Richmond society, Cornelia reported that "a thousand compliments were paid to sister Ellen on her appearance and a great many witty speeches made. . . ." Cornelia herself had loosened her corsets. Ellen had spent two hours struggling with Cornelia's hair. She "found it impossible . . . after two hours of vexation to herself and torment to me. . . . You may suppose I had a very humble opinion of my own attractions." However, Cornelia was not too humbled to make fun of a "Miss Henrietta Henningham Codrington Carrington Venable Watkins." After a few weeks she found "the people were not such fools as I thought them at first." She danced two reels. Even so, society, or "dissipation," as Ellen called it, was not really her thing. Her real interests were in observation, of the steamboat, a fascinating novelty, and in seeing as much as possible of what she referred to as "architectural details."[9]

If such a thing as a feminist had then existed, Cornelia would have become one. She was a better draftsman than her grandfather, and today would surely have been a professional architect. Some nine years after her debut with sister Ellen in Richmond she wrote to Nicholas to congratulate the Trists on the birth of a daughter: "You will not love her the less for being so unfortunate as to be born a woman,"[10] a misfortune which Cornelia herself probably felt acutely.

The sisters, so different and yet so much alike, were not always congenial. Cornelia suspected Ellen of "an affectation of superiority." Martha must have expressed a hope that they would get on better together, for Ellen wrote her of "the slow but sure advancement of the union you have sometimes spoken to me of." [11] This greater closeness was achieved at Poplar Forest, the retreat in Bedford County where family members could be alone, and in command of their own time and quiet occupation.

Chapter 28

Poplar Forest

*The best dwelling house in the state, except that of Monticello;
perhaps preferable to that, as more proportioned to the faculties
of a private citizen.*

TO BOTH RANDOLPH and his father-in-law debts remained pressing, and notes impossible to curtail. Jefferson was still seriously in arrears, but he knew that he could get his debt "accommodated," that is, he could borrow again. The men who transacted his business in Richmond, at first George Jefferson and then Bernard Peyton, often carried him on their books, not an uncommon practice in the plantation economy. The sale of land appeared to both these Virginia farmers as a sure resource and an ample security.

At the time of his retirement Jefferson had written Randolph of his plan to sell various tracts, even the land at the Natural Bridge that he had once bought for no other reason than sheer delight in this phenomenon of nature.[1] In this letter he confessed: "I know nothing of management." It was with a sense of relief that in 1815 he turned over most of this plantation business to young Jeff Randolph.[2] Other concerns, at which he was surely more skilled, were pressing upon his attention.

In 1817 both men took what appears in retrospect to have been a fatal step. Randolph was forced to borrow from the Richmond branch of the Bank of the United States, of which Wilson Cary Nicholas was president, and where Jefferson also had notes outstanding. As security Randolph gave a deed of trust to Edgehill, made out to his son Jefferson Randolph and to Samuel Carr as security for the loan. In so doing the father showed a perfect ignorance of the character of the son. But before we judge too hastily of the wisdom, or lack of wisdom, of this act it is worthwhile to look back to the previous year to discover that originally he had had a different course in mind.

In a letter to one of his creditors he revealed that once again, as he had done in the aborted plan to move to Mississippi in 1801, he had attempted to relieve himself of dependence on Edgehill. At this time, 1816, before taking out that fatal mortgage, he had had an opportunity to sell part of this home farm for "a fair price . . . without delay." Martha had talked him out of it:

I am desirous of selling here [Varina, for which there was no buyer] to gratify my wife who wishes to keep Edgehill, unbroken, for her sons. . . . The desire of my wife has not prevailed without some conflict. I can make much more here [at Varina]. . . . Besides this place suits my health best. I was born at Tuckahoe, which is not as healthy. I never left it till sixteen years old, and had the ague and fever every year, until I got too strong for it, which took place about twelve. My constitution is suited to the river. This has been one cause in the delay in making up my mind, which you have noticed. . . .[3]

As usual the colonel has confided unnecessarily in his correspondent, but this letter, never before published, shows that it was Martha's influence, rather than sheer thoughtlessness, which finally caused him to give his son Jeff this handle on Edgehill.

Jefferson, also in debt to the Nicholas bank, was now asked for what would seem to be almost a *quid pro quo*. In any event he seemed unable to refuse a request to endorse two notes for Nicholas, of $10,000 each, and this at a time when by his own admission he could not have laid his hand on more than $50 in cash. He was already involved in the great project of his old age, the founding of Central College, later to be known as the University of Virginia. He was still engaged in building at Poplar Forest, nor was he able to curtail the ruinous hospitality so constantly demanded of him at Monticello. Poplar Forest may actually have represented an attempt at retrenchment, but if so it was of little avail.

This Bedford County retreat was to become, with the University, the architectural triumph of his old age. This becomes very evident when we realize that Poplar Forest was begun when he was sixty-three, and the University when he was seventy-four, while the rotunda at the University was actually built when Jefferson was eighty years old.[4] We may forgive him letting his grandson Jeff assume those financial burdens which could have harassed the private man.

Nor was he at all modest about Poplar Forest, which he intended for the inheritance of Maria's son Francis Eppes. He had written the boy's father: "When finished it will be the best dwelling house in the state, except that of Monticello; perhaps preferable to that, as more proportioned to the faculties of a private citizen."[5] He was sparing no pains to improve this house and the land around it. Hugh Chisholm, who had worked at Monticello, laid the brick walls, but perhaps as a move of economy it was John Hemings to whom he confided the fine interior woodwork.

Unlike Monticello, Poplar Forest was the result of a single inspiration, possessing the same unity of design that we see at the University. The house is a perfect octagon, placed on a knoll among a grove of poplars. Porticoes, back and front, each cover only a single side of the octagon. From the front he could overlook red clay fields to the mountains. Although the slope is not steep Jefferson achieved two levels through judicious excavation. The lawn behind the house was lowered by a few feet so that both the upper and lower floors open at ground level. This device, unique in Jefferson's building, welds his house to the landscape. The rooms are all octagonal with the exception of the central dining room that opened through a pyramidal ceiling to a large skylight. There has been no attempt to dominate the landscape; a homely tranquility reigns under the poplar trees. Only, as Frederick Nichols has put it, there is the perfection of pure geometric form.[6]

The road from Monticello to "the Forest" first wended its way south, crossing the slow-flowing James at Warren, through the flat country of Buckingham and Appomattox, then turning west through Campbell County toward the mountains. Some seventy miles all told. From the beginning of construction in 1806 until well up in his seventies Jefferson was undaunted by the two or three days spent on this journey. Particularly in winter, roads could be impassable; once at Poplar Forest, one's isolation was complete. During

Randolph's absence on the Canadian campaign of 1813, Jefferson wrote Ellen for word of her father, for "I shall see no newspaper until I get Back."[7] Even in summer there could be hardships more painful to the owner than the isolation which he really sought. "I have not seen a pea since I left Albemarle," he wrote Martha, "and have no vegetable but spinach and scrubby lettuce."[8]

Privacy was the great luxury enjoyed there, but privacy never meant for Jefferson separation from the comfort of his family. Coming in pairs, the granddaughters took turns keeping their grandfather company. Apparently, to these young ladies neither the journey nor the visits were an unadulterated joy. Cornelia described one of these as she experienced it with Ellen in 1821. Jefferson at this date was seventy-eight, but if *he* complained, we have no record of it.

We are arrived here fatigued to death as usual my dear Virginia, after the most tedious journey that ever was made. I am sure I almost died on the road from impatience. We got to Warren in the height of the rain that fell the day we left you, and were detained there all night, in consequence of which, and the roads being in the most detestable order, we could not get to Hunters the next day as we intended, and spent the night at horrid old Floods, between the sheets that Dr. and Mrs. Flood had been sleeping in for a month I am sure, not *between* them exactly, for finding the counterpane clean we pinned the top sheet down close all round and laid upon that, doing ourselves up hand foot and face in our clothes so that our skins at least should not be defiled by touching pitch. . . . Strange to say everything else in the house had the appearance of having been cleaned not more than a week before. . . . The roads for the greater part of the way were so bad that Bill [the coachman] more than once stopped and said he thought that if he ventured any farther we should certainly be upset, and once Burwell was obliged to dismount and hold up the carriage to prevent it from going over. When we arrived here we found Mr. Yancey gone to Liberty Court (*16* miles off) and the keys of the house could not be obtained until his return; Burwell had shaken open the front door so that we could enter to get into several of the rooms of the house, but our chamber door, in which room all the bedding was, was locked. Besides nothing either to eat or drink could be obtained, and to make the matter worse the hard weather had killed almost everything in the garden. We satisfied our hunger with the wracks of our travelling provisions, and whatever old Hannah and Burwell could find . . . [from when] the house was shut up last year. . . . We were more hungry and tired than nice though, you may suppose, and at night were very contentedly about to stretch off upon the outside of the beds which had a single blanket laid over the mattress, when the keys arrived, and in a moment we had tea and wine, and comfortable beds."[9]

Cornelia feared that "two months here will seem like two years," but she has brought "a great supply of books." Ellen, older and more her grandfather's companion, found compensations. After dinner Jefferson would have the chess table, especially constructed by John Hemings for the purpose, brought out under the trees, and he and Ellen would sometimes play, and often chat together. On these occasions the old gentleman seemed to relax. He would reminisce about his own early home and, Ellen remembered, would speak of his favorite sister Jane, of her wit and her musical gift. They had often sung together. He would even speak of his wife, long dead, of whom so little is recorded. "On one occasion," Ellen said, "I was complaining of a rude speech that had been made to me. . . . 'Your Grandmother,' said he, 'was one day spoken to by a lady acquaintance in an impertinent and improper manner when she answered, I make no reply to that speech. I had rather receive two such affronts than offer one.'"[10] The world belongs to the living, Jefferson would say, but to this granddaughter he would open ever so slightly a door upon the past.

Poplar Forest encouraged intimacy; even the servants seemed closer here to family life than they did at Monticello. There the service activities took place out of sight and hearing in the offices under the south walkway. Like the granddaughters at Poplar Forest, the faithful Burwell was always present, and so, very often, was John Hemings. They too would have much preferred to be at home. Ellen's letters are full of messages from one Hemings to another, from John to his wife Priscilla, and from Burwell to Critta. Ellen wrote to Virginia: "Burwell has had another attack, but is better. When you write pray mention Critty and his children and say how they are, it will be very gratifying to him. . . . John Hemings begged it of me as a very particular favor to give his news to Aunt Priscilla, to say he was doing well but 'mighty tired of the Forest and wished himself at home.' Any message that she may send him it will give me great pleasure to receive from you—for Johnny is one of my prime favorites and more so now than ever since I have witnessed his kind attention to Burwell."[11]

There is a lovely description of housekeeping at the Forest. Jefferson, although always courteous and serene, had very fixed ideas of how a house should be run. It cannot have been easy to keep house for a man who designed his own bedroom curtains. Even Martha, presiding efficiently at Monticello, had had her troubles. There was, for example, the affair of the closet. It appeared that Martha did not share her father's high opinion of alcove beds. In 1822 she wrote her daughter Virginia: "I have at last succeeded in having my alcove turned into a closet. . . . I laid regular siege to Papa who bore it in dignified *silence* for some time, but I gave it to him for breakfast, dinner and supper, and breakfast again until he gave up in despair at last and when it is painted it will not disfigure the room at all . . ."[12]

At the Forest Ellen as housekeeper was quite helpless: "We have lived altogether on chickens, being unable to keep pork meat for want of ice. We get snow enough from Mr. Radford's . . . to give us hard butter and cool wine. Whilst Israel, Cornelia and myself were chief butlers, Grandpapa insisted on our using that cooler (*refrigerator*, I believe he calls it), which wasted our small stock of ice, and gave us butter that runs about the plate so that we could scarcely catch it, and wine about blood heat—but on Burwell's recovery he soon scouted it . . . and we have been quite comfortable ever since."[13] It seems that Burwell had only to speak to exert his authority.

In the summer of 1819 one might have expected nothing worse than a failed refrigerator, or a round of visits on a hot day, but worse was soon to befall.

Chapter 29

1819—The Paper Bubble Burst

Land in this state cannot now be sold for a year's rent.

EIGHTEEN NINETEEN WAS a year of disaster. A wave of speculation, particularly in western land, had followed the war of 1812. To say the least, Americans had not mastered the art of banking. The First Bank of the United States, never a favorite of Mr. Jefferson's, had expired in 1811, but to the enemies of banking this was no consolation. State banks, private banks, all sorts of banks, proliferated; it required no capital to start a bank. Specie payments were suspended, and, as might be expected, prices soared.[1]

What was somewhat euphemistically referred to at the time as "the foreign contagion" now came into play. The price of cotton on the Liverpool market soared, then dropped disastrously with no warnings that the Americans could see. In 1818 it was quoted at 32.5 cents a pound; one day in 1819 it dropped to 26 cents and continued to fall until it reached 14.3 cents. The whole western world was beginning to suffer from a postwar decline in prices. At the same time, European agriculture was beginning to revive with the peace, with a consequent decrease in demand for American exports. As Jefferson wrote his old friend John Adams, "the paper bubble is then burst."

Men like John Jacob Astor who had been speculating heavily in discounted bank stock now felt the need to retract. The chosen instrument of reform was the Second Bank of the United States, and its measures were draconian. Payment in specie was once more demanded, and loans were called in. Industry may survive such rigors; they are in any case used to operating on short-term credit. For the planter it is quite different; he can pay but once a year, when his crop goes to market, and hardly then if he has had a bad year. Many a planter faced ruin, or, as Jefferson put it, "a general revolution of property in this state."[2]

Sitting under the trees at Poplar Forest, Jefferson had the happy faculty of distracting his mind from problems such as these. With Ellen at his side he could discuss such matters as whether, given the opportunity, one would wish to live one's life over. The two were sitting together on such a tranquil day in August when a letter was handed him. It was from Wilson Cary Nicholas informing his old friend that he, Nicholas, was bankrupt.

Jefferson, for once, made no effort to conceal the position that confronted him. Ellen wrote her mother that

Grandpapa's spirits were most visibly affected when he heard the news although it came to him softened by a solemn promise from Colonel Nicholas himself, that he should not lose a dollar. He placed, I think, considerable reliance on this promise, but the *possibility* of such an overthrow of his affairs . . . made a deep impression on him; he *said* very little, but his countenance expressed a great deal. He mentioned the circumstance of his endorsement to me (which I was before perfectly ignorant of) and also Colonel Nicholas's promises.[3]

That same day Jefferson renewed "the two notes of $10,000 for which I am by endorsement responsible to the United States Bank." As a third party to this endorsement he named his grandson, to whom he would "convey lands amply sufficient for this debt, to him in trust for its payment."[4] Less than three months later even this inveterate optimist admitted the sad truth that "Lands in this state cannot now be sold for a year's rent," although he still hoped that "our legislature [may] have wisdom enough to effect a remedy by gradual diminution only of the medium [paper money]."[5] Yet no one knew better than Jefferson himself that the trouble lay deeper, and that a one-crop economy would always be subject to these fluctuations.

Ellen had long been aware of her father's "pecuniary embarrassments," but those of her grandfather came as a shock. She wrote to her mother:

At present all my thoughts center in my dear grandfather; let his old age be secured from the storms which threaten us all, and I would willingly agree to abide their peltings. I am almost ready to fix my ideas of right and wrong on this single point; to believe everything honorable which can save him—everything base, vile and dishonorable that tends to obscure the evening of such a life.

You say nothing of poor Jane, nor how she bears these accumulated distresses. . . .[6]

Ellen referred to Jeff's wife, who was, of course, the bankrupt's daughter. Jane, in fact, came to the first meeting with Jefferson after the disaster in deepest distress and with many misgivings. She need not have feared. He folded her in his arms. It was his part to comfort her without a thought of his own trouble.

Meanwhile Jeff and his devoted wife Jane were leading a quite different life than that lived at Monticello. They had moved to Tufton, one of Jefferson's four contiguous farms. Jeff tells us in his memoir: "My grandfather was uneasy until I moved to a farmhouse of his, one mile from Monticello on the same side of the river. He forthwith had an easy graded road made from Monticello directly to my house. . . . His ideas and mine not agreeing about farming I rented his farms." Jeff noted here that his grandfather's expenses at Monticello often much exceeded the rent. The young couple themselves then followed the only practice that made solvency possible on a Virginia farm; they labored morning, noon, and night, and Jane certainly worked every bit as hard as her husband.

Jeff had a carefully laid-out schedule, followed by all, black and white, on the plantation. On each of the four large farms,

. . . a middle aged woman cooked for the laborers and milked a half a dozen cows and made butter. She had two and a half days task of wool in the week. The children were all brought to her house every morning to be taken care of while their mothers were out, she employing as help all old enough. Every Saturday they brought their work and butter to my wife. Cotton warp was purchased and this made a thick warm cloth for clothing the negroes. There was the utmost punctuality in the discharge of their duties. They were a fat, cheerful set, proud to have to report to their mistress who always addressed them kindly and cheerfully, she having to superintend the clothing of a hundred negroes, seeing that their clothing was properly made and comfortable. . . . She deliver[ed] out to each farm its weekly ration of bacon: herself at daylight every morning in her dairy. These were the duties more or less of every "aristocratic" mistress of a family in Virginia. . . .

Fortunately through my mother's training I had a hardy temperament and indomitable will—could sleep anywhere, eating anything and never tiring. To ride from early dawn to eve in continuous rain or snow, not dependent upon the weather, never halting for it. If I was twenty-five miles from home at dark, regardless of road or weather I always went home, fording or swimming in the night swollen bridgeless streams. What was my life was more or less the life of every Virginia farmer. Our mode of living was plain, abundant and comfortable. We had abundance of necessaries, few luxuries of dress, furniture or diet. I had an application to become a candidate for the legislature; it so disturbed my grandfather that I had to assure him that I never would think of public life as long as he lived.[7]

This was the sacrifice the necessity of which was so regretted by this hardy Virginia farmer. Although life at Monticello was less austere, Martha, now assisted by the girls, had much the same tasks to perform. In her *Domestic Life* Sarah Nicholas Randolph described Martha as sitting like an ancient Greek matron watching over the work of her handmaidens. Sunday, Martha said, was no day of rest for her, because on that day she received the requests and complaints of all the old women on the plantation. For the women the task was like that of superintending a small factory, presiding over this outsize housekeeping. The men at least had overseers, but this was not true of the women, who all appeared to have "carried the keys" and the burden of the innumerable dependents.

Life at Monticello, if a busy one, did offer space and considerable comforts. The house at Tufton was, to say the least, cramped. Although Jeff could describe their manner of living as "plain, abundant and comfortable," Jane's family thought otherwise. A sister, looking back, did not wear Jeff's rose-colored glasses. She reminded Jane of a time when "the common comforts of a plenty of meat and wood" were lacking. She asked, ". . . was it one or two frocks a week that Pat and Margaret [the children] used to wear?

Whichever it was I remember full well how awfully dirty they were, and how the flies congregated around Pat when I would be hearing her lessons. . . . yet . . . you were happy."[8]

Yet . . . it was not the sort of life calculated to make a hard-working son tolerant of an improvident father.

Chapter 30

Governor Randolph

Little better than a signing clerk . . .

WHEN AT HOME RANDOLPH worked as hard as his son, but he was not often at home. Even when he was not politicking, or off to the wars, or abroad attempting to borrow money, his farms were so scattered as to make their operation difficult and ineffective. In 1819, the year of all years in which he might have elected to stay on his farm, this Virginia farmer decided to run for the office of governor of his state.

At this period the governor was elected by the General Assembly rather than by popular vote. Randolph's financial position was now so shaky as to leave him open to attack. In the letter of 1816 to Taylor he had mentioned being "villainously slandered" by some persons in connection with his credit, and these slanders followed him at the time of the 1819 election in the House of Delegates. Randolph, in a moment of anger, had accused his creditors of usury, and this had been made the subject of a strong report by W. C. Rives of Nelson County. Joseph C. Cabell was supporting his friend Randolph because, as he wrote John Hartwell Cocke, "I am incapable of standing coldly by and see a dagger aimed at the bosom of an honorable although imprudent man."[1] In spite of this just analysis of the colonel's character, Cabell does not appear to have doubted his fitness for office as governor of the commonwealth. Perhaps a really good candidate was hard to find.

However that may have been, the election of a governor was an important occasion, and the hour of Randolph's nomination in the House was tense indeed. The whole Senate appeared at the Bar of the House; the lobby and galleries were crowded. In the presence of so august an assembly, the member nominating Randolph, a Mr. Chamberlayne, threw down the gauntlet of defiance. He said if a certain report injurious to the character of Colonel Randolph was not there repeated, he should hold it to be false.

The silence of death prevailed throughout the House for some minutes. No one rising, the ballot was commenced. Randolph's election proceeded without further difficulty.

The governor-elect had certainly made no enviable record in the field of politics. His achievements had been as a scientific farmer and as an amateur physician and botanist. As a private citizen it came naturally to him to follow Jefferson's example in exalting Nature's God, a God that unfortunately scarcely resembled the Biblical God worshipped by his fellow countrymen. In his inaugural address the governor apostrophized "the author and sovereign of nature perpetually displayed in the endless variety of visible works . . . as they are unfolded to man by the still more wonderful power and ingenuity of his own mind. . . ." These words were suspect enough, but certainly the burgeoning politician did not have to add that "silent admiration" should be substituted for "labored praise, or ceremonious worship." This was to offend every churchman, which was to say virtually every man, among his colleagues.

Another issue, as sensitive in its own way as religion, was next on his agenda. Randolph did not believe in the immediate feasibility of emancipation, but he did support colonization, the gradual removal of free Negroes to Africa or, preferably, to Santo Domingo. The latter, he pointed out, "separated by a sufficient space of sea . . . might even encourage an advantageous commerce." He called upon the legislators to have "a generous regard for the interests of distant posterity."[2] This call, too, fell upon deaf ears. Almost at once he had established himself as opposed to the views of the majority of his colleagues.

Another, and principal, cause of dissension was the division of power between the governor and his council of state. It may be that Randolph had not made a close study of the Virginia constitution before assuming office. The constitution had been framed by men who had just taken over from the power of an overbearing royal executive, and they had not been about to encourage its reappearance in any executive office of their own creation. Clauses affecting the power of the governor were almost all couched in the negative; he could hardly take any independent action without the advice and consent of this body, the self-perpetuating and deeply entrenched Council of State.

The constitution stipulated that "the Governor shall not prorogue or adjourn the Assembly during their sitting, or dissolve them at any time." Surely this was a very essential aspect of the negation of the executive power. The power of appointments, that is, of patronage, was almost totally in the hands of the Assembly. The Council of State was to consist of eight members. "They shall annually choose out of their own members a President," who was authorized to preside over the council in the governor's absence. Although the Assembly was clearly supreme over both the governor and his council, the division of power between the two executive branches was somewhat cloudy. Certainly Randolph and his council held radically different views of what that division should be.[3]

The governor contended that "the initiation of all business is in the presiding officer at that time, to whom application must be made if a Councilor wishes any particular business to be taken up, and at whose discretion it rests to prefer one subject or anther. . . . In the case of appointments, which the Governor is required to make by advice of the Council, he must either have a voice, or he can take no part whatever, and becomes a passive instrument to sign the commission by their order. . . ." To Randolph's increasing frustration this last was what usually took place. The council was dominated by a small clique, and in fact began meeting independently, in the governor's absence.

The governor had gone to Richmond with high hopes, both of the usefulness he might be to his country and of the pleasure that in this case he, and no one else, might be able to offer his family. He had always enjoyed his daughters, and they, in their turn, were fond of their father. During the first summer in Richmond we find him full of plans for the girls' pleasure:

The steamboat goes at six o'clock tomorrow morning very punctually. I have sent to Varina already to give notice that we are coming. Phil will attend you with the carriage very early. To arrive in time you must be up by four o'clock. We will set out for Varina from the steamboat, on board of which we will breakfast, as we may not reach Varina sooner than nine o'clock. This novelty is worth your seeing, in my opinion. Besides there is beautiful scenery on the river and I hope the day will be fine which will make it surely agreeable.

. . . if Booth does not . . . come to town again I will wait with pleasure that you may see his acting. . . . We must see the Richmond Vauxhall [pleasure gardens] some day next week, and the Penitentiary. Also the new canal and locks at Westham. But the unhealthy season is fast approaching. There is more malaria produced in an hour now than was in a week when Ellen was down. We must not trust it too long.

I am much afraid the little carriage may be wanted at Belvidere [home of David Meade Randolph]. . . . I have this moment been disappointed in my last ordinance to procure one larger that we might invite some of your companions. Adieu my dear girls for tonight.[4]

About the steamboat Cornelia had written earlier to her sister Virginia: "I should be inconsolable if I were in your place for not being able to attend that party in the steamboat, the dear delightful steamboat. To have gone sixty miles down the river . . . and with a band of music!"[5] By July it must have been enjoyed by all, as were the Richmond Vauxhall and perhaps Booth, if that celebrated man had in fact returned to Richmond. Even the penitentiary, where reform and a new design had been undertaken by the governor, was no doubt an edifying sight.

For the governor such pleasures were counterbalanced by constant friction with his council. He was elected to a second term as the candidate least objectionable to the legislature, and now, in his second inaugural, he made no bones about stating his own views upon this sensitive matter. A letter that Martha wrote to her good friend Nicholas Trist shows that she supported her husband in this quarrel. Young Nicholas, not yet married to his beloved Virginia, was at this time studying law in New Orleans. Martha wrote:

If you take the *Enquirer* you will see that the Governor and his council have brought their quarrel to an issue at last. His cause might have stood by its own merit, for everybody who understands the subject at all, says that his construction of the constitution was unquestionably the true one, but during the reigns of the many *Rois fainéants* who come into office, they have been in the habit of taking the reins of government entirely into their own hands, and thereby reducing the Governor to a mere signing clerk. When therefore a good Governor is elected who is really competent and determined to do his duty and to permit them only to advise upon such business as he *thinks proper* to lay before them, there will always be a struggle more or less according to circumstances. They are *constitutionally* insignificant and useless therefore as a *body*. They have always been, and always must be, contemptible.

Who were the people "who understood the subject at all" she does not say, but they probably did not include her father. Jefferson had always scrupulously avoided the appearance of exerting political influence upon his sons-in-law, and although Randolph often promoted his father-in-law's projects in the Assembly, he clearly did not employ the skillful indirection which Jefferson himself might have used under similar circumstances. As for Martha, there is no record that Jefferson ever discussed such matters with his daughter. He had defined her role long ago. It was her part to smooth her husband's furrowed brow on his return from the political arena. Unfortunately Martha was not very good at this role, although no doubt her husband required more than the usual amount of soothing. She admits as much to Nicholas: "His friends regret the occurrence from the *warmth* he has carried into it, self command you know was never his characteristic virtue."[6]

Martha's one visit to the capital occurred early in the governor's second term. A family of obstreperous small boys, and the additional responsibility of an aging father, kept her pretty well tied to Monticello. It was with a truly holiday spirit that she wrote to Virginia of this visit, "Can you figure to yourself *me*, my dear

Virginia, in a beautiful white crape *robe*, a lace turban and ruff fashionably drest and looking like a lady?!! . . . We are going to another party tomorrow."[7] The young Stevensons (Isaac Coles's sister Sally was now married to Andrew Stevenson, Speaker of the House) were giving the most brilliant parties that season. Gay as she undoubtedly was, Martha does not neglect to assure her daughters: "Many persons have inquired after Ellen and yourself both, but I have talked so much of myself that I forgot everybody else. . . ."

Pleasure, so well deserved, simply beams from this letter, but even so, Martha, always a success wherever she appeared from Paris to Washington, does not appear always to have melted the hearts that her husband had alienated. Colonel David Campbell, who had served with Colonel Randolph in Canada, wrote his brother that Mrs. Randolph "was a vain and sarcastic woman."[8] She had entertained him while the governor, "playing the great man," had retired to his study. Randolph had his own prescription for getting along in society. He wrote an anonymous correspondent: "As violent resentment is less injurious to health in my temperament than deep and permanent vexation of mind, I have never taken much pains to govern myself. . . ."

Chapter 31

Ellen

If she had been a man she would have been a great one.

MARTHA'S RESPONSIBILITIES at Monticello kept her from returning to the governor's mansion in the difficult winter of his second term. On her first visit she had had the windows washed, draperies mended, and rugs "shaken out," but after this the governor's house relapsed into its previous condition, the neglected retreat of a very solitary man. He could have the company of his wife only by the rugged expedient of riding all Saturday night on his gaunt but tireless steed, appropriately named Dromedary, to spend Sunday with his family. On Monday, the eighty-mile ride had to be done again on the return trip to his increasingly frustrating duties at the capital.[1]

Martha seemed sincerely to regret not being able to join him, but as *some* member of the family must always be with her father, she preferred that the girls rather than she herself should enjoy the pleasures of Richmond. She had to be aware of all these marriageable young ladies at home at Monticello, who, it was becoming increasingly evident, would not have a penny to sweeten their charms. Richmond was an opportunity for the girls, and *someone* must stay at Monticello. Martha might spread herself very thin, but there was never any doubt in her mind where her own highest duty lay.

She cheered her own low spirits with reports from the girls: "Ellen's letters have actually kept me alive this winter." As for her sisters, "do ask those poor sluts if it is possible that they should not have made one poor solitary conquest."[2] Such pleasantries, with their eighteenth-century bite, were typical of Martha's style, and certainly were not taken seriously by the independent Randolph girls. They responded with spirited accounts of paying formal visits in a broken-down carriage. With it all, as Martha said, they had "the advantage of your promised *thirty cents* per annum." Husbands, she admitted, were in short supply.

Ellen indeed had made many conquests, but Martha wondered if this particular daughter would ever marry. Some years before she had written to her old friend Mrs. Trist that "Ellen fulfills the promise of her childhood . . . she is to her grandfather the immediate jewel of his soul."

Ellen remained at home, apparently in no hurry to marry. "Indeed," Martha wrote, "after her sister's fate I almost wish that she never may." [3]

Ellen had had her pick of the most eligible men not only of Albemarle and Richmond, but of Washington, Baltimore, and Philadelphia. That Ellen remained single at twenty-eight unquestionably calls for an explanation. What, in fact, outside of marriage was open to the young ladies of Monticello? No matter what their gifts, which were in Ellen's case extraordinary, no career or even occupation of interest was open to them. Jefferson declared that had Ellen been a man, she would have been a great one. Intellectual gifts allied to personal charm, what more could one need? Only unfortunately their possessor was the wrong sex. "A cold mountain nymph," cried Francis Walker Gilmer, most persistent of rejected suitors, but Ellen was not frigid, or even cold—she was, quite simply, bored.

At first, for Ellen as for her mother Monticello itself had been enough. Who would not have envied her, seated under the trees at Poplar Forest, beside the wisest, most charming man of the age? As she had matured she had become, in a very real sense, her grandfather's companion. In that private scene at Poplar Forest the man who had buried so completely even the memory of a once-beloved wife could speak of her to the girls. With Ellen conversation was not limited to family anecdotes, but took off naturally into the realm of ideas. The famous Adams-Jefferson dialogue concerning the desire to live one's life over originated under the trees at Poplar

Forest. In 1825 when Ellen as a bride had visited Jefferson's old friend in Quincy, she had repeated a conversation with her grandfather on this fascinating subject; the New England philosopher at once picked it up, and the two old men had pursued the theme in their own letters.[4]

But of what use to open one's eyes on the world if one was a young woman to whom much of that world must remain out of bounds? The strain was severe, and by 1819 Ellen was already feeling its effect. At Monticello the handsome, sensitive Gilmer pressed his suit in vain: "She must be colder than polar snow, and harder than everlasting granite, if she do not feel some tenderness for the early and romantic devotion with which I admired her."[5] He solaced these pains by remarking on her character: "too irregular and eccentric, like her father." Ellen herself was aware of an erosion. She wrote her mother, still at this time her principal confidante: "I am becoming more and more sensible of the changes which my character and feelings have undergone . . . company and conversation in which I once delighted have lost their power to charm. . . . I frequently receive attentions which it is not in my power to return *solidly*. . . . I am often gratified and envied at the same time."[6]

As for poor Francis Walker Gilmer, by 1823 she can say that he is "fast degenerating into a sour morose *old bachelor*." By which time, of course, Ellen thinks of herself as an old maid, but not, she hopes, an ill-tempered old maid.[7]

All her feelings came out in a letter to Nicholas Trist, the favorite correspondent and confidant of the Monticello women. In two of the letters of this time to Nicholas, she turned her keen powers of analysis upon herself. In January she wrote to this intelligent and understanding friend:

I indulge in no longing or listlessness, my habits are those of steady occupation, and I walk a great deal, this I learnt in Washington . . . what then, will you ask, is the matter? . . . It is a general sense of oppression, a weariness of life, an almost total loss of interest in anything that I can do myself or that is done around me; it is the perpetual intrusion into all my plans and employments of that harassing and discouraging reflection, which I believe is conveyed by the Latin words *cui bono*, of what use is all this. . . . My occupations are what they have always been, but their 'salt and savour' is gone.

What follows shows the force of her effort to apply to her own life the example of her grandfather's rationality and self-discipline, and how it must fail, given the lack of substance for rationality to work on:

The experience of a few years past has very much weakened the confidence I formerly felt in the supremacy of mind over matter. My philosophy at one time had something of the stoic character. I fancied that self-command might be carried to so high a degree as to constitute almost an entire self-dependence, and that the mind in the full possession and free exercise of her powers, enjoyed a controul almost complete over our inward feelings and habits of thought, and although she could not alter the nature of external circumstances, she so far influenced and modified their aspect, as to render us in a very great degree independent of them. I believe now that our actions may be regulated by reason, that use may exercise a controul over our feelings, whether they be the effect of constitutional or temporary causes, sufficient in a great measure to prevent their interference with the performance of our duties, and that the mind may be brought to such a state as to regulate the manners and preserve in them that equanimity necessary for the comfort of our friends and associates, but that even to effect this implies a vigorous mind and considerable force of character, and that as for regulating the principles on which our own happiness depends 'cette fiere raison dont on fait tant de bruit' has been too well described by Mde. Deshoulieres 'Toujours impuisante et severe / Elle s'oppose a tout, et / ne soumettre a rien.'

. . . But I am apologising for a dismal letter by one more dismal still . . .[8]

Whatever were her private trials, successes, or failures, Ellen continued to charm visitors to Monticello, particularly those enlightened ones from the cooler northern climes. Ellen's reputation had in fact, spread to Boston. A young visitor, Elliot Cresson, shown around Monticello by Ellen, was absolutely overcome by her charm, but felt it would be "insane to venture" a proposal.

A sort of quiet self-possession had been the fruit, after all, of that rigorous struggle with her own restlessness. It was not to be long before another visitor, Joseph Coolidge, was to find himself considerably bolder.

Ellen was a superb analyst of character. Henry S. Randall, one of the first—but certainly not the least—of Jefferson's biographers, owed everything of this nature to his long and fruitful correspondence with Ellen. In spite of all her care for female modesty, for one would as soon appear naked in public as see one's name as "author" upon the printed page, Ellen could not resist speaking out for her own area of expertise. She wrote Randall: "You are inquiring . . . as you are bound to do, most minutely and particularly into all the details of private life, and in order to understand him you must understand those by whom he was surrounded." She could even suggest that he abridge the finished work and prepare a one-volume edition for the general reader, "leaving out what is chiefly useful to the student of history."[9]

For very many years none of the many people who have written about Jefferson looked as closely, or as honestly, at personal character as did this granddaughter. Of her father, to whom she was devoted, she was able to say: "With some noble qualities . . . and naturally warm affections, [he] was jealous, suspicious, irascible and violent." But why? How? Wormley, "attached and faithful servant," had let drop a word that suggested something tragic in the relations of Thomas Jefferson and Thomas Mann Randolph. This was the tragedy that Ellen never quite faced up to or, if she did, she did not confide in Randall.

Chapter 32

Missouri—"A Firebell in the Night"

I am your servant, John Hemings.

ALTHOUGH NATURALLY A severe blow, the Nicholas failure does not seem to have destroyed Jefferson's congenital optimism in regard to his financial affairs. He had turned all these problems over to his grandson, in order to work on what he described as "this immortal boon to our country,"[1] the University of Virginia. It was this institution which was to supply that cadre of educated men that Jefferson felt necessary to the survival of democracy, and to this object he meant to devote the rest of his life.

More disturbing than any difficulties of his own was the crisis now arising over the admission to statehood of the territory of Missouri, usually referred to simply as "the Missouri question." His old opponents, the northern Federalists, had sponsored a move in Congress to free all slaves in that territory on its admission to the Union. More than once during the troubled year of 1820, Jefferson wrote painfully long letters on this subject—painful because of a stiffening wrist which made all writing difficult. To the old statesman, with his amazing prescience, this crisis was a harbinger of things to come, ultimately a blow to the Union itself.

He put it unequivocally in an oft-quoted letter to John Holmes, the congressman from Maine: "I consider it at once as a knell of the Union. . . . A geographical line, coinciding with a marked principle, moral and political, once conceived and held up to the angry passions of men, will never be obliterated. . . ."[2] It was not a gradual emancipation to which he objected; it was the precedent of federal authority imposed upon a state which he saw as possibly leading to a general emancipation, and certainly to that "geographical line" which would be fatal to the Union.

Painful wrist or not, he continued this letter to Holmes, for several pages: ". . . The cession of that kind of property [slaves], for so it is misnamed, is a bagatelle which would not cost me a second thought, if, in that way, a general emancipation and *expatriation* could be effected; and gradually, and with due sacrifices, I think it might be. But as it is, we have the wolf by the ears, and we can neither hold him, nor safely let him go. Justice is in one scale, and self-preservation in the other. . . ."

The italics are Jefferson's own. To modern ears this emphasis on expatriation could seem to vitiate his liberalism. Perhaps the majority of people in both North and South at this period visualized the new nation as homogeneous and white. Our own view, so aptly expressed today by the Rev. Jesse Jackson as a *rainbow* coalition, was certainly not generally held in Jefferson's time. To Jefferson particularly his concept of "the people" speaking with virtually one voice depended on a degree of homogeneity; democracy as he saw it must rest on this character of the people who should exercise it. Later on in this same year he went even further in a letter to Albert Gallatin, saying that in the event of a general emancipation "all whites south of the Potomac and the Ohio must evacuate their States, and most fortunate those who can do it first."[3]

If Jefferson was serious in this opinion, and there is no reason to think that he wrote frivolously, it must mean that in his opinion a general emancipation without *expatriation* would bring either black violence or at best a form of general economic ruin. Almost forty years before, he had set down the famous passage in the *Notes on Virginia*: "I tremble for the future of my country." He spoke now an equal and even more immediate warning. Missouri, and the whole vexed question, was "a firebell in the night." Jefferson was proved right in his anticipation of the anguish of civil war as the ultimate consequence of the slavery evil. What is not always realized was that he was also right in his belief that the Southern economy, geared as it was to the institution of slavery, was simply not capable of a sudden total transformation.

One problem endemic to the slave economy was the lack of a home market of any size for imported goods. Imports could not balance the export crop; southern trade was increasingly going through New York or New England ports. Middlemen were absorbing profit, northern-sponsored tariffs were raising the cost of imported goods, and perhaps most irksome of all was the central Bank's unsympathetic attitude to long-term loans, which were the only kind that the planters wanted. Such was the classic economic bind from which the South suffered. The whole section, and Jefferson with it, suffered from the single-crop system which he had so long deplored, and which was, in fact, so greatly at variance with his ideal of a society of independent yeoman farmers.

After the war and its abrupt termination of slavery, economic ruin became all too apparent. The price system did not permit the support of a free population of blacks in any adequate manner. Besides those capable of earning a living, there were as many again of children and old people, always a charge on the labor force, whether free or slave.[4] That a gradual emancipation might have saved the grief and long travail to come was the earnest belief of the few, but as Jefferson himself clearly saw, even this was to be a forlorn hope. Nothing now could save the South without radical economic change. All this, of course, was clearer in Virginia than in the Deep South, where cotton still prospered, at least for most of the time. It was, in fact, the sectional division that Jefferson so presciently feared.

Randolph, as governor of Virginia, had made a valiant effort. Quixotic as always, and often more liberal than Jefferson himself, he might have been expected to go the whole way and to propose a general, albeit gradual, emancipation. It would have been perhaps a hopeless, but at least a potentially effective, measure. But in public as in private life Randolph had hesitated and could not bring himself to make the decisive, and admittedly unpopular, leap. In his inaugural address he suggested the liberation of "a fair proportion of slave youth."[5] Jefferson had never given up his proposition of liberating "all born after a certain date." In the letter to Gallatin he called the governor's plan "ineffectual," although a move in the right direction. That it was, in fact, too late for any plan to meet with the approval of the gentlemen in Richmond soon became evident. The South had already made slavery her own "peculiar institution"; the drama must be played out to the bitter end, almost, indeed, as though these gentlemen had sought their self-destruction.

The old man, prey to ambivalence and even to despair, could cry out to Holmes: "I regret that I am now to die in the belief, that the useless sacrifice of themselves by the generation of 1776, to acquire self-government and happiness to their country, is to be thrown away . . . and that my only consolation is to be, that I live not to weep over it."

But despair had never held Jefferson for long. He could still work for the future, still put his faith in the youth for whom he was building his University. It was at this time that he designed his architectural masterpiece, the complex of colonnades and pavilions that was to be his "academical village." Closer to his own family was the building at Poplar Forest. It is here, in a series of letters to and from his master builder, John Hemings,[6] that we can most closely approach Jefferson's own relationship with that "misnamed sort of property," one of his own slaves.

John is a phonetic speller, but otherwise a letter writer of clarity and force. The letters show that he was a skilled craftsman, and that he was able to work from drawings.

JH TO TJ, POPLAR FOREST, NOV. 2, 1819

Sir: I am going on as you request with the blinds one pair at a time. I am now got 20 single flights rady for hangin. There is only enough to close 10 windows. I have pine enough to do the hole of them. I don't think you ever get the locks and hinges for these stiar way doors. If you had you did not leve them out hear. . . . we have had no rain to make ets way through the celing. . . .

JH TO TJ, NOV. 18, 1819

. . . Along about midnight it come up a brisk rain, and it woked me and I got up, and lite a candel and went upstairs, and it was lekin badly and I sot up untel day light, and went on the roof of the house to take off the shutters and rased up; the plank, and examoned. . . .

TJ TO JH, NOV. 27, 1819

I am very glad indeed that the cause of the leak is discovered. Miss no opportunity of every possible further search whenever rain falls. . . .
    Write to me every Wednesday.

JH TO TJ, NOV. 29, 1821

Sir, I am sorry to complain to you so near the close of my work, above all things on earth I hate complaints. . . . the moment your back is turned from the place Nace takes everything out of the garden and carries them to his cabin and buries them in the ground and says that they are for the use of the house. I don't set up myself for the things that are made for your table but as common a thing as [illegible] which we are suffering for the want of now. . . . [T]he pipel tels me that he is making market of them at the first opportunity. . . . In my situation I am at work in the morning by the time I can see and the very same at night. . . .

Sir, I am your faithful servant,
John Hemmings

JH TO TJ, TUESDAY, DEC. 11, 1821

. . . the skylight has made all the improvement imagenible. I have finish the rooms all to a little of the fir base which I shall git done in a day now. The boys is dressing the shingles and the other jobs before me.

I am your servant,
John Hemings

After December 1821 we have no letters until April 1825. By this time Jefferson was already suffering from dysentery, "a tedious case, confined to the house upward of three months." The letters now develop a warmth of feeling, especially on John's part.

TJ TO JH, APR. 17, 1825

. . . You will have to make up your mind to go once more to Bedford, to put up the entablatures of the parlour. . . . You have the drawings. We may be able to do this work next summer perhaps. Your friends here are well, and I wish you well.

JH TO TJ, JULY 23, 1825

Dear Sir: I hope this [illegible] may find you well, and in good health. We begin to tin the west side of the house and we have youst 5½ boxes. We shd in a few days finish that side except the Potcos. The rouft is [blot] that I am fost to employ both of the boys. . . .

JH TO TJ, AUG. 11, 1825

Dear Sir: I hope you are well. We have got through the 15 boxes and it will take 10 boxes more to finish the house. . . . We have go about preparing the chines raling and puting up the ornaments of the hall. Marster F. Eppes was saying something abot tining the flot rouft over the hall. You and him can deeside it between you how it shol be done. Sir Plese to send the tin off soon as you can. The flat rouft will take [blot] boxes. That in all their tin in Lynchburg at 15½ dollars wich is much nearer if it could be got.

I am your obedient servant.
Jon hemings

JH TO TJ, SEPT. 18, 1825

. . . Dear Sir, I hope you well.

JH TO TJ, SEPT. 28, 1825

Sir I hope this may find you well with all my heart for it is my wish. I shall be don my work on Saturday 7th of October. . . . Sir plese to odder the mules . . . the odd one off plese for me to ride. . . .

I am your humble servant
John Hemmings

Jefferson's letters to this key servant are businesslike, rather lacking in sentiment, as were his relations with all his workmen, black and white. Two of his Hemings servants he described as "affectionate"; these two were James and, later on, Burwell. John's own last letter to Jefferson we may certainly describe as "affectionate," if from his side only.

After his return from Poplar Forest, John set to work to make a writing desk for his friend Ellen, who had been married in the previous year to Joseph Coolidge of Boston. The writing desk, along with all her belongings, was lost when the packet boat carrying them burned at sea. Jefferson wrote her at length of John's distress: "John Hemings was the first who brought in the news. . . . He was au *desespoir*! That beautiful writing desk he had taken so much pains to make for you! Everything else seemed as nothing in his eye, and that loss was everything. Virgil could not have been more afflicted had his Aeneid fallen a prey to the flames. I asked him if he could replace it by making another. No; his eyesight had failed him so much, and his recollection of it was too imperfect."[7]

John, we know, was a cabinetmaker of considerable skill. Besides Ellen's desk he had once built the body of an elegant carriage to Jefferson's specifications, and he had rebuilt Maria's harpsichord when it had been allowed to fall apart at Millbrook after her death. When plagued by rheumatism at Poplar Forest, Jefferson sent for his "siesta chair" from Monticello, also the work of John. It may be that John was able to tune the harpsichord, although it is possible that Martha went with him to perform that office.

Ellen had declared that John was a favorite of hers, and the sentiment was certainly returned. There is another letter to the family in John's hand:

JH TO SEPTIMIA, POPLAR FOREST, AUGUST 28, 1825

Dear Miss Septima. Your letter came to me on the 23rd and happy was I to embrace it to see you take it upon yourself to writ to me and let me know how you Grand Papa was. Glad am I to hear that he is no worst—I hope you ar well and all the family. Giv my love to all your Georg Wyth Randolph specaly. I should get don the house on tusday that is tining [tinning] it. We have all the garrets to do wich is one hundred feet long.

The rest of the letter is concerned with the details of building, closing with the hope "I shal be able to com home by the 25th of November if Life Last."[8]

John, we know, was entrusted with "putting up the entablatures in the parlor." For the friezes at Poplar Forest Jefferson employed the same fine workman who was doing the ornamental work at the University, William J. Coffee. Some years before Coffee had done the charming little busts of the Monticello family. Now Jefferson paid him well, $100 in 1823, to mold and cast the friezes at the Bedford house.[9] A letter to Coffee describes his pleasure and his sense of freedom in the design of this house: "In my middle room at Poplar Forest I mean to mix the faces and ox skulls, a fancy which I can indulge in my own case, although in a public work I feel bound to follow authority strictly."[10]

There is no doubt that John Hemings was an essential part of the Monticello "family." Where he had learned his forceful English is not clear; it probably came naturally, but reading and writing would have been a different matter. Ellen gives a hint when she wrote her sister of her desire to "befriend and educate as well as I can" one of Burwell's children.[11] If formal education was not available to the blacks, the process of learning could never have been discouraged at Monticello. Nor was it possible to think that John Hemings could not have made his own way. It was not the individual slave but the mass that Jefferson felt was unprepared to enter the white society, and, even more pertinent perhaps, that the white society was not prepared to accept.

Chapter 33

Pecuniary Disaster

Put not your trust in Princes.

ALTHOUGH RANDOLPH AND his father-in-law were alike in foreseeing a possible civil war, they differed predictably in their personal response. Jefferson could only thank God that he would not see the day of reckoning in his own lifetime, while Randolph took an almost lighthearted view of coming catastrophe. He wrote to young Nicholas Trist, then a cadet at West Point, to recommend the science of gunnery: "It is impossible that the slave system should continue, without some check on their increase, and not in the end produce a great, long, and obstinate struggle. I shall not live to see it; but I should much rather it should happen in my time than in that of my descendants. . . ." (Randolph would have been pleased, and certainly not surprised could he have known that his youngest son, George Wythe Randolph, was to be secretary of war in the Confederacy.)

"I have enough fondness for the Art of War," he told Trist, "to desire to take part in any kind of War, if it be but inevitable." [1] For many years, in fact, he had considered that "to die in the field is the greatest good that can befall man."

Randolph had left the governor's office amid a noisy public quarrel with his council of state. True to his thesis that outbursts were less injurious to his health than long-sustained vexation, he had even carried his outrage into the streets of Richmond. This undignified exit did not prevent his running for the General Assembly in the spring of 1823. His *idea* of a political career as the *summa bonum* of human existence was too deeply entrenched for any reverse to terminate. As in personal quarrels, his ability to cheer up and bounce back remained undiminished.

The harassment of debt was not so easily dismissed. While still in the governor's chair, he had complained that his creditors made life a "torment." Now strong in body and strong in the consciousness of his disinterested love for his family, as though these factors alone were enough to gain him credit, he went to New York to borrow money. Never one to conceal his most private feelings even in negotiating a mortgage, he wrote to Henry Remsen, a New York merchant to whom Jefferson had introduced him, in the fall of 1823:

I must be allowed to express the very strong sentiment of gratitude to you for the most important favor to my numerous and excellent family of a wife, six daughters and five sons, which I most sincerely and warmly feel and shall ever cherish in an honest and constant heart. As for myself I am alltogether indifferent as to the good or evil which may be in fate for me. . . . I live only for them. . . . I am quite a robust man, and a very experienced farmer, therefore with the excellent farming means I have by long toil become possessed of may yet succeed in clearing the estate of my family from its encumbrances.[2]

The loan offered by Remsen proved to be only a partial and temporary relief. By the spring of 1824 Randolph took the last fatal step toward ruin: he gave his son Jefferson Randolph a deed of trust to Varina and Edgehill, in return for the son's assumption of his father's total debt, amounting to more than $23,000. Jeff, already in charge of his grandfather's affairs, was now the man in control of his father's as well. Jeff Randolph, the hard-working, hard-boiled realist, was now the man at the helm.[3]

With Jeff's trusteeship the whole sad tale of his father's financial dealings had come to the surface, apparently for the first time. Martha poured out her heart in a letter to Nicholas Trist that clearly shows how little she had been aware of the state of their affairs:

The derangement of Mr. Randolph's affairs of which I have long known enough to weigh heavily upon my spirits, but it is within this last two or three months only that I have been aware of the extent of the ruin that awaits us from that quarter. Jefferson and myself have both strenuously urged the immediate settlement of his affairs and the honest payment of his debts. During my father's lifetime there can be

no great change in our situation, and there are resources in his possession the value of which are incalculable. Once clear of debt and there
are many ways in which a man of his experience and talents may
support himself and a family who already have a home and the
comforts of life found them. I have the sad consolation of thinking
that we have nothing to reproach ourselves with, for never have we
spent the half, and many years not the fourth of his income. But
securityships which throw him into the hands of usurers have under-
mined an estate that without that, would have maintained us in
affluence and provided for our children. He has in better times made
$10,000 from his estate, and in the worst, $3000. I believe the expenses
of both plantations and his family included have never been beyond
$2000 and much oftener under, and this after the sale of one plantation
land and Negroes all of which went to pay his securityships. But
enough. You will yourself feel the necessity of confining this within
your own breast—as the thing is not yet known and Mr. Randolph
still has hopes of a loan that will give him a chance (he hopes) to
recover.[4]

For the first time in her life Martha is dealing in figures; neither
her husband nor her father had ever confided them to her before.
Such total ignorance would be unusual today, and even among
Martha's contemporaries there were many women who took a
more active part in their husbands' affairs. The vigorous letters of
Hetty Carr are a case in point, but Martha had learned this strict
division between the role of the sexes directly from her father. Even
in this letter of disillusionment she does not cry out, "If I had only
known!" or regret her own past ignorance. She points out, on the
contrary, that in her role of household manager she has been
beyond reproach; nor does she break the old habit of relying on her
father. She exhibits a truly Jeffersonian optimism when she speaks
of "resources . . . the value of which are incalculable." Her son Jeff,
on the contrary, was apt to calculate them to the last penny.

After a lifetime of public service Jefferson himself, with his
almost mystical reliance on the people he had served, may have
been counting in the final analysis on less material resources. The
great humiliation of his last years was to be the discovery of how
frail indeed was this reliance. A few months before Martha's letter,
this had come home to him when he had attempted to repay what

was at least a moral obligation. Bernard Peyton, his man of business in Richmond, had extended Jefferson credit far above and beyond the call of duty, and now Peyton asked him to use his influence to obtain for him a job, the postmastership of Richmond. Under these circumstances Jefferson turned to the influence which, up until now, he had so scrupulously avoided using. The current president, James Monroe, had the postmastership in his power to give. Jefferson must have been aware that he had made Monroe what he was, pushing the second-class man into the first rank. Now in his need he wrote Monroe, putting this request in the strongest possible terms: "In a conversation with you . . . some two or three years ago I mentioned to you that there would be one single case, and but one in the whole world into which I should go with my whole heart and soul, and ask as if it were for myself. It was that whenever the Post Office or Collector's Office at Richmond, either of them should become vacant, you would name Colo. B. Peyton to it, and preferably to the P.O. . . ."[5] He sent a copy of this letter to Peyton, saying that "if I am anything in Washington the request must prevail."

Monroe refused him. In a letter to Jefferson, dated August 26, 1824, Monroe announced the appointment of ex-governor Preston, stressing the fact that Preston had "been seriously wounded in an action on the northern frontier." In fact Preston had sustained a broken leg. At the end of Monroe's letter there appeared a most enigmatic sentence: "It is proper for me further to add, in profound confidence, that among the other applications, one has been made by a person of great consideration, respecting whom, in competition with any other person, I cannot consult you." This mysterious person was Thomas Mann Randolph. Feeling himself on the brink of "inevitable ruin," he had pulled out all the stops in an effort to gain this same appointment, with its greatly needed salary of $2,000 per annum. Randolph had not confided in his father-in-law, and Jefferson appears not to have understood in the least what person had been meant by Monroe's reference to that mysterious other applicant. The wound to Jefferson was deep, so deep that he could wonder to another correspondent that the claim of a broken leg should outweigh his own lifetime of service to his country.[6] In this episode there is something of Elizabethan tragedy: "Put not your trust in Princes." Saddest of all, perhaps, was the growing failure of communication between these members of a beleaguered family. It was a harbinger of events to come.

Chapter 34

Mrs. Coolidge

GEORGE TICKNOR TO THOMAS JEFFERSON, BOSTON, MARCH 27, 1824

Dear Sir:

Allow me to ask your kindness and hospitality . . . for a young gentleman of education and fortune . . . who is well known to all of us for his excellent and amiable character, and who, by a residence of several years in Europe, has recently completed the course of instruction he had so well begun at home.

Do me the favor to present him to Governor Randolph, Mrs. Randolph and their family . . .[1]

Thus introduced by George Ticknor, Joseph Coolidge made his appearance at Monticello. In addition to the attributes described by his friend, we have it on no less an authority than Lord Byron that Coolidge was intelligent, very handsome, and "mighty fond of poesy." Walter Muir Whitehill tells us that Coolidge had gone to Europe after graduating from Harvard, not so much to complete a course of instruction as "to see what he could and to meet whom he might," which had led to a visit to the poet, then sojourning in Italy. What particularly had impressed Byron was that his young admirer "had obtained a copy of my bust from Thorwaldsen in Rome to send to America. I confess I was . . . flattered. . . . It must have been expensive though."[2] A romantic lover of poetry who could afford to buy a bust from Thorwaldsen! Joseph Coolidge was exceptional indeed.

It was a visit of only two weeks, but two weeks can rarely have been better spent. The young man who had come to pay homage to the great philosopher and democrat stayed to fall in love with that philosopher's "dearest jewel." Jefferson had not been unaware of the romance in their midst; it must have been plain to all as the young people strolled about the mountain together, in that beautiful Albemarle spring. Perhaps they sat in the little temple, above the just-blooming fruit trees.

At last Ellen had met a man who seemed to know who he was, and where he was going. The sensitive Gilmer had been gifted and adoring, but insecure. He was the son of that society which Ellen had already felt to be closing in around her. Coolidge sprang from a line of successful Boston merchants; he believed, and I think he made Ellen believe, that the future belonged to him. It was an aura irresistible to the young woman who had once asked herself *cui bono?* Besides he was handsome, and he had the passion for poetry that Ellen had had as a girl, and had perhaps almost forgotten. When he left Monticello he had spoken to Martha: "I confessed to Mrs. Randolph the interest her daughter had inspired." Martha had not unnaturally suggested that perhaps two weeks was too short a time in which to conclude such a momentous question. Coolidge acquiesced. An exchange of letters followed, letters which were eminently satisfactory to the correspondents. How far Ellen followed her natural bent for self-analysis in these letters we shall perhaps never know, for diligent research has failed to turn them up. They must have been either lost or destroyed, probably the latter, as Ellen may well have followed the pattern set by her grandfather, and apparently also by her mother, in destroying letters between husband and wife.

By October the Boston side of this correspondence wrote to Monticello to ask if he might return to renew his suit. "I do not presume that you now hear for the first time," he wrote Jefferson, "of my attachment to a member of your family, but respect and gratitude alike forbid me to ask again the protection of your roof without confessing the true motive of my visit." Such letters are difficult to write, and no matter how formal, they are revealing of character. Young Mr. Coolidge had successfully steered between the Scylla of over-confidence and the Charybdis of sycophancy. He closes his letter: "Apart from the interest which I feel in you, Sir, as the cherished relative of one who under every circumstances will be dear to me, may I not be permitted to assure you of my unfeigned regard?"

Jefferson, who had once so seriously erred in his estimate of Martha's suitor, was on this occasion absolutely right. He answered that he "was satisfied no two minds could be formed, better compounded to make each other happy." As for a financial provision for the young couple, Jefferson said quite simply that Ellen's family could do nothing to help them at the present time, but at this date (October 1824) he still had confidence that "My property is such that after a discharge of these encumbrances [his debts] a comfortable provision will remain for my unprovided grandchildren." Coolidge could hardly have known at the time that quite apart from the lack of "comfortable provision" a descent of dependent relatives was to be Ellen's marriage portion. Even so, although often plagued, the groom seems never for an instant to have regretted his bargain. Ellen, dependent relatives or not, was all that he desired.

Ellen's financial problem was more immediate; it had to do with a trousseau. Her father, desperate as his financial position now was, had exerted himself on her behalf, but there was a limit not only to his funds, but to his knowledge of the latest in feminine fashion. Ellen wrote to Margaret Nicholas in Baltimore: "In Boston I am told there will be a campaign of parties . . . *you* will know far better than I, what I shall want to make a *genteel* appearance. . . . It is bad enough to go to him utterly without fortune, and it would be *too* bad, for him to have to *dress* me." Ellen can send $85 at once. "All my plain clothes, linen, petticoats, stockings, both silk and cotton, thread cambric pocket handkerchiefs, white cambric frocks, etc., my father got in Richmond for me. What I want from Baltimore is all in the *dress* line."[3]

At the close of his cordial letter of invitation to Ellen's Boston suitor, Jefferson had referred to the great event so shortly expected at Monticello. This was "the visit of my antient friend Gen'l La-Fayette. The delirium which his visit has excited in the North envelopes him in the South also."[4] In this description Jefferson was recognizing the symbolic role played by Lafayette for the American people. It was already achieved, and destined to survive for at least another century. In 1917 American doughboys stepping onto

French soil were represented as saying, "Lafayette, we are here!" Jefferson himself, marked by the daily toil and compromises of politics, and subject always to the minute inspection of history, did not serve the purpose of myth as well as Lafayette. This in spite of the fact that Jefferson's own view of his relation to his fellow citizens partook so largely of this mystical element. It was his fellow citizens to whom he felt responsible, and to whom, in the last analysis, he confided his place in the history of the republic. His confidence in what he called the "republican mass of our country" was not lip service only.[5] He *believed* in them, he trusted them, and it was to them that he turned in the difficult last year of his life.

It was fitting, indeed, that the two "antient friends" and comrades-in-arms should meet, not in privacy, but in the full euphoria of a public event. Jeff Randolph, who had a considerable part in engineering the occasion, described the meeting as it occurred on Monticello's east lawn:

The lawn on the eastern side of the house at Monticello contains not quite an acre. . . . The barouche containing LaFayette stopped at the edge of this lawn. His escort—one hundred and twenty mounted men—formed on one side in a semi-circle extending from the carriage to the house. A crowd of about two hundred men who were drawn together by curiosity to witness the meeting of these two venerable men, formed themselves in a semi-circle on the opposite side. As LaFayette descended from the carriage, Jefferson descended from the steps of the portico. . . . Jefferson was feeble and tottering with age— LaFayette permanently lamed and broken in health by his confinement in the dungeon of Olmetz. As they approached each other, their uncertain gait quickened itself into a shuffling run, and exclaiming, "Ah, Jefferson!" "Ah, LaFayette!" they burst into tears as they fell into each other's arms. Among the four hundred men witnessing the scene there was not a dry eye—no sound save an occasional suppressed sob. The two old men entered the house as the crowd dispersed in profound silence.[6]

It was an occasion of almost religious awe.

Inside the house there was immediate relaxation; private friendship took over. James Madison arrived late for dinner, in time for dessert, no doubt one prepared in the French style. After the cloth

had been removed and the wine served, the younger guests, Joseph
Coolidge and Ellen among them, gathered round, listening to the
conversation of the two old men. After this the public dinner at the
Rotunda which took place the next day may have been an anticlimax, but an anticlimax of a formidable character. Four hundred
guests were fed at tables placed in three concentric circles under the
dome of this recently completed building at Jefferson's University.
Although some of the guests, Joseph Coolidge among them, were
aware of the architectural triumph of the building around them,
the keynote on this occasion had obviously to be patriotic fervor.

The most important toast of that day was "To Thomas Jefferson
and the Declaration of Independence—alike identified with the
cause of liberty." Valentine Southall, as presiding officer at the feast,
read Jefferson's reply, for the old man declared that his voice was
not up to such an effort:

Born and bred among your fathers, led by their partiality into the line
of public life, I labored in fellowship with them through that arduous
struggle which, freeing us from foreign bondage, established us in the
rights of self-government. . . .

I joy, my friends, in your joy, inspired by the visit of this our ancient
distinguished leader and benefactor. . . . To these effusions for the
cradle and land of my birth, I add, for our nation at large, the aspirations of a heart warm with love of country, whose invocations to
heaven for its indissoluble union, will be fervent and unremitting
while the pulse of life continues to beat, and, when that ceases, it
will expire in prayers for the eternal duration of its freedom and
prosperity.[7]

When Valentine Southall sat down, the applause must have
nearly lifted the roof of the dome, nor can we read the words today
without joining in that fervent prayer.

Among the four hundred at dinner no women were present.
The ladies had been entertained outside, in the galleries and ar-
cades of the pavilions.[8]

When, in fact, Ellen took the irrevocable step of committing
herself to becoming Mrs. Joseph Coolidge, Jr., of Boston is not clear,
although most likely it occurred during this memorable visit. The

wedding itself took place the following spring. In contrast to those at Boston the festivities at Monticello were probably rather casual. Joseph's parents, although cordially invited, were not able to come down for the occasion. The groom brought a Mr. Harrison Ritchie with him to serve as best man, and no doubt Virginia, not yet married to her faithful Nicholas, would have been her sister's maid of honor, as far as this role was customary at the time. Few formal arrangements could have been made, for no one knew when the Reverend Frederick Hatch, described as a "circuit preacher," would be able to show up at Monticello. The Reverend Mr. Hatch may not have been unaware that the funds derived from the seizure of church lands in Albemarle after the Revolution now appeared as the first item in the endowment of the new University.[9]

In 1824 there was no church building of any denomination in the village of Charlottesville, and the churches in the county were all but abandoned. The fact that Jefferson in this very year was designing an Episcopal church for erection in Charlottesville must have soothed the clergyman's feelings, but would not have made his schedule of services, from home to home and courthouse to courthouse, any less demanding. Monticello must wait its turn. Mr. Hatch arrived unexpectedly, with only two hours to spare, at a time when many of the wedding party, including the best man, were off on an early morning fox hunt.[10] Luckily the groom was not a fox hunter. He and Ellen stood up together in the drawing room at Monticello, and Mr. Hatch declared them man and wife. Ellen's hands trembled to such an extent that she could barely hold a prayer book.[11]

Once married Ellen surely ceased to have tremors, for on a very extensive wedding trip through New York and New England they continued to pursue Joseph's ambition to see everything and meet everyone. It was a strenuous trip, and Ellen proved ready to absorb a multitude of new impressions, all apparently in favor of New England. She wrote her grandfather: "I should judge from appearances that they are at least a century in advance of us in all the arts and embellishments of life." She has seen but one drunken man, and he a South Carolinian! The journey has given her "an idea of prosperity and improvement, such as I fear our Southern States cannot hope for, whilst the canker of slavery eats into their hearts and diseases the whole body by this ulcer at the core." [12]

Jefferson missed this granddaughter sorely. "We did not know," he wrote, "until you left us, what a void it would make in our family," but when it came to the serious comments in her letter he backed away. "I have no doubt that you will find . . . the state of society there more congenial with your mind, than the rustic scenes you have left: although these do not want their points of endearment. Nay, one single circumstance changed, and their scale would hardly be the lightest. One fatal stain deforms what nature had bestowed upon us of her fairest gifts." But he avoids Ellen's far more pointed indictment, passing immediately to the safer area of "I am glad you took the delightful tour, etc." [13]

Lafayette and his young friend Fanny Wright pressed him far harder on the same subject. Rather surprisingly Jefferson admired this outspoken young woman; her unbridled enthusiasm for the American experiment may have reminded him of his own youth. At any rate he answered her representations in the cause of emancipation in the same manner that, nearly a decade before, he had answered Edward Coles. This young man had done on an individual scale what Fanny Wright later attempted as a communal experiment: [14] he had freed his own slaves. Edward was the brother of Isaac Coles, already mentioned in these pages. He had conducted an extensive correspondence with Jefferson on the subject of emancipation. [15] Jefferson had then replied, in effect, I am too old. But on this occasion he indulged in what was, for him, an unusual twist of humor: ". . . at the age of eighty-two, with one foot in the grave, and the other uplifted to follow it, I do not permit myself to take part in any new enterprises." [16]

Ellen, in a later comment on Fanny, was less courteous than her grandfather: "A disgrace to her sex—invites public attention with a rhinoceras, etc." [17] The allusion to a rhinoceros is a bit obscure, but in any case Fanny had committed the unforgivable female sin, she had allowed her name to appear in print!

Ellen did, in fact, find some difficulty in the numerous adjustments that Boston required of her. "I do not think that she is so much pleased with Boston or its inhabitants, as I thought she would have been," wrote Joseph to her grandfather.[18] Ellen was homesick. Like every Virginian who has left home, she was always to feel herself an exile, a happy and fortunate one, perhaps, but an exile nonetheless.

Chapter 35

The Battle of Edgehill

Broke to atoms, in mind, body and estate.

IN THIS SAME YEAR of 1824 the battle of Edgehill was joined in earnest. We remember that Randolph had been forced to reveal *all* his debts, and that both Martha and Jeff had believed that all should be paid off. Jefferson too found himself in serious difficulties that summer. He was compelled to ask his Richmond agent, Bernard Peyton, to negotiate another bank loan, and to allow his account with the ever-patient Peyton to remain unpaid.[1] Under these circumstances Jeff's mind was made up, he would take all these debts upon his own shoulders, and to this end he was perfectly ruthless in liquidating his father's assets. Edgehill was to be offered for sale the following August.

Randolph had once himself desired to sell Edgehill, but, in response to Martha's wishes, he had given up the idea. Of late years its fields, its crops, and its Negroes, interwoven as they were with all his best endeavors, had become his dearest possession. If Jeff had been willing to compromise, the fearful family battle that followed might have been avoided, but Jeff was not. In one letter to his wife Jeff spoke of having advised his grandfather to "give up his property to his creditors and to look to his children [i.e., Jeff himself] for support."[2]

Very early on Jeff appears to have determined to save Edgehill from the wreckage, for the benefit of himself, and of his own and his mother's family. His mother-in-law, the redoubtable Peggy (Mrs. Wilson Cary) Nicholas deplored in one letter Jeff's impropriety in actually commencing some building on the Edgehill property before he had acquired it by legal purchase in the sale of January 1826.

Randolph's reaction to this prospective sale may be imagined. Once again, as in 1791, father and son battled over the ownership of Edgehill, but this time the battle was far bloodier. It was fought to the death, for the father was hardly to survive it. His contention, as explained in three long letters to his friend Francis Gilmer, was that Edgehill should only be held liable for a *portion* of his debt, that of the immediate mortgage held by an outside party on the property. To that end he himself suggested a division of the farm into five pieces, so that the sale of one alone might settle the claim against him. This was quite contrary to the security he had given Jeff, who had taken over the *whole* of his father's debts in return for a lien on the whole of Edgehill. Later Randolph was to complain bitterly that this division of the property destroyed its value; and no one since then seems to have noticed that, far from being a nefarious scheme of Jeff's, it had originally been his father's own suggestion.

In any case Jeff turned down his father's contention that only a part of the property need go in the contemplated sale. Nor was he any more open to pleas that his father might be permitted to retain a few acres next to the mountain for a vineyard, or to take timber for a sawmill that he meant to put up on the property. Jeff set his face like stone against any such arrangements. He made his own plans clear: he intended to grow tobacco and breed Negroes to pay the debt in time. He would raise the necessary money for the purchase by selling his own property at Pantops, which he had previously bought from John Eppes. "How can I wish him success in that scheme?" his father asked. Father and son were not "within a thousand years of agreement," and the more they discussed these matters the worse things got.

The saddest part of it all was that in the very midst of his violence Randolph understood his own fate. Like Job he protested the sale of every slave; every bushel of wheat seemed to be torn from his own heart. He found it "more than I can bear with fortitude sufficient to suppress feelings or retain expressions of resentment; which do more harm than good allways, but to a man harassed as I am bring his fate more certainly and speedily." He sees what he is doing but cannot help himself; he is out to self-destruct.[3]

Was Randolph aware that, like Samson, he might bring the pillars of the temple down with him? Martha made her choice, if a choice it can be called. As she had outlined in her letter to Nicholas Trist, she had concurred in the decision to leave her father's property in the care of trustees for her benefit, rather than have it go directly to her, because, in the latter case, it would have been subject to the claims of her husband's creditors. Actually if she wanted a roof for herself and the children, no other course was open to her. But the realization of this hard fact was not acceptable to the disinherited one. He absented himself from Monticello during the day, only to return at night to destroy Martha's hard-earned rest, and to abuse his son. Relatives and neighbors described him as "more cruel, barbarous and fiend-like than ever."[4] He was, indeed, a very sick man.

The public reason that he later gave was that after his misfortune he had left Monticello to avoid the supercilious looks of Mr. Jefferson's various guests.[5] Actually he could not stand the position of utter dependency, now obvious for all to see. Up till then it could always be glossed over, or possibly even reversed. Francis Gilmer found him "broke to atoms, in mind, body and estate."[6] The only legal authority he had left was over the minor children, and he hastened to exercise it by forbidding Martha to allow Tim and the little boys to cross the property line to visit Jeff's family at Tufton.

Jeff's wife, dear motherly Jane, could still hope that the colonel's bark might be worse than his bite, and that he still might be reconciled to his son.[7]

Although Randolph succeeded in obtaining a delaying order in 1825, Edgehill was finally sold on January 2, 1826: the buyer, as he had suspected, was Thomas Jefferson Randolph.[8] The battle of Edgehill was over at last, leaving deep and permanent wounds behind. Jefferson applied what balm he could: "It is now that the value of education will prove itself to you, in the recourse to books of which it has qualified you to avail yourself, and which, aided by the conversation and endearments of your family, and every comfort which the place can be made to afford you. . . ."[9] The prescription was not only ineffective; it was impossible to swallow.

Up until now Martha had been able to stand by her husband. By making this impossible he made her suffer, beyond what even her strong heart was able to bear. Ellen was not there to see, but the other girls, Virginia in particular, could not look back on those days without real grief and revulsion. Never again, said Virginia, should her children consent to see their mother "sinking under such treatment." [10]

How much, if at all, did Martha understand what had happened to her husband? His sister Nancy, "the poor afflicted victim" of Bizarre, and incidentally of her own selfish passions, had long depended on the generosity of her elder brother. Even with semi-strangers it appeared to have fortified his ego to have signed their notes. Moreover, buried deep in this stormy marriage under layers of dependency and real love, there must have been hostility on his part. Deepest of all was the fear of facing success, the need for a valid excuse. How otherwise could he face the fact that no matter what he did, or how he might prosper, Martha would not leave her father's house? One day, he may half-consciously have thought, it will be my home, my family, and now his own son had usurped that place. "Like Lear," Gilmer had said, Randolph might "roam the world, houseless and penniless." [11] But after all Lear had only been deluded; Randolph had his own furies, from whom death alone might now release him.

Kitchen, Monticello—*Lindsay Nolting*

Anne Cary Bankhead, terra cotta
bust by William J. Coffee, 1818—
Thomas Jefferson Memorial Foundation

Interior of dome—*Andrew Johnson, Thomas Jefferson Memorial Foundation*

"Sy Gilliat, or the Banjo Man," oil on canvas, c. 1810—*Valentine Museum*

Poplar Forest—*Stevens & Co.*

Thomas Mann Randolph: artist unknown
—*Alderman Library*

Thomas Jefferson Randolph, by Charles Willson
Peale, oil on canvas, 1816—*Thomas Jefferson Memorial Foundation*

Ellen Wayles Coolidge: artist unknown—*Mrs. John S. Eddy*

Nicholas Trist, by John Neagle, c. 1835—*Thomas Jefferson Memorial Foundation*

Martha Jefferson Randolph, by Thomas Sully,
1836—*Thomas Jefferson Memorial Foundation*

April 18ᵗʰ 2 o'clock in the morning Friday

To my five daughters I wish to bequeath my property in the funds.
To Benjamin & Lewis the two negroes now in Benjamins possession.
my five remaining negroes Emily I wish liberated as soon as you break
up house keeping here; Martha Ann at the death of her old grandmother, in the mean time to live with her and take care of her. To
Betsy Hemmings. Sally & Wormley I wish my children to give their
time. If liberated they would be obliged to leave the state of Virginia
To my dear George I have nothing but my love to leave, and in any
division made of my books that he should have a share.
In dividing the plate among you, I wish Jefferson to have the
cassroles, & Mr. Coolidge the duck. To Nicholas I leave my
fathers clock.

written by mama's request

Codicil to will of Martha Jefferson Randolph, April 18, 1834
—*Edgehill-Randolph Papers*

John Hemings to Septimia Randolph,
Poplar Forest, August, 28, 1825: holograph
letter—*Pauline Page: Alderman Library*

Monticello gravestone: "THE SED IS PLACED AT THE
HEAD OF MY DEAR AFFECTIONATE WIFE PRISCILLA HEMINGS
DEPARTED THIS LIFE ON FRIDAY THE 7TH OF MAY 1830.
AGE 54."—*Edwin S. Roseberry: Thomas Jefferson Memorial
Foundation*

Cornelia Jefferson Randolph, terra
cotta bust by William J. Coffee,
1818—*Edwin S. Roseberry: Ms. Louise
Kirk*

Watercolor by Cornelia Randolph. Cornelia painted this nostalgic view
looking back at Monticello from Edgehill—*Thomas Jefferson Memorial
Foundation*

Chapter 36

A Glorious Day on Which to Die

TRY AS MARTHA DID to keep these scenes of conflict from her father, he saw it all. Added to his knowledge of Martha's suffering, which he was powerless to allay, there was his own desperate financial condition. For himself, he said, it was a matter of indifference what might be in store, but he realized that the fate of Martha and her children was at stake. For the first time in eighty-two years he was kept awake by "painful thoughts." And then suddenly, as Martha described it, "like an inspiration from the realms of bliss," came the idea that might save them all: a lottery![1]

Jefferson had always relied on the sale of his land to pull him out of any financial crisis, but now lands in Virginia were selling for only a third or a fourth of what they would have brought when the debt was incurred. A "fair value" was impossible to obtain on the current market—but might not the sale of lottery tickets achieve this end, the return from the tickets equal to "a fair value" for the land offered? The trouble was that lotteries, once freely resorted to in Jefferson's youth, were now looked on askance, at least in the case of a private individual. A special dispensation from the Virginia legislature was now required before a lottery could be held in the state.

At first Jefferson had no doubt that the permission would be forthcoming. That he might be turned down hardly occurred to him, but he had failed to realize the full impact of changing times. The economic base of the country was changing, and along with it ideas of fiscal right and wrong were changing, too. With a higher regard for money values went a new condemnation of games of chance. The old philosopher at Monticello pointed out that chance was simply another name for those events in nature which so far we have failed to understand. For those less enlightened a reliance on chance appeared to flout the new industrial ethic, that only by hard work and outsmarting one's neighbor did one get on in the world.

Jefferson laid stress on the fact that a lottery, while hurting no one, was the only way of getting "fair value" for his land. But what was fair value? During all these years Virginia planters had been exhausting their land and exploiting their slaves. That Jefferson himself had forborne to carry these practices to an extreme did not alter the fact that the bottom had now dropped out of the market for Virginia land. Even far more thrifty and prosperous farmers than Jefferson were suffering. John Coles of neighboring Estouteville summarized his accounts as follows:

Col. John Coles worked in the years 1816-17-18 & 19 22 hands, and for these four years the gross am't of his sales was $24,507.80—or say $280 per hand.

In the years 1820-21-22-23-24 & 25 he worked 30 hands, the gross am't of sales being only $25,323.05 for those six years, or say $140 per hand.[2]

A decline of one-half.

What then can we mean by fair value? Jefferson was right in a sense when he had pointed out to his son-in-law that the soil and the crops still produced on it were no longer considered wealth, which now depended on the money market, on, indeed, bits of "scrip," i.e., depreciated paper. This was admittedly in the short run, but time for an eighty-three-year-old man could hardly be anything else. Even in the long run he was suffering grave doubts as to the future of the South, and even of the Union. Fair value was a moot question in times such as these.

He was on far more solid ground when he wrote of the lottery scheme as representing a return by his fellow citizens for sixty-four years spent unremittingly in their service. How, he not unjustly asked, could his case set an unwise example, for how many men could bring forth such a claim? This claim, so self-evident, had to be presented to the legislature where there were new men, and new political axes to grind. Men like Joseph C. Cabell knew that the old man at Monticello was even then spending the last ounce of his failing strength in the service of his state's University. Cabell fought valiantly on behalf of the lottery, but there was no way of concealing the opposition in the legislature.

To Jefferson, already prostrated with the onslaught of his final illness, this was a shattering blow. For all this time his belief in his relationship with his fellow citizens had sustained him; now he had put it to the test, and it appeared to have failed him. To his friend Cabell he poured out the full measure of his distress: "If refused [permission for the lottery] I must sell everything here, perhaps considerably in Bedford, move thither with my family where I have not even a log hut to put my head into. . . ."[3] He had already given the house at Poplar Forest to Maria's son Francis Eppes, and had refused Francis's immediate offer to return it to his grandfather.

To Jeff he wrote:

It is part of my mortification to perceive that I had so far over-valued myself as to have counted on it with too much confidence. I see in the failure of this hope, a deadly blast of all my peace of mind, during my remaining days. . . . I am overwhelmed at the prospect of the situation in which I may leave my family. My dear and beloved daughter, the cherished companion of my early life and nurse of my age, and her children, rendered as dear to me as if my own had lived with me from their cradle, left in a comfortless situation, hold up to me nothing but future gloom, and I should not care if life were to end with the line I am writing; were it not that in the unhappy state of mind which your father's misfortunes have brought upon him, I might yet be of some avail to the family.[4]

When Jeff showed this letter to Randolph Harrison, Harrison threw it down half-read, and burst into tears.

On the day, February 10, that the Lottery Bill was reported in the House Jefferson's oldest granddaughter, Anne Cary, lay dying at her home, Carlton, near Monticello. Jefferson had been too ill to go to her, and when he did go on the eleventh he found her already "speechless and insensible."[5] It was in the midst of this personal grief that the news arrived. The Lottery Bill had passed, but even this was a qualified victory. The greatest blow had only been postponed. Jefferson learned that Monticello itself must be included in the prize. When Jeff told him this, the old man turned pale. He must have time, he said. He must consult Mrs. Randolph.[6] Martha had been with him in the first house, in the days of his hope and his grief; only Martha had been with him in Paris; and only Martha shared the whole strength of his feeling, that Monticello *was* his personal life. It would remain with them for the duration of his life, then it would have to go.

It was only too clear that nothing else remained to be done. Now around the central figure of Jefferson a Greek chorus of relatives raised their voices, bewailing the fate of the Monticello family. "Poor old man," wrote one of the Carr women. "I believe he flatters himself that the state will buy it [Monticello] from whomever wins it."[7] This conjecture perhaps was true, for Jefferson could still exercise his native ability to rise above disaster, even to close his eyes to what to others seemed clear. Only perhaps he might not be there; all now hung on the frail thread of that ebbing life.

"Poor Mrs. Randolph," lamented Mrs. Carr, "to have Col. Randolph aggravate her distress is too bad." And in fact since Anne's death Randolph had been virtually out of his mind. He continued to absent himself in the daytime, and to come home at night to harass his wife and abuse his son, "more like a demon than a man." It was not possible to conceal it all from the dying man.[8]

Meanwhile, Jeff was pushing the lottery scheme as best he could. Support must be won for the sale of tickets, and from the beginning the project was plagued by ambivalence and confusion. Once Jefferson's plight was made public, offers of volunteer contributions had come in, and there was some question whether or not these might be accepted, as they would tend to interfere with the sale of lottery tickets. Bernard Peyton was not exaggerating when he spoke of how much depended on Jefferson's life. A public that would come to the support of Thomas Jefferson could hardly be expected to feel the same way about the aristocratic Randolphs. While the lottery delayed, the days of life were running out.

When Jeff returned from a trip promoting the lottery in late June, he found Jefferson ill and in great distress about his daughter. "It is an agony," he told Jeff, "to leave her in the situation she is now in. She is sinking every day under the suffering she now endures;

she is literally dying before my eyes."[9] He made Jeff promise never to leave her, that he would always be on hand to give her any comfort and assistance that he could. Jeff promised at once.

As the end drew near Jefferson composed himself: "I commit my soul to my God," he told Jeff, "and my child to my country."[10] Martha stayed at his side during the day, but he would not permit her to sit up at night. That was traditionally the task and privilege of the men of the family, of Jeff and of Nicholas Trist, and of his servant Burwell. Jeff wrote to his wife at Tufton: "After passing a very good night my grandfather sank rapidly. . . . My mother perfectly conscious of his situation. I hope will bear it. I will hang out a white towel or sheet upon the thorn bush upon the brow above Priscilla's house to let you know when it is over."[11]

On Monday, July 3, Jefferson slept all day, and on waking, thinking the morning had come, he said, "This is the fourth of July." When offered laudanum he shook his head, "No, doctor, nothing more." Now his sleep was disturbed, and once he sat up in bed, crying out, "The Committee of Safety ought to be warned." At fifteen minutes before midnight those about him stood noting the minute hand of the watch. At 4 : 00 A.M. he called the servants in attendance in a strong clear voice. He did not speak again. Jeff wrote that at "about ten he fixed his eyes intently upon me, indicating some want, which, most painfully, I could not understand." Burwell stepped forward, and adjusted the pillow to its accustomed height. Jefferson seemed satisfied. He ceased to breathe, without a struggle, fifty minutes past meridian.[12]

On the same day, in Quincy, Massachusetts, his "antient friend," John Adams, also lay upon his deathbed. There too, they had watched the clock. As death drew near Adams murmured, "Jefferson still survives." But it was not so. The white handkerchief already fluttered from the thorn bush above Aunt Priscilla's house.

Without doubt the two old men had willed it so. It was a glorious Fourth indeed, the fiftieth anniversary of the Declaration. A glorious day on which to die.

Chapter 37

The Black Family Scattered

JEFFERSON'S WILL HELD no surprises for the family. He had given Poplar Forest to Francis Eppes, which perhaps he might not have done if he had been fully aware of the desperate situation soon to face his daughter. All the rest of his property was left in trust for Martha, under the trusteeship of Jefferson Randolph, Nicholas Trist, and Alexander Garrett, to be in effect during the lifetime of her husband. The purpose of this provision was, of course, to prevent the claims of Randolph's creditors, which would have been legally good against any property in his wife's name. The debt on Jefferson's estate alone amounted to $107,273.[1] Jeff, who had taken over this enormous indebtedness, was named as sole executor. Randolph had never broken completely with Jefferson. He now swore never to set foot in Monticello, to be dependent upon the "executor," by which name alone he now bitterly referred to his son.

Nicholas Trist, who after all the long years of their engagement had been married to Virginia in the autumn of 1824, was to be in charge of the Monticello house. The men decided, with Martha's agreement, that the furniture and slaves must go; it was the only way to cut down the expense that they no longer had funds to cover, and every penny that could be raised was needed to cover debt. The sale was held on January 15, 1827, by which time Martha and the younger children had departed for Boston. Cornelia and Mary stayed on at Tufton, where for five days they heard every detail of the sale, glad at least that their mother need not be present to bear this final trial.[2]

Such an event brought home, as nothing else could have done, the underlying horror of slavery. Mary wrote to reassure Ellen that, so far as she could determine, all but one of those sold had gone to people in the neighborhood, so that they would not be too far separated from friends and family. Yet in the end the fact remained: humanity, long-sustained good treatment, even affection could not mask the brutal reality of chattel slavery.

It has often been asked, and may still be asked, why Jefferson, as Washington had done, did not free all of his slaves instead of the chosen few who were, in fact, freed by his will. The answer, of course, is in that brutally unadorned word: chattel. Washington's estate was solvent, and he was free to dispose of his property as he wished. His slaves were, in fact, freed after his wife's death. Jefferson's position was quite different; at no time in that long and brilliant career had he ever been free of debt. Jefferson Randolph was legally and morally responsible to his creditors to realize what he could out of the wreckage of the estate, and his creditors were not above pushing him to the last penny. In terms of property, slaves were as important as land; in fact, one form of property hardly existed without the other. But there was a further consideration. Even if Jefferson's estate had been free of any liens whatsoever, there was, by the time of his death, an insuperable obstacle to the freeing of a body of slaves. By the law passed in 1806 all slaves must leave the state of Virginia within a year of obtaining their freedom. Edward Coles, for example, had been able to free his slaves only by the expedient of conducting them personally to Illinois, which he was able to do because, in the first place, he was not dependent on them for a livelihood, and because he had, in addition, the sort of family backing and political influence which enabled him to obtain a post in the territory.

At no time was such a choice open to Jefferson. Once he had assumed a role in the public life of his state, or, indeed, had accepted his wife's inheritance with its accompanying debt, he was inexorably bound to the system he both feared and hated. There were, however, options, means of ameliorating the worst evils of chattel slavery even beyond the obvious ones of individual responsibility and good treatment. Jefferson, as we know, had made a habit of permitting slaves able to survive on their own, to "walk away." In addition to being "well fed and well clothed, good year or bad year," many Jefferson servants, Mammy Ursula and John Hemings among them, received cash payments for work performed.[3] There was also the device of giving a slave "his time." Under this arrangement he was not legally free, but could hire himself out and keep the return for his labor for himself. Financial pressures seem to have prevented Jefferson from indulging in this practice to any extent, had he wished to do so, although we remember that Robert Hemings had bought his own freedom with money paid him by an employer. Jefferson had hired him out to a Dr. Straus so that Robert could be near his wife, apparently not foreseeing that he would later be asked to give up Robert altogether. He did not, however, refuse Robert his freedom, as of course he could have done.

Such options, however, were not open to the man who died bankrupt at Monticello. Some wills of the period make particular mention of slaves already given to family members. Some of the Monticello house servants fell into this category. Significantly Sally Hemings was among them, but Jefferson forbore to mention individual slaves in his will other than the five to whom he solemnly and earnestly undertook to give their freedom.

I give my good, affectionate, and faithful servant Burwell his freedom, and the sum of three hundred dollars, to buy necessaries to commence his trade of glazier, or to use otherwise, as he pleases.

I give also to my good servants John Hemings and Joe Fosset, their freedom at the end of one year after my death; and to each of these respectively, all the tools of their respective shops or callings; and it is my will that a comfortable log house be built for each of the three servants so emancipated on some part of my lands convenient to them with respect to the residence of their wives, and to Charlottesville and the University where they will be mostly employed . . . of which houses I give the use of one, with a curtilage of an acre to each, during his life or personal occupation thereof.

I give also to John Hemings the services of his two apprentices Madison and Eston Hemings, until their respective ages of twenty-one years, at which period respectively I give them their freedom; and I earnestly and humbly request of the legislature a confirmation of the request of freedom to these servants, with permission to remain in this state, where their families and connections are. . . .[4]

Even this provision, minimal as it was, might have embarrassed his executors. The Monticello slave auction was not held under a court order, but as Jeff Randolph had assumed his grandfather's debts he was responsible to his creditors for the liquidation of the estate. A list of this 1827 auction of Monticello slaves and one of a second auction in 1829 bear out Mary's conclusion.[5] There are no familiar household names in these lists. Out of the thirty-two sold in 1829 eight were bought by Jefferson Randolph himself. Of the twenty other purchasers the great majority bore recognizable local names, such as Dr. Dunglison who bought Waggoner David.

Others close to the family remained in their charge. Their future had been left to the good conscience of Martha and the girls. Martha's husband, excluded from Jefferson's will as a measure to protect her from her husband's creditors,[6] was now completely alienated and withdrawn from family affairs. The responsibility for their few remaining slaves seems to have been Martha's alone. That she did indeed take this charge seriously may be seen in a letter to her son Ben, then living at his wife's home at Redlands. The letter faces up squarely to the conflict inherent in this situation. Pressed for cash as she was, Martha had to weigh the needs of her children, particularly of her daughters, literally for the clothes upon their backs, against the welfare of those slaves whose "hire" was an appreciable part of the income at her disposal. That it was a continuing problem may be seen from this letter to Ben, dated from Boston.

I have no doubt dear Benjamin, but that you have made the best possible arrangement, in hiring the servants. I have two objects particularly in view paramount to every other, to ensure their being kindly treated and in families where they would be in the least danger from local situation of being corrupted; for that reason I look on the neighborhood of a village and the University as bad, probably you will laugh at my scruples and think I have forgotten strangely the existing state of things, but I have not, it is exactly because I remember too well the laxity of principle so prevalent upon that subject, that I feel anxious that these poor uneducated creatures should be placed in situations as little exposed to temptation as possible. I have always felt an awful responsibility on their account, and regret to think how illy I have discharged my duties toward them. You are right in supposing the interests of my children the first and dearest object in my life, and I would lay down *my own* life with joy to ensure prosperity and happiness to them, but I have no right to sacrifice the happiness of a fellow creature *black* or *white*, for that makes no difference in religion, or what is a part of it, sound morality. But I should not consider giving Martha Ann to Lewis as ever endangering her happiness, to the contrary Elisabeth [Lewis's wife] is a sweet amiable girl and very pious, and Lewis himself is one of the kindest and best, of the human family. Separating her from her family is an evil, yet it is one that we are all exposed to in this life. I have no hesitation therefore in making him the gift and thank you dear Benjamin for the suggestion, and as Lewis will return again to the States next year she will probably soon see her friends again, will have a kind and excellent master & mistress and delightful climate [Lewis was in Arkansas]: but I wish her to be informed of it, that it may not fall like a clap of thunder upon her at the moment of separation, and beg you dear son to see to it and to write to Lewis if you know where he is. Lavinia's hire will be most acceptable to Mary, for my expenses last year were greatly beyond my income, and we shall be extremely straitened for the whole of the present year, and perhaps a part of the next, therefore the $15 are as great a *blessing* to us, as a mouse was to the old woman's cat in Pilpay. It will come very safe in a letter, & *united states* bank notes pass everywhere without discount.[7]

In addition, of course, there was the fate of the slaves freed by Jefferson's will, every one of whom was descended from the remarkable Betty Hemings, although only Madison and Eston, Sally's sons, also possessed the Wayles blood. John Hemings was Betty's son by the white builder Joseph Nielson; Burwell and Joe Fosset were Betty's grandsons by her daughters Mary and Bett, both of whom had been by black fathers before Betty had made her Wayles connection.[8] By no means did these five represent the whole Hemings connection; they were those whom Jefferson believed could go it alone in the white world.

In the case of John Hemings, who had been so essential to Jefferson in his own building operations, freedom came late. He had been Ellen's favorite Johnny, and Ellen, indeed, was a favorite with John. He had made her that beautiful desk as a wedding present, which had later been lost when the packet boat bearing

Ellen's possessions to Boston had been burned at sea. After Jefferson's death he had undoubtedly remained close to the Monticello family. There is no record of John Hemings ever having worked at the University. As Jefferson Randolph was building himself a new house at Edgehill, naturally enough John was working there. That he did end his days at Monticello is likely, for his wife Priscilla is buried there. Priscilla had been the younger children's mammy, and although James, the unmarried brother, had asked for her, Martha had promised that she might go with her husband.[9] Martha kept her word, for on the slope southeast of the house where some of the cabins had stood there was a crude headstone: THE SED IS PLACED AT THE HEAD OF MY DEAR AFFECTIONATE WIFE PRISCILLA HEMINGS DEPARTED THIS LIFE ON FRIDAY THE 7TH OF MAY 1830. AGE 54.[10]

Madison, as we know from the recent publicity given by Fawn Brodie to the account of his life published in the *Pike County Republican* of 1874, continued to practice his trade of builder, and died many years later in Ross County, Ohio. Eston, too, moved from Virginia to Ohio; and was last heard of in Wisconsin.[11]

Burwell, it would appear, was in no hurry to leave Monticello. Cornelia wrote to Ellen: "He has taken pleasure in trying to keep the house clean, and even the yard, he has attempted to keep in some kind of order." And again, "Burwell has made Monticello look well and homelike."[12] It must have been a labor of love, for no funds remained to pay for help. Burwell was earning his living, as Jefferson had foreseen, by practicing his trade of glazier at the University. He had also been a house painter at Monticello. As an expert in this field we hear of him hired by Isaac Coles during his extensive additions to the Coles house at Enniscorthy in 1832.[13] In 1829 he wrote Ellen that "Mr. Clay named him to a place at $16 a year."[14] Obviously Burwell, perhaps closest to Jefferson of all the Hemingses, had no difficulty in making his way in that white world. Joe Fosset, the restless one, went north. As a blacksmith he, too, was well equipped to follow a trade.

There were others, not freed, still belonging to the family. Among these was Sally, the center of all that discussion and speculation in our own day. Was she, or was she not, Jefferson's mistress? And what happened to her after his death? The first of these questions can now be seen in a new perspective, in the light of additional knowledge, up until now shrouded in mystery, of what happened to her just preceding and after his death.

First of all Sally did not "belong" to Jefferson; she was considered in the family as the property of his granddaughter Ellen. This becomes clear at the time of Ellen's marriage. Sally, in fact, had been Ellen's maid for virtually the entire time of Jefferson's retirement. This, and Ellen's legal ownership, comes to light in a letter that Ellen wrote to her mother in 1825, while she and Joseph Coolidge were still on their wedding trip. They had been discussing the disposition of Sally with their lawyer:

Mr. Bullfinch, the lawyer, is drawing up a power of attorney which Joseph will sign empowering Jefferson to dispose of Sally and to protect her. Her own wishes, you know, my dear mother, must direct the disposition that is made of her, for I would not for the world that after living with me for fifteen years any kind of violence should be done to her feelings. If she wishes to be sold let her choose her own master; if to be hired she should have the same liberty, or at least not to be sent anywhere she is unwilling to go; but why should I say anything to you on this subject, who are the very soul of gentleness and humanity.[15]

A few months before the Coolidges' marriage, Mr. Thomas Key had arrived from England to take up the professorship of mathematics at the new University, and shortly after the letter from Ellen giving Jeff her power of attorney, he hired out Sally to the Keys. A letter dated April 1826 describes a visit from Sally to Monticello, and it was obviously not the first time that such a visit had occurred. Mary wrote to Ellen: "Your maid Sally was here lately with Mrs. Key, begged me also to deliver a message of love to her mistress and to say how much she wanted to see you and the baby both. [Ellen's first child had arrived.] She thinks of you with much affection and I always have a long *chat* with her on your account as often as she comes here. She makes a very good nurse, and Mrs. Key seems to have perfect confidence in her ability and fidelity."[16]

Obviously Sally had been absent from Monticello, possibly for as long as a year and certainly for some months before Jefferson's death. In this hitherto unpublished letter of Mary Randolph's we see her as a fond and trusted friend of the family, something that we have had no opportunity to observe before.

The Keys lived on Pavilion VIII on the East Lawn at the University, but they, or at least Mr. Key, were not happy in their situation. Key had attempted earlier to resign from the faculty, and by July 1827 he was definitely preparing to depart for England. Mrs. Key must have wished to keep Sally with them, because there now ensued complicated negotiations, conducted principally through correspondence with Nicholas Trist, for the purchase of Sally. Mr. Key said that he wished to liberate Sally. His first proposition was an even trade for his boy Morris. Nicholas communicated this offer to Ellen, who consented on the condition that (1) the measure met with Sally's approval and (2) that she was to be liberated. However, these negotiations ran into a snag when Jefferson Randolph, Ellen's brother, discovered that the boy Morris "labored under an infirmity," and that the exchange would be unequal.

Another professor at the University, Dr. John Patton Emmet, had also wanted to buy Sally. At this point Nicholas Trist had felt free to discuss the situation with Emmet, who offered $400 for her and expressed a willingness to hire Sally pending the negotiations with Key. In order to settle the matter Trist offered to meet with Key on the University grounds. There was considerable urgency, as Key was leaving town the following day. The negotiation that followed took place on Saturday, July 21, 1827, and was conducted by means of notes recorded in the Trist Papers of that date. We may say that the exchange was lively in the extreme.

Note #1, Trist to Key (not recorded), must have contained Trist's offer to meet with Key, and probably also contained his rejection of the deal concerning the boy Morris.

Notes #2 & 3, both from Key to Trist, explained that he had simply meant to give Sally "for her own use" whatever money he might have received for Morris. This sounds like an afterthought, because clearly he had originally hoped to trade Morris for Sally.

He now offered to meet Emmet's price of $400, but in this case could not undertake to free Sally. He inferred that Trist had not made it clear to Emmet that Sally's consent was a condition of her sale.

Sally was sent for. Trist explained to her that if she were freed (as Key had told her he planned to do) that it was his belief that she would be forced to leave the state.

Note #4, Trist to Key: Sally's answer "is that, under the circumstances, she wishes to be bought by Mr. Key. My reply is to let Mr. Key know that I am ready to conclude the sale." However, the note does not stop here. Trist gave full rein to his indignation at Key's imputation that he would have sold Sally to Emmet without her consent. This, he says, is "an utter and impudent falsehood." If this note had been delivered a duel would have appeared imminent, but Trist withheld it, and in its place sent Note #5, offering Key an opportunity to retract his objectionable remarks concerning Sally's consent, or lack of it, in the conversation with Emmet, which Trist interpreted as impugning his veracity.

The two men now meet, Trist accompanied by a friend, Professor Davis, in the office of the bursar, Mr. Brokenbrough. Key assures Trist that he had not meant to doubt his veracity. Trist accepts this, but demands a written statement from Key that he will free Sally if she is sold to him. This statement, witnessed by Brokenbrough, is entered under this date in the Trist Papers. The exchange is not yet over, for Key apparently does not know how to leave well enough alone. He explains that he still thinks that Trist had made more of a point of Sally's consent when discussing the sale with him than he had in the deal with Emmet. Trist answers that whatever Key may have *thought* is a matter of complete indifference. Trist and Davis then walk out of the room.[17]

A letter from Joseph Coolidge to Trist of August 17 shows that Coolidge was aware of these negotiations, and that he expected to receive some funds on Sally's account,[18] but there is strong later evidence that the sale did not go through. On July 29 Mary had written to Ellen: "The Keys are gone [back to England]. . . . Sally is going into Dr. Emmet's service when he returns from New York with his bride. I do not know on what grounds she counts on remaining in the state for the law forbidding it was expressly explained to her when she had her choice to make between freedom and continuing to belong to you. The price given for her is considered a very good one in these times."[19]

Although the Emmets remained at Morea, their home near the University, it seems that Sally must have been returned, or remained, in the Randolph family. This is substantiated by a curious document found in the Edgehill-Randolph Papers. The year is not given, and was later misattributed to 1836, but the date is given as *Friday*, April 18. We may refer to the Perpetual Calender and discover that April 18 in fact fell on a Friday, not in 1836, but in 1834. In addition this most interesting paper is dated from Washington.

In 1834, Martha, then living in Washington where the Trists were now making their home, was taken ill in the night. The slaves still belonging to the family, all of those, in fact, that they had not wished to sell, were now hired out, and the small sums thus derived were applied to the use of the girls. Martha, in sudden alarm, thought of Sally and Wormley and Betsey, slaves who had never been freed, but who should be given "their time." So in the middle of the night, two o'clock in the morning of April 18, 1834, Martha dictated a brief statement to her daughter Virginia:

APRIL 18TH 2 O'CLOCK IN THE MORNING FRIDAY

To my five daughters I wish to bequeath my property in funds. To Benjamin and Lewis the two negroes now in Benjamin's possession. Emily I wish liberated as soon as you break up housekeeping here; Martha Ann at the death of her old grandmother, in the meantime to live with her and take care of her. To Betsy Hemings, Sally and Wormly I wish my children to give their time. If liberated they would be obliged to leave the state of Virginia. To my dear George I have nothing but my love to leave, and in any division made of my books that he should have a share. In dividing the plate among you, I wish Jefferson to have the casseroles, and Mr. Coolidge the duck. To Nicholas I leave my father's clock.

written by Mama's request.[20]

This is virtually the same as the more formal will drawn in January 1836 and probated in November of that year.[21] However, Betsey, Sally, and Wormley are not mentioned in the latter will, which suggests that these three were by then happily accounted for. Betsey was the beloved mammy at the home of Francis Eppes at Millbrook in Buckingham County. In a letter from Ellen Coolidge of March 1855 to Jefferson's biographer Henry Randall, we learn that Wormley "continues as a servant in the family." At this time he was with "Mrs. Ruffin, one of my brother's married daughters." In July Ellen wrote again to Randall: "I have just heard of Wormley's death. He survived his young, and most excellent mistress, Mrs. Ruffin, just one year."[22]

Betsey, we know from her well-tended tombstone at Millbrook in Buckingham County, lived until 1857. The inscription reads: "In memory of our Mammy Betsey Hemings, who was mother, sister, and friend to all who knew her. She departed this life on the 26th of August, 1857, in Millbrook, aged 75 years. The pure in heart shall see God."[23]

It may be of interest that the grave of John Wayles Eppes, nearby, has been utterly abandoned, while that of Betsey Hemings has been lovingly maintained by Hemings kin who live in the neighborhood during the summer months.

Sally may have died by then; her son Madison Hemings told the editor of the *Pike County Republican* that she had died in 1835. However, in July of that year Sally is again mentioned as belonging to the family. Martha at this time was in Boston with Ellen. Ill and harassed by debt, she wrote to Virginia referring to the hiring out of various slaves "which will assist their various mistresses. . . . I presume Mr. Smith will make some arrangement about Sally which will accommodate Cornelia. . . ."[24]

Sally was sixty-two years old. It seems clear that she had never been freed, or even given her "time." Death overtook her at last, probably at the home of her son Madison. Martha had written "I am truly sorry that I possess such property, if I could afford it I would liberate every one of them."[25] Wherever the truth of the matter lies we must remember that only a few years before Sally had preferred bondage among those she knew, rather than freedom in a strange country. Significantly, neither Martha nor the girls show any sign of remembering the scandal and the scurrilous verses that had been circulated at that time. It is as though Sally herself had never had anything to do with all that.

Chapter 38

The End of the Story

WHEN THOMAS MANN RANDOLPH left Monticello after Jefferson's death, he did not consider that he had left his wife, nor had Martha, after her very real suffering at his hands, totally abandoned her husband. Although he had written Nicholas, "I do not consider myself a member of the family at all, and cannot reside at Monticello again," he had nevertheless stopped a letter to his lawyer "which has thrown Mrs. Randolph into such agitation." From a distance, at least, he could be considerate of her feelings. At about the same time that Martha had escaped to Boston with the children, Randolph had gotten a job. From James Barbour, secretary of war in the John Quincy Adams cabinet, he managed to obtain a commission on the boundary survey between northern Florida and the state of Georgia.[1]

In the actual field work of this expedition the colonel conducted himself well. But on his return he played true to form; he ruined his chances of further employment with public complaints of his treatment by Adams and Barbour. At one point he had written a letter to Henry Clay with the intention, apparently, of provoking that blameless official to a duel.[2] He was no longer really responsible for his actions. He was holed up in a little five-room house in North Milton, in abject poverty. The ex-governor of his state was deprived even of the right to vote, as he no longer met the property qualifications. It was at this point that he wrote to Martha, in Boston, two letters which in fact were never shown her.

Joseph Coolidge had made his wife's mother welcome, but Randolph had been more than he could swallow. After all Coolidge was a businessman with a reputation for respectability, and the idea of the fiery colonel's arrival, as he wrote Nicholas Trist at Monticello, "makes me shudder." [3] "The object," he wrote, "should be to keep Him from Monticello . . . and Her here with her children. . . . This morning there have come to hand two letters from Him." [4] Pressure was put on Martha to remain in Boston. To effect this object, and to keep her apart from her husband, Coolidge clearly withheld these letters. On December 5 she wrote to Jeff, "I have not heard a word from him since I left Monticello."

From Boston, Coolidge wrote that "She submits implicitly to what is proposed [to her], excepting that she wishes to pledge herself that, at a future day, he shall again be received at Monticello, and that she shall, even now, contribute to his support: against such a pledge I have earnestly protested!'"

In the meantime Randolph was writing wistful letters from Milton to the girls at nearby Monticello, particularly, it would seem, to Mary. In September he wrote a letter in childish writing, with large blots. "Will my dear Mary let George [perhaps a servant] know when she heard from her Mama and how all were at Monticello now." [5] There is a fat cow at his door, and she is very much on his mind. If they can have her slaughtered at Monticello before the cold weather they could divide the meat between them.

At times this man who could no longer live successfully with his fellows could yet think rationally, and enjoy observation of natural phenomena. "Did you observe," he wrote Mary, "the aurora borealis last night?" The light had shone into his room until two o'clock in the morning. He detects a relationship between electricity and magnetism, which he seriously discusses with the young ladies at Monticello. [6] At the same time he is capable of writing an utterly irrational letter to the editor of the *Richmond Enquirer*. He has been told that somewhere in the paper, he will not trouble himself to look up the back issues, that he has been insulted, and he wishes to challenge any and all responsible to an immediate duel. [7]

Perhaps he was drinking. In any case the letter to the *Enquirer* was written when winter weather and abject poverty, even the lack of a second blanket for his bed, were driving Randolph to his knees. An effort to find shelter at Charles Bankhead's Carlton had come to nothing. Martha, unaware of his extremity, had at least seen to it that Nicholas Trist should urge his return to Monticello. The colonel resisted these approaches, but at last, by March 10, he "begs to be informed whether he may be allowed to occupy again the North Pavilion . . . for his funds are getting too low for any tavern." [8] Nicholas sent back word at once: the North Pavilion was at his service.

Randolph, as always, was aware of his own limitations; this time he was determined to stay within them. He informed Nicholas: "For the family at Monticello, every member of it, I feel and take pleasure in cherishing a most sincere and genuine affection [Jeff, of course, was at Edgehill] . . . but I have no disposition for society at present. I must acknowledge that it is painful to me in a family because it constantly recalls past scenes. . . . I must live by myself to be tranquil, and tranquility is indispensable to me as I am now." [9]

Martha's view of all this was realistic. She herself was never again to have a permanent home. Indeed she would not have had even the smallest income in her own name if the states of Louisiana and South Carolina had not nobly come to her aid with a gift of $10,000 each. No money came legally to her from the estate, for the debt was not cleared in Jeff's lifetime. In the meantime the money from the two generous states was invested in a loan to the University. Her responsibilities, as we know, were great: two unmarried daughters, three sons, James, Ben, and Lewis, to launch upon the world; and the two children, Septimia and George. The Coolidges, the Trists, and Jeff Randolph and his stalwart wife Jane did what they could, but what they could was limited; it amounted to little more than offering her a home under their own roof, so she continued to move about from one home to another.

Under these circumstances she was yet determined "Never to abandon him [Randolph] to poverty, nor as long as my situation can be endured to propose a separation. In that, however, I must be determined by circumstance." She, no more than her husband, could face a repetition of the dreadful scenes of 1826. But there could be no question of abandoning him: "There can be no doubt *there*, so long as the property is vested in *me*, and *he* is destitute." [10]

Even Virginia had her doubts, as we have seen, but it was

Martha's determination that at last brought Randolph back to Monticello, at least as far as the North Pavilion, where he remained in dignified isolation. His stay there was to be brief, only a little more than three months passed before death came to release him at last. Perhaps he, abandoned, had enjoyed the spring in that half-abandoned place. Certainly he did enjoy his death. We cannot resist saying that he made a production of it. Martha found his illness hard to take seriously at first. "How hard hearted," she wrote Ellen, "my incredulity now appears." Although she had nursed him devotedly, from five in the morning till nine at night, gratifying his every wish, still it had been from duty only. She never believed until the last five days that there was any danger. On Sunday John Hemings came over from Edgehill to see the sick man, and on Monday morning Randolph had Martha send a message to Jeff. He wished to have a last interview with all the men in the house. Now for the last time he could enjoy the pleasures of confession, and give rein to those magnanimous feelings that he had always believed were native to him, but that he had never been able to sustain in life.

Martha described the scene in her letter to Ellen: "He offered and begged of him [Jeff] mutual forgiveness. He said it was folly for a dying man to talk of forgetting, but that *he* [Jeff] would live for many years, and begged that everything might be forgotten. He said in presence of us all 'an honester man exists not.' He exculpated him entirely, and again asked his forgiveness. [Did Randolph see something of his own blind stubbornness in this son?] He said something kind and affectionate to each of the gentlemen, spoke of me as his adored wife and his children with great affection. He seemed to wish to atone for the errors, blunders, he called them, of his past life. . . ." [11]

This is a straightforward description, and Martha does not give it undue weight. During his illness there had been "the same *suspicion*, impatience, and propensity to *argue* upon the most trifling circumstance as there had ever been," but now she can rejoice that she sacrificed her wishes. . . ." Here a part of the letter has been cut away, so we are not sure what her wishes may have been, but a later fragment makes clear that Martha had no illusions, and that she suffered no real grief. A few weeks later she wrote again to Ellen: "After the first burst of grief was over tranquility was soon restored. . . . I think with you that returning health would have brought with it the same passions and jealousies, and that confidence, so completely destroyed, could never have revived." She did not even mourn for the man that had been.

The children, who after all had not suffered as Martha had, spoke more kindly of their father—all but Jeff, who composed an epitaph which seemed to be in praise of himself, rather than of the deceased. For Martha there was but one person for whom all her grief, as all her passionate love, had been reserved. During that first year in Boston after her father's death she had moved in a dream: "One image has possession of my brain, in company or alone, sleeping or waking, it is always there." [12] Was it a comfort then to Martha to reflect that the image which haunted her would become a part of our national memory?

But, she wrote Jeff, he must not think that she did not exert herself. She sewed, she read, she even went out in company; for the sake of the girls she maintained a cheerful front. That May she returned to Monticello. The sale had delayed so long that some of the family almost hoped that the final parting need not take place. Cornelia felt it particularly. The house, in its desolation, spoke to her. To her the prospect was never more beautiful: ". . . whether in the morning when the landscape is covered by a soft mist and you look to the east and see the blue horizon disappear behind those beautiful Edgehill and Shadwell mountains, or in the evening when the deep indigo and bold outline of the Blue Ridge shows against the bright gold colored or orange western sky." At night she would sometimes sit on the stones at the end of the barn and look back at "the pillars of the house gleaming from the deep shade of the trees." It was Cornelia's own private love affair, with a place, not a man, for this lovely girl was never to marry.

"Carrying the keys," that is, the housekeeping, in an all but empty house had been quite different after all the servants had gone, but Cornelia never minded. Some of the old servants, freed or not, had stayed about the place. John Hemings, working for

Jeff at the new house, was near, as was Burwell. Mammy Ursula had never left. It was the family who now moved about. Mammy's death in 1830, full of years as she must by then have been, awakened in Cornelia all the old nostalgia: "Should we ever visit Monticello again her loss will cause a painful addition to the feeling of loneliness and desolation . . . finding the old servants about us when we went there it did seem something like home. . . ."[13]

Martha and the girls were with Jeff at Edgehill when the final blow fell. "There is some prospect of selling Monticello," Martha wrote. "I thought I had made up my mind upon that subject, but I find when it comes to the point that all my sorrows are renewed and that it will be a bitter bitter heartache." Cornelia lamented that they were at Edgehill. Any place, she wrote, would have been better than being there, in full sight of Monticello. "The very beauty of the country adds to it," to the regret, the sense of loss. Monticello was sold in 1831 to a Charlottesville druggist, for $9,000.

From Martha's bedroom window on the southwest corner of the house at Edgehill one had only to look out to see the "little mountain." It was here that she wrote her own farewell:

I will still think of thee, as in times gone by when I looked from the terrace of Monticello and thought "all the kingdoms of the world and the glory thereof" lay spread before me. Every feature of that landscape has its own spell upon my heart, can bring back the living, breathing presence of those long mingled with the clods of the valley, can renew (for a moment) youth itself. Youth with its exquisite enjoyments, its ardent friendships, and Oh! dearer than all, its first, purest, truest love!

M. Randolph
Edgehill, October 2, 1833[14]

From the southwest lawn Cornelia painted a watercolor of their lost mountain. People were leaving their native state, and Cornelia asked, Why? Her watercolor gave no answer. "Whatever be the cause," she wrote, "whether our slaves or the hard laws made against us by Congress I am not wise enough to know."

Martha could have told her. To Nicholas Trist she had said it. "Land and Negroes in Virginia are to nine persons out of ten *certain ruin*, and to all certain expense, and uncertain profit, and trouble, and vexation of spirit, that wearies one of life. . . ." [15]

Slaves and family, all were gone from Monticello. Priscilla Hemings's is the only black grave recorded there. The white graves cluster around the single monolith which marks the grave of Thomas Jefferson. Martha lies at his feet.

Notes

CHAPTER 1

1. *The Eye of Thomas Jefferson*, ed. Howard Adams (Washington: National Gallery of Art, 1976), xxxvi. Hereafter cited as *Eye*.

2. Ibid., 3.

3. *Thomas Jefferson's Farm Book*, ed. Edwin Morris Betts (Charlottesville: University Press of Virginia, 1976), 254, 255.

4. Mrs. Drummond to TJ, Williamsburg, March 12, 1771. In *The Papers of Thomas Jefferson*, ed. Julian Boyd (Princeton: Princeton University Press, 1950), 1:65. Hereafter cited as Boyd.

5. Thomas Jefferson, *Notes on the State of Virginia* (Philadelphia, 1788), 163.

6. Colin Rowe, *The Mathematics of the Ideal Villa* (Cambridge, Mass.: MIT Press, 1976), 3.

7. Fiske Kimball, *Thomas Jefferson, Architect* (New York: Da Capo Press, 1968), 23.

8. "Unconnected Thoughts on Gardening," *The Works of William Shenstone, esq.* (London, 1764), 2:129.

CHAPTER 2

1. Henry S. Randall, *The Life of Thomas Jefferson* (1858; rpt. New York: Da Capo Press, 1972), 1:64, 65.

2. *The Selected Writings of Thomas Jefferson*, ed. Adrienne Koch and William Peden (New York: The Modern Library, 1944), 3.

3. *Thomas Jefferson's Garden Book*, ed. Edwin Morris Betts (Philadelphia: The American Philosophical Society, 1944), 16.

CHAPTER 3

1. TJ to Francis Eppes, Oct. 10, 1775 (Boyd, 1:247).

2. TJ to John Randolph, Nov. 29, 1775 (Boyd, 1:269).

3. TJ to Francis Eppes, Nov. 7, 1775 (Boyd, 1:252).

4. Marie Kimball, *Jefferson: The Road to Glory* (New York: Coward McCann, 1943), 306.

5. TJ to John Page, July 30, 1776 (Boyd, 1:483).

6. TJ to John Hancock, Oct. 11, 1776 (Boyd, 1:524).

7. *Garden Book*, 72–75.

8. Helen Cripe, "Music: Thomas Jefferson's 'delightful recreation,'" *Antiques*, July 1972, 125.

9. James A. Bear, Jr., "The Furniture and Furnishings of Monticello," *Antiques*, July 1972, 113.

10. Wallace Gussner, *Furniture in Williamsburg and Eastern Virginia* (Richmond: The Virginia Museum, 1972), 27.

11. "Memoirs of a Monticello Slave, as dictated to Charles Campbell by Isaac," *Jefferson at Monticello*, ed. James A. Bear, Jr. (Charlottesville: University Press of Virginia, 1967), 3, 4, 20. See also John Coles Account Book, Manuscript Department, Aldermen Library, University of Virginia.

12. Marie Kimball, *Jefferson: War and Peace* (New York: Coward McCann, 1947), 141.

13. TJ to David Jameson, April 26, 1781 (Boyd, 5:468).

14. Kimball, *Jefferson: War and Peace*, 239.

15. TJ to Lafayette, Aug. 4, 1781 (Boyd, 6:112).

16. TJ to James Monroe, May 20, 1782 (Boyd, 6:184).

17. Boyd, 6:197n.

CHAPTER 4

1. Sarah N. Randolph, *The Domestic Life of Thomas Jefferson* (1871; rpt. New York: Ungar, 1958), 63.

2. TJ to Castellux, Nov. 26, 1782 (Boyd, 6:203).

3. TJ to Elizabeth Eppes, Oct. 3 (?), 1782 (Boyd, 6:198).

4. *Selected Writings*, ed. Koch and Peden, 193.

5. TJ to Martha Jefferson Randolph, Philadelphia, Jan. 16, 1792. *The Family Letters of Thomas Jefferson*, ed. James A. Bear, Jr. (Columbia, Mo.: University of Missouri Press, 1966), 93.

6. TJ to Marbois, Dec. 5, 1783 (Boyd, 6:371).

7. TJ to Martha Jefferson, Nov. 28, 1783 (Bear, *Family Letters*, 19).

CHAPTER 5

1. Randolph, *Domestic Life*, 73.

2. Ibid., 74, quoting Martha Jefferson Randolph, "Memoir."

3. Ibid., 76.

4. Daniel Boorstin, *The Lost World of Thomas Jefferson* (Boston: Beacon Press, 1948), 36, quoting lecture read by TJ to the Philosophical Society, Philadelphia, Mar. 10, 1797.

5. TJ to David Rittenhouse, Jan. 25, 1786 (Boyd, 9:216).

6. *Eye*, 125.

7. Ibid., 274.

8. TJ to Jean Nicolas Demeunier, June 26, 1786 (Boyd, 10:63).

9. TJ to Brissot de Warville, Feb. 11, 1788 (Boyd, 12:578).

10. Enclosure in letter to George Wythe, Sept. 17, 1787 (Boyd, 12:130).

11. TJ to Edward Bancroft, Jan. 26, 1788 (Boyd, 14:492, 493).

12. Jefferson's Account Books, bound typescript, Manuscript Department, U. Va. See, among other pertinent entries, Jan. 1, 1788.

13. Bear, *Family Letters*, 36.

14. Abigail Adams to TJ, July 6, 1787 (Boyd, 11:551).

15. Elizabeth Langhorne, "The Other Hemings," *The Albemarle Magazine*, Oct.-

Nov. 1980, 61, and James Bear, "The Hemings Family of Monticello," *Virginia Caval-cade*, Autumn 1979, 81.

16. TJ to William Short, May 7, 1784 (Boyd, 7 : 229).

17. Boyd, 14 : 426n.

18. Bear, *Family Letters*, 39.

19. TJ to Mrs. William Bingham, May 11, 1788 (Boyd, 13 : 151, 152).

20. Bear, *Family Letters*, 34, 37.

21. Elizabeth Tufton to Martha Jefferson, Aug. 13, 1789 (Edgehill-Randolph Papers, U. Va.).

22. *Eye*, 142.

CHAPTER 6

1. Edward Dumbauld, *Thomas Jefferson, American Tourist* (Norman, Okla.: University of Oklahoma Press, 1976), 87.

2. Ibid., 74.

3. Edward Dumbauld, "Jefferson and Adams' English Garden Tour," in *Jefferson and the Arts: an Extended View*, ed. William Howard Adams (Washington, D.C.: National Gallery of Art, 1976), 157.

4. Ibid., 148.

5. Ibid.

6. TJ to Maria Cosway, Oct. 12, 1786 (Boyd, 10 : 443–53).

7. Cosway to TJ, Nov. 17, 1786 (Boyd, 10 : 538, 539).

8. TJ to Cosway, Apr. 12, 1788 (Boyd, 13 : 104).

9. Cosway to TJ, Apr. 29, 1788 (Boyd, 13 : 115).

10. *Eye*, 95.

11. Ibid., 117.

12. F. J. B. Watson, "Americans and French Eighteenth-Century Furniture in the Age of Jefferson," *Jefferson and the Arts*, 277.

13. Granquist, Charles L., "Thomas Jefferson's 'whirligig chairs,'" *Antiques*, May 1976.

14. TJ to Martha Jefferson Randolph, Oct. 18, 1808 (Bear, *Family Letters*, 351, 352; and *Eye*, 324).

15. *Eye*, 204.

16. TJ to Martha Jefferson, May 21, 1787 (Bear, *Family Letters*, 41).

17. TJ to John Jay, Sept. 17, 1789 (Boyd, 15 : 437).

18. *Eye*, 204.

19. Ibid., 46.

20. Helen Cripe, *Thomas Jefferson and Music* (Charlottesville: University Press of Virginia, 1974), 49, 52.

21. *Seeds of Liberty*, ed. Max Savelle, chap. on "Music" by Cyclone Covey (New York: Knopf, 1948), 52.

CHAPTER 7

1. James A. Bear, Jr., *Report of the Curator, 1979* (Thomas Jefferson Memorial Foundation, Monticello, Va.), 20.

2. William H. Gaines, Jr., *Thomas Mann Randolph, Jefferson's Son-in-Law* (Baton Rouge: Louisiana State University Press, 1966), 23, 24.

3. TJ to Thomas Mann Randolph, Jr., Nov. 25, 1785 (Boyd, 9 : 60).

4. TMR, Jr., to TJ, Aug. 16, 1786 (Boyd, 10:260).

5. TJ to TMR, Jr., Aug. 27, 1786 (Boyd, 10:307).

6. TMR, Jr., to TJ, Apr. 14, 1787 (Boyd, 11:292).

7. Martha Jefferson Randolph, "Reminiscence of Thomas Jefferson," Edgehill-Randolph Papers, U. Va.

8. TJ to Mme. de Corny, Apr. 2, 1790 (Boyd, 16:290).

9. TMR, Sr., to TJ, Jan. 30, 1790 (Boyd, 16:135).

10. TJ to TMR, Sr., Feb. 4, 1790 (Boyd, 16:154, 155).

CHAPTER 8

1. Merrill Peterson, *Thomas Jefferson and the New Nation* (New York: Oxford University Press, 1970), 410.

2. Dumas Malone, *Jefferson and the Ordeal of Liberty* (Boston: Little, Brown, 1962), 182; and James T. Flexner, *The Young Hamilton* (Boston: Little, Brown, 1978), 440.

3. TJ to TMR, March 16, 1792. Dumas Malone, *Jefferson and the Rights of Man* (Boston: Little, Brown, 1951), 436.

4. Malone, *Rights of Man*, 339.

5. Adrienne Koch, *Jefferson and Madison: The Great Collaboration* (1950; rpt. New York: Oxford University Press, 1969), 132, 133.

6. Bear, *Family Letters*, 93.

7. Ibid., 114.

8. Ibid., 68, 71.

9. TMR, Jr., to TJ, Apr. 23, 1790 (Boyd, 16:370).

10. Bear, *Family Letters*, 51.

11. TJ to Thomas Mann Randolph, Sr., July 25, 1790 (Boyd, 17:275).

12. TJ to TMR, Jr., July 25, 1790 (Boyd, 17:275).

13. TJ to TMR, Sr., Oct. 22, 1790 (Boyd, 17:123).

14. Gaines, 33.

CHAPTER 9

1. Bear, *Family Letters*, 72.

2. John Gregory, *A Comparative View of the State & Faculties of Man with Those of the Animal World* (London: Printed for J. Dodsley in Pall-Mall, 1777), 29–31, 45, 46.

3. Bear, *Family Letters*, 75.

4. Ibid., 72.

5. TJ to TMR, Jan. 18, 1796 (TJ Papers, Library of Congress microfilm, U. Va.).

6. TJ to Mary Jefferson Bolling, Oct. 31, 1790 (Boyd, 17:656).

7. A. R. Morris to St. George Tucker, March 2, 1815 (Tucker-Coleman Papers, The Swem Library, College of William and Mary, Williamsburg, Va.).

8. Anne R. Morris to St. George Tucker, March 20, 1815 (Tucker-Coleman Papers, Wm. and Mary).

9. *The Papers of John Marshall*, ed. Charles Cullen and Herbert A. Johnson (Chapel Hill: University of North Carolina Press, 1977), 2:168–78.

10. Anne Morris to St. G. Tucker, Feb. 9, 1815 (Tucker-Coleman Papers, Wm. and Mary).

11. Bear, *Family Letters*, 116.

12. Ibid., 118.

13. Morris to Tucker, Dec. 13, 1814 (Tucker-Coleman Papers, Wm. and Mary).

CHAPTER 10

1. Gaines, 34.
2. TJ to Bowling Clark, Sept. 21, 1792 (*Farm Book*, 13).
3. *Farm Book*, 255. Quoted from *Notes on the State of Virginia*.
4. TJ to Benjamin Vaughan, June 27, 1790 (*Garden Book*, 152).
5. *Garden Book*, 183.
6. Martha Jefferson Randolph to TJ, Jan. 15, 1795 (Bear, *Family Letters*, 131).
7. For the Hemings family tree, see *Jefferson at Monticello*, ed. Bear, 24.
8. *Farm Book*, 58.
9. Ibid., 43.
10. Ibid., 6.
11. MJR to TJ, Jan. 30, 1800 (Bear, *Family Letters*, 183).
12. TJ to Maria Jefferson Eppes, February 12, 1800 (Bear, *Family Letters*, 185).
13. Ellen Wayles Coolidge Memoir (Coolidge Papers, U. Va.).
14. Bear, *Family Letters*, 113.
15. *Garden Book*, 194. TJ to TMR, June 30, 1793.
16. Gaines, 37. TMR to TJ, Oct. 31, 1793 (Massachusetts Historical Society).
17. Account Books, U. Va. Manuscript Department.
18. Gaines, 38.

CHAPTER 11

1. Frederick D. Nichols, "Jefferson: The Making of an Architect," *Jefferson and the Arts: An Extended View*, ed. William Howard Adams, (Washington: National Gallery of Art, 1976), 175.
2. Ibid., 171.
3. Marie Kimball, *Jefferson: The Scene of Europe* (New York: Coward McCann, 1950), pp. 56–58.
4. *Garden Book*, 173.
5. TMR to TJ, May 8, 1793 (Massachusetts Historical Society, Boston).
6. *Garden Book*, 224.
7. Ibid., 228.
8. Kimball, *Jefferson: The Scene of Europe*, 57.
9. *Garden Book*, 249.
10. *Farm Book*, 460.
11. Monticello Construction File (Jefferson Memorial Foundation), Aug. 1800.

CHAPTER 12

1. TMR to Peachy Gilmer, July 4, 1818 (Virginia State Library, Richmond, Va.).
2. TJ to TMR, Nov. 25, 1785 (Boyd, 9:59).
3. Recollections of Dr. Massie (Virginia Historical Society, Richmond).
4. TJ to TMR, Apr. 9, 1797 (Edgehill-Randolph Papers, U. Va.).
5. "The Commonplace Book of Thomas Mann Randolph, Jr.," Manuscript Department, Alderman Library, U. Va.
6. TJ to TMR, July 14, 1794 (Mass. His. Soc.).
7. Joseph C. Robert, *The Story of Tobacco in America* (New York: Knopf, 1952), 72, 45–48.

8. Andrew Drummond to John Coles, April 5, 1780 (Smith Carter Papers, U. Va.).

9. Samuel Eliot Morison, *The Oxford History of the American People* (New York: Oxford University Press, 1965), 326.

10. Gaines, 41, 42.

11. *Farm Book*, 273.

12. TMR to TJ, Apr. 12, 1800 (Mass. His. Soc.).

13. Bear, *Family Letters*, 154.

14. Thomas Jefferson Randolph Memoir (Edgehill-Randolph Papers, 1861, U. Va.).

15. TMR to TJ, Jan. 10, 1800 (Mass. His. Soc.).

16. MJR to TJ, Jan. 30, 1800 (Bear, *Family Letters*, 182).

CHAPTER 13

1. Malone, *Jefferson and the Ordeal of Liberty*, 502.

2. Ibid., 505.

3. Gaines, 46.

4. MJR to TJ, rec'd. July 1, 1798 (Bear, *Family Letters*, 166).

5. TJ to Mary Jefferson Eppes, Jan. 4, 1801 (Bear, *Family Letters*, 191).

6. MJE to TJ, Jan. 24, 1802 (Bear, *Family Letters*, 217).

7. Mary Jefferson to TJ, Aug. 28, 1790 (Bear, *Family Letters*, 65).

8. TJ to Mary Jefferson, July 4, 1790 (Bear, *Family Letters*, 60).

9. TJ to MJE, March 3, 1802 (Bear, *Family Letters*, 219).

10. MJE to TJ, Feb. 2, 1801 (Bear, *Family Letters*, 194).

11. Richard Beale Davis, *Francis Walker Gilmer* (Richmond: The Dietz Press, 1939), 373.

12. Ibid., 373.

13. Randolph, *Domestic Life*, 301.

14. "Memoirs of a Monticello Slave," in *Jefferson at Monticello*, ed. Bear, 16, 17.

15. Ellen Wayles Coolidge to Henry S. Randall, May 16, 1857 (Coolidge Papers, U. Va.).

16. TJ to John W. Eppes, Oct. 9, 1801. Norma B. Cuthbert, "Thomas Jefferson's Legacy to His Grandson," *The Huntington Library Quarterly* 6 (May 1943): 336.

17. MJE to JWE, Jan. 21, 1802 (Eppes-Randolph Papers, #7109, U. Va.).

18. MJE to JWE, Nov. 25, 1802 (Eppes-Randolph Papers, U. Va.)

CHAPTER 14

1. Bear, *Family Letters*, 153, 154.

2. Fawn Brodie, *Thomas Jefferson: An Intimate History* (New York: Norton, 1974), 473.

3. "Memoirs of a Monticello Slave," in *Jefferson at Monticello*, 4.

4. Edmund Bacon to TJ, 1809, Mass. His. Soc. .

5. Coolidge Collection, Mass. His. Soc.; also Marie Kimball, *Thomas Jefferson's Cook Book* (Charlottesville: University Press of Virginia, 1976), 37.

6. *Farm Book*, 15, 16.

7. Winthrop D. Jordan, *White over Black* (Chapel Hill: University of North Carolina Press, 1968), 143.

8. TJ to Mary Jefferson, May 25, 1797 (Bear, *Family Letters*, 145).

9. TJ to William Evans, Feb. 22, 1801; Evans to TJ, Feb. 27, 1801; TJ to Evans, March 31, 1801 (Coolidge Collection, Mass. His. Soc.).

10. Maria Jefferson Eppes to TJ, Apr. 21, 1802 (Bear, *Family Letters*, 224).

11. TJ to Evans and Evans to TJ, November 1802 (Coolidge Collection, Mass. His. Soc.).

12. Thomas Jefferson Randolph Memoir (Edgehill-Randolph Papers, U. Va.).

13. Malone, *Jefferson the President: First Term* (Boston: Little, Brown, 1970), 212.

14. Ibid., 497, 498.

15. Brodie, 544, 545.

16. Douglas Adair, "The Jefferson Scandals," typescript, Alderman Library, U. Va.

17. Brodie, 370.

18. Ellen Wayles Coolidge to Henry S. Randall, June 11, 1857 (Coolidge Papers, U. Va.).

19. Account Book, Oct. 12, 1801. Typescript vol. at U. Va.

20. Frederick D. Nichols and James A. Bear, Jr., *Monticello, a Guidebook* (Monticello: Thomas Jefferson Memorial Foundation, 1967), 22–24.

21. TJ Memo (Coolidge Collection, Mass. His. Soc.).

22. Mrs. William Thornton's Diary, vol. 1, Library of Congress.

23. Col. John Coles to TJ, Sept. 1804 (Library of Congress). Also TJ to Jas. Dinsmore, Sept. 25, 1805 (Library of Congress).

24. TJ to J. Dinsmore, June 8, 1805 (Mass. His. Soc.).

CHAPTER 15

1. Malone, *Jefferson the President: First Term*, 320.

2. Ibid., 284.

3. Dumbauld, *Thomas Jefferson, American Tourist*, 239.

4. TJ to Stevens Thomson Mason, Oct. 27, 1799. *Garden Book*, 267.

5. Randall, 3:327.

6. TJ to Edward Bancroft, Jan 26, 1788 (*Farm Book*, 10).

7. "The Private Life of Thomas Jefferson," by the Rev. Hamilton Wilcox Pierson, in *Jefferson at Monticello*, 89.

8. TJR Memoir (Edgehill-Randolph Papers, U. Va., 1867), 89.

9. Recollections of Dr. Massie, Virginia Historical Society.

10. TMR to TJ, March 6, 1802 (Mass. His. Soc.).

11. TJ to TMR, March 12, 1802 (Mass. His. Soc.). For the Louisiana situation, see Malone, *Jefferson the President: First Term*, 254, 255.

12. TMR to TJ, March 20, 1802 (Mass. His. Soc.).

13. TMR to TJ, Oct. 29, 1802 (Mass. His. Soc.).

14. Ellen Wayles Coolidge Memoir (Coolidge Papers, U. Va.).

CHAPTER 16

1. TJ to Jean Baptiste Say, March 2, 1815 (*Garden Book*, 543).

2. Bear, *Family Letters*, 213.

3. Ibid., 193, 223.

4. TJ to MJR, Feb. 5, 1801 (Bear, *Family Letters*, 195).

5. MJR to TJ, Oct. 29, 1802 (Bear, *Family Letters*, 238).

6. MJE to TJ, Nov. 5, 1802 (Bear, *Family Letters*, 239).

7. Margaret Bayard Smith, *The First Forty Years of Washington Society*, ed. Gaillard Hunt (1905; rpt. New York: Ungar, 1965), 34, 35.

CHAPTER 17

1. Malone, *Jefferson and the Ordeal of Liberty*, 176.
2. Bear, *Family Letters*, 249, 250.
3. Jack Eppes to TJ, March 9, 1804; Eppes to TJ, March 11, 1804; TJ to Eppes, March 15, 1804; Eppes to TJ, March 19, 23, 26, 1804; TJ to James Madison, Apr. 13, 1804 (Jefferson Microfilm, U. Va.).
4. Jefferson Memorandum Book, April 17, 1804 (Manuscript Department, U. Va.).
5. *Worthy Women of Our First Century*, ed. Mrs. Owen J. Wister and Miss Agnes Irwin (Philadelphia: J. B. Lippincott Co., 1877), 35–38.

CHAPTER 18

1. Smith, *First Forty Years of Washington Society*, 49, 50.
2. Thomas Jefferson Randolph Memoir (Edgehill-Randolph Papers, U. Va.).
3. *Worthy Women*, 39.
4. The Coles Diary, courtesy Mrs. Philip McKagen.
5. Ellen Wayles Coolidge, Memoir, Coolidge Collection, U. Va.
6. Malone, *Jefferson the President: First Term*, 379; and *Worthy Women*, 39. For general rules of etiquette, see Randall, 2:667.
7. Smith, *First Forty Years of Washington Society*, 46.
8. *Worthy Women*, 39.
9. Ibid., 29.
10. Ibid., 40.
11. Ibid.

CHAPTER 19

1. *Collected Papers of the Monticello Association*, ed. George Green Shackelford (The Monticello Association, 1965), 137.
2. Malone, *Jefferson the President: Second Term* (Boston: Little, Brown, 1974), 74, 75.
3. William Plumer, *Memorandum of the Proceedings of the United States Senate, 1803–1807*, ed. Everett S. Brown (New York: Macmillan, 1925), 269, 270.
4. The Debates and Proceedings of the Congress of the United States (Gale and Seaton, Government Documents, 1934), April 1806.
5. *Richmond Enquirer*, June 24, 1806. Letter from Isaac Coles.
6. *Annals of the Congress, 9th Congress, 1st Session*, 1105, 1106.
7. TJ to TMR, June 23, 1806 (Edgehill-Randolph Papers, U. Va.).

CHAPTER 20

1. For a general account, see "The Murder of George Wythe," J. P. Boyd and W. E. Hemphill, *William and Mary Quarterly*, 3rd series, XII, Oct. 1955.
2. Malone, *Jefferson the President: Second Term*, 135–40.
3. Plumer, *Memorandum*, 523, 622.
4. Diary of Isaac Coles (private collection).
5. Malone, *Jefferson the President: Second Term*, 277.
6. TJ to TMR, Feb. 10, 1807 (Mass. His. Soc.).
7. Isaac Coles Diary.

CHAPTER 21

1. Malone, *Jefferson the President: Second Term*, 410.
2. TJ to TMR, Nov. 30, 1807. Cited in Malone, *Jefferson the President: Second Term*, 469.
3. Bear, *Family Letters*, 277.
4. *Garden Book*, 338.
5. Bear, *Family Letters*, 318.
6. *National Intelligencer*, June 26, 1807.
7. Gaines, 69.
8. Malone, *Jefferson the President: Second Term*, 434.
9. TJ to TMR, Jan. 31, 1809 (*Garden Book*, 405).

CHAPTER 22

1. *Eye*, 26.
2. *Garden Book*, 26, 27.
3. Dumbauld, "Jefferson and Adams' English Garden Tour," 149.
4. *Eye*, 328.
5. Jefferson to William Hamilton, July 1806 (*Garden Book*, 322–24).
6. Smith, *First Forty Years of Washington Society*, 73.
7. Thomas Whately, *Observations on Modern Gardening* (London: T. Payne, 1770), 50.
8. Dumbauld, "Jefferson and Adams' English Garden Tour," 143.
9. Bear, *Family Letters*, 101.
10. *Garden Book*, 360.
11. *Eye*, 319.
12. *Garden Book*, 113.
13. F. Kimball, *Thomas Jefferson, Architect*, fig. 161.
14. M. Kimball, *Jefferson: The Scene of Europe*, 146.
15. *Garden Book*, 316.
16. Smith, *First Forty Years of Washington Society*, 65.
17. Bear, *Family Letters*, 308.
18. Ellen Wayles Coolidge to Henry S. Randall, 1856. Randall, 3: 347.
19. William Beiswanger, "A Temple in the Garden," Dedication of the Garden Pavilion at Monticello (1984), 7, 8.

CHAPTER 23

1. TJ to MJR, Philadelphia, May 17, 1798 (Bear, *Family Letters*, 162).
2. TJ to Ellen Wayles Randolph, Washington, Nov. 27, 1801 (ibid., 212, 213).
3. Ellen Wayles Coolidge to Henry S. Randall (Randall, 3: 348, 349).
4. Randall, 3: 350.
5. Cripe, 59–62n.
6. Bear, *Family Letters*, 475.
7. Cripe, 40.
8. Samuel Mordecai, *Richmond in Bygone Days, by an Old Citizen* (Richmond: George M. West, 1856). 178 seq.
9. Randall, 1: 70.
10. John Hervey, *Racing in America* (New York: privately printed by the Jockey Club, 1944), 1: 117.
11. Bear, *Family Letters*, 82.

CHAPTER 24

1. Cornelia Randolph to Virginia Randolph, December 27, 1821 (Edgehill-Randolph Papers, U. Va.).
2. Interview with Garland Monroe, in *Weevils in the Wheat, Interviews with Virginia Ex-Slaves*, ed. Charles L. Perdue, Jr., Thomas E. Barden, and Robert K. Phillips (Charlottesville: University Press of Virginia, 1976), 214, 215.
3. Author's interview with Joseph Agee, descendant of Coles family slaves, 1984.
4. Monroe Interview, *Weevils in the Wheat*, 214, 215.
5. Sally Ashton Interview, *Weevils in the Wheat*, 14.
6. "Memoirs of a Monticello Slave," in *Jefferson at Monticello*, 22.
7. *Mary Chestnut's Civil War*, ed. C. Vann Woodward (New Haven: Yale University Press, 1981), 213, 214.
8. For the folklore material quoted in the rest of this chapter see *Folklore and Folklife in Virginia*, ed. Charles L. Perdue, Jr., "Black Music and Tales from Jefferson's Monticello," by Elizabeth Langhorne (Charlottesville: The Virginia Folklore Society, 1979), 1:60–67.
9. *Selected Writings*, ed. Koch and Peden, 279.

CHAPTER 25

1. TJ to Anne Randolph Bankhead, Dec. 29, 1809 (Bear, *Family Letters*, 394).
2. Ellen Wayles Coolidge Memoir (Coolidge Papers, U. Va.).
3. Gaines, 83, 84.
4. TMR to Francis Walker Gilmer, June 11, 1809 (Library of Congress Microfilm, M109, U. Va.).
5. TMR Will, March 16, 1813 (Library of Congress Microfilm, U. Va.).
6. Gaines, 84.
7. Ibid., 89–91.
8. Ibid., 92.
9. TJ to William P. Newby, June 21, 1815 (*Garden Book*, 546).
10. TJR Memoir (Edgehill-Randolph Papers, U. Va.).
11. *Farm Book*, 460.
12. Ibid., 22, 23.

CHAPTER 26

1. EWR to MJR, March 2, 1814 (Coolidge Papers, U. Va.).
2. EWR to MJR, March 30, 1814 (Coolidge Papers, U. Va.).
3. EWR to MJR, Jan 28, 1818 (Coolidge Papers, U. Va.).
4. *Life, Letters and Journals of George Ticknor* (Boston: Houghton Mifflin, 1909), 1:34 seq.
5. "The Private Life of TJ," in *Jefferson at Monticello*, 101.
6. Dumas Malone, *The Sage of Monticello* (Boston: Little, Brown, 1981), 176.
7. MJR to Mrs. Trist, May 31, 1815 (Vir. His. Soc.).
8. TJ to Dr. John Bankhead, Oct. 28, 1815 (Edgehill-Randolph Papers, U. Va.).
9. MJR to TJ, Nov. 20, 1816 (Bear, *Family Letters*, 417).
10. Gaines, 108.
11. Hetty Carr to Dabney S. Carr, Feb. 5, 1819 (Carr-Cary Papers, U. Va.).
12. TJR Memoir (Edgehill-Randolph Papers, U. Va.).

13. TJ to Wilson Cary Nicholas, March 18, 1819 (TJ Papers, Library of Congress Microfilm, U. Va.).

CHAPTER 27

1. EWR to MJR, Sept. 27, 1816 (Coolidge Papers, U. Va.).
2. EWC Memoir (Coolidge Papers, U. Va.).
3. EWR to MJR, March 1816 (Coolidge Papers, U. Va.).
4. EWR to TMR, Mar. 26, 1816 (Coolidge Papers, U. Va.).
5. EWR to MJR, May 1, 1816; Dec. 30, 1816, Dec. 29, 1818 (Coolidge Papers, U. Va.).
6. Nicholas P. Trist to MJR, Sept. 10, 1818 (Trist Papers, Southern Historical Collection, University of North Carolina at Chapel Hill).
7. MJR to Nicholas P. Trist, Sept. 20, 1818, and NPT to MJR (Trist Papers, UNC).
8. David Meade Randolph to NPT, Nov. 6, 1818 (Trist Papers, UNC).
9. Cornelia to sisters, Dec. 14, 19, 1817, and Jan. 28, 1818 (Trist Papers, UNC).
10. Cornelia Randolph to NPT, May 20, 1826 (Coolidge Papers, U. Va.).
11. EWR to MJR, July 18, 1819 (Coolidge Papers, U. Va.).

CHAPTER 28

1. *Eye*, 337, 338; and TJ to TMR, Jan. 17, 1809 (*Farm Book*, 333).
2. *Garden Book*, 546, 552.
3. TMR to Thomas Taylor, Feb. 24, 1816 (Virginia Historical Society, Richmond).
4. Nichols, "The Making of an Architect," in *Jefferson and the Arts*, 163.
5. TJ to John Wayles Eppes, Sept. 18, 1812 (*Garden Book*, 488, 489).
6. Nichols, "The Making of an Architect," 177.
7. Bear, *Family Letters*, 404.
8. TJ to MJR, June 6, 1814 (Bear, *Family Letters*, 405).
9. Cornelia Randolph to Virginia Randolph, April 20, 1821 (Trist Papers, UNC).
10. Ellen Wayles Coolidge Memoir (Coolidge Papers, U. Va.).
11. Ellen to Virginia, May 4, 1819 (Jefferson-Coolidge Papers, U. Va.).
12. MJR to Virginia Randolph Trist, Jan. 10, 1822 (Trist Papers, UNC).
13. Ellen to Virginia, Aug. 24, 1819 (Jefferson-Coolidge Papers, U. Va.).

CHAPTER 29

1. R. Hildreth, *Banks, Banking and Paper Currencies* (1840; rpt. New York: Greenwood Press, 1968), 67.
2. Malone, *The Sage of Monticello*, 312. TJ to John Adams, Nov. 7, 1819, in *The Works of Thomas Jefferson*, ed. Paul Leicester Ford (New York: G. P. Putnam, 1905), 12:144, 145. George Dangerfield, *The Awakening of American Nationalism, 1815–28* (New York: Harper Torchbooks, 1955), 72–78, 86.
3. EWR to MJR, Aug. 24, 1819 (Coolidge Papers, U. Va.).
4. TJ to Joseph Marx, August 24, 1819 (Ford, 12:134, 135).
5. TJ to John Adams, Nov. 7, 1819 (Ford, 12:144, 145).
6. EWR to MJR, Aug. 24, 1819 (Coolidge Papers, U. Va.).
7. TJR Memoir (Edgehill-Randolph Papers, U. Va.).
8. Sarah E. Nicholas to Jane Hollins Randolph (Randolph Papers, U. Va.).

CHAPTER 30

1. Joseph C. Cabell to John Hartwell Cocke, Dec. 12, 1819 (Cabell Papers, U. Va.).
2. TMR Address to the Legislature, Dec. 4, 1820 (Journal of the General Assembly of Virginia, Richmond, 1820).
3. *A Collection of All Such Acts of the General Assembly of Virginia of a Public and Permanent Nature, as are now in force, with a Table of the Principal Matters,* Richmond, 1803.
4. TMR to My Dear Girls, Saturday Evening, July 28, 1820 (Trist Papers, UNC).
5. Cornelia to Virginia Randolph, May 19, 1820 (Trist Papers, UNC).
6. MJR to NPT, June 8, 1822 (Trist Papers, UNC).
7. MJR to Virginia, Dec. 13, 1820 (Trist Papers, UNC).
8. David Campbell to Maj. John Campbell, Jan. 22, 1821 (Duke University Library, Durham, N.C.).

CHAPTER 31

1. Gaines, 122.
2. MJR to Virginia, Jan. 10 and Feb. 14, 1822 (Trist Papers, UNC).
3. MJR to Mrs. Trist, May 31, 1815 (Vir. His. Soc.).
4. Malone, *The Sage of Monticello*, 491–93.
5. Francis Walker Gilmer to Dabney Carr, March 4, 1820 (Virginia State Library).
6. EWR to MJR, Richmond, Apr. 9, 1819 (Coolidge Papers, #9090, U. Va.).
7. EWR to NPT, Aug. 11, 1823 (Trist Papers, UNC).
8. EWR to NPT, Jan. 20, 1823 (LC).
9. EWC to Randall, 1856 (Letter Book, Coolidge Coll., U. Va.).

CHAPTER 32

1. Malone, *The Sage of Monticello*, 383.
2. TJ to John Holmes, April 22, 1820 (Ford, 12:158).
3. TJ to Albert Gallatin, Dec. 26, 1820 (Ford, 12:187, 188).
4. Randall, 3:327.
5. Gaines, 125.
6. Jefferson Correspondence with John Hemings (Library of Congress microfilm, U. Va.).
7. Bear, *Family Letters*, 461.
8. John Hemings to Septimia Randolph, Aug. 28, 1825 (Meikleham Papers, U. Va.).
9. Thomas Jefferson's Memorandum Book, entry for March 22, 1823 (courtesy Lucia Stanton, Monticello Research Assistant).
10. TJ to William J. Coffee, July 10, 1822 (Building File, Monticello).
11. Ellen Wayles Randolph to Virginia Randolph, Aug. 31, 1819 (Coolidge Papers, U. Va.).

CHAPTER 33

1. TMR to NPT, June 5, 1820 (Trist Papers, UNC).
2. TMR to Henry Remsen, Dec. 3, 1823 (Hench Coll., U. Va.).
3. Malone, *The Sage of Monticello*, 453.
4. MJR to NPT, Apr. 4, 1824 (Trist Papers, UNC).

5. TJ to James Monroe, Feb. 20, 1824 (Ford, 12: 343–345).
6. TJ to Bernard Peyton, Sept. 3, 1824 (Mass. His. Soc.).

CHAPTER 34

1. George Ticknor to TJ, March 27, 1824 (TJ Papers, LC).
2. Walter Muir Whitehill, *Collected Papers of the Monticello Assoc.* (Monticello Assoc., 1965), 89, 90.
3. EWR to Margaret Nicholas, March 26, 1825 (Edgehill-Randolph Papers, U. Va.).
4. TJ to Joseph C. Coolidge, Oct. 24, 1824 (Ford, 12: 381–384).
5. TJ to Thomas Jefferson Randolph, Nov. 24, 1808 (Bear, *Family Letters*, 365).
6. TJR Memoir (Edgehill-Randolph Papers, U. Va.).
7. *The Complete Jefferson*, ed. Saul K. Padover (New York: Duell, Sloan, & Pearce, 1943), 447, 448.
8. Malone, *The Sage of Monticello*, 405n.
9. George Maclaren Brydon, *Virginia's Mother Church* (Philadelphia: Church Historical Society, 1952), 2:503.
10. Report to the Monticello Association, 1932, Alderman Library, U. Va.
11. EWC to Virginia (now Mrs. Nicholas Trist), May 9, 1826 (Coolidge Papers, U. Va.).
12. EWC to TJ, Aug. 1, 1825 (Bear, *Family Letters*, 454).
13. TJ to EWC, Aug. 27, 1825 (Bear, *Family Letters*, 457).
14. Frances Wright, *Views of Society and Manners in America* (Cambridge, Mass.: Harvard University Press, 1963), 269.
15. Elizabeth Langhorne, "Edward Coles, Thomas Jefferson, and the Rights of Man," *Virginia Cavalcade* 23 (Summer 1973): 30–36.
16. TJ to Miss Fanny Wright, Aug. 27, 1825 (Ford, 12:410).
17. EWC to MJR, June 6, 1830 (Coolidge Papers, U. Va.).
18. Harold Coolidge, "An American Wedding Journey," *The Atlantic Monthly*, March 1929, 354–366.

CHAPTER 35

1. Malone, *The Sage of Monticello*, 449.
2. TJR to Jane Hollins (Mrs. TJ) Randolph, Dec. 7, 1826 (Edgehill-Randolph Papers, U. Va.).
3. TMR to Francis Walker Gilmer, June 21, July 9 and 12, 1825 (Gilmer Papers. U. Va.).
4. Ellen Carr to Jane Hollins Randolph, July 22, 1826 (Edgehill-Randolph Papers, U. Va.).
5. TMR note appended to letter from TJ, Jan. 8, 1826 (Edgehill-Randolph Papers, U. Va.).
6. Francis Walker Gilmer to Peachy R. Gilmer, June 19, 1825 (Vir. His. Soc.).
7. Jane Hollins Randolph to Cary Anne Smith, June 27, 1826 (Edgehill-Randolph Papers, U. Va.).
8. Malone, *The Sage of Monticello*, 472.
9. TJ to TMR, Jan. 8, 1826 (Ford, 12:432, 433).
10. Virginia Trist to EWC, March 19, 1828 (Coolidge Papers, U. Va.).
11. F. W. Gilmer to P. R. Gilmer, June 19, 1825 (Vir. His. Soc.).

CHAPTER 36

1. Malone, *The Sage of Monticello*, 473.
2. Elizabeth Langhorne, K. Edward Lay, and William D. Reiley, *A Virginia Family and Its Plantation Houses* (Charlottesville: University Press of Virginia, 1987).
3. TJ to Joseph C. Cabell, Feb. 7, 1826 (Ford, 12:451).
4. TJ to Thomas Jefferson Randolph, Feb. 8, 1826 (Randall, 3:531).
5. Bear, *Family Letters*, 470.
6. Hetty Carr to Dabney S. Carr, March 13, 1826 (Carr-Cary Papers, U. Va.).
7. Jane Margaret Carr to Dabney S. Carr, Feb. 27, 1826 (Carr-Cary Papers, U. Va.).
8. Ibid.
9. Jane Hollins Randolph to Cary Ann Smith, June 27, 1826 (Edgehill-Randolph Papers, U. Va.).
10. TJR to Dabney S. Carr, July 11, 1826 (Carr-Cary Papers, U. Va.).
11. TJR to Jane Hollins Randolph, July 2, 1826 (Edgehill-Randolph Papers, U. Va.).
12. Randolph, *Domestic Life*, 428.

CHAPTER 37

1. Malone, *The Sage of Monticello*, 511.
2. Mary Jefferson Randolph to Ellen Wayles Coolidge, Jan. 25, 1827 (Coolidge Papers, #9090, U. Va.).
3. Jefferson's Account Book, March 30, 1812 (U. Va.).
4. Ford, 12:482, 483.
5. List of slave auction, Jan. 1, 1829 (#8937, Manuscript Department, Alderman Library, U. Va.).
6. Malone, *The Sage of Monticello*, 488.
7. Martha Jefferson Randolph to Benjamin Franklin Randolph (Smith-Carter Papers, U. Va.). Incorrectly dated Jan. 27, 1838. Correct to Jan. 27, 1836, when Martha was still living and Lewis Randolph was in Arkansas, as referred to in the letter.
8. "Memoirs of a Monticello Slave," in *Jefferson at Monticello*, 25, 26.
9. Martha Jefferson Randolph to Septimia Randolph, Jan. 29, 1829 (Meikleham Papers, U. Va.).
10. This stone was found by Mr. Bear on the south-east slope of Monticello Mountain. As of 1985 it is stored in the Archaeological Laboratory at Monticello.
11. Brodie, 473–476.
12. Cornelia Randolph to Ellen Wayles Coolidge, May 18, 1827 (Coolidge Papers, U. Va.).
13. Isaac Coles to Joseph C. Cabell (private collection).
14. Ellen Coolidge to Martha Jefferson Randolph, Oct. 28, 1829 (#9090, Coolidge Papers, U. Va.).
15. Coolidge, "An American Wedding Journey," 358, 359.
16. Mary Randolph to Ellen Coolidge, April 16, 1826 (Coolidge Papers, U. Va.).
17. Correspondence Key to Trist and Trist to Key, numbered notes, July 21, 1827 (Nicholas P. Trist Papers, vol. 4, 1826–1828, Library of Congress).
18. Joseph Coolidge to Nicholas Trist, Aug. 17, 1827 (Trist Papers, LC).
19. Mary Randolph to Ellen Coolidge, July 29, 1827 (Coolidge Papers, U. Va.).
20. Codicil to Will of Martha Jefferson Randolph, April 18, 1834 (Edgehill-Randolph Papers, U. Va.).
21. Albemarle County Will Book 12, 270.

22. Ellen Coolidge to Henry S. Randall, March 13, 1855, and July 13, 1855 (Coolidge Papers, U. Va.).

23. Inscription taken by the author in 1983.

24. Martha Jefferson Randolph to Virginia Trist, Boston, July 15, 1835 (Trist Papers, UNC).

25. Martha Jefferson Randolph to Nicholas Trist, April 17, 1833 (Trist Papers, UNC).

CHAPTER 38

1. Gaines, 167.

2. Ibid., 181.

3. Joseph Coolidge to Nicholas Trist, Aug. 17, 1827 (Trist Papers, LC).

4. Joseph Coolidge to Nicholas Trist, Aug. 13, 1827 (Trist Papers, LC).

5. TMR to Mary Jefferson Randolph, Sept. 24, 1827 (David Campbell Collection, Duke University).

6. TMR to Mary, Sept. 20, 1827 (Trist Papers, UNC).

7. TMR to *Richmond Enquirer*, Jan. 18, 1828 (Edgehill-Randolph Papers, U. Va.).

8. TMR to NPT, March 10, 1828 (Trist Papers, Book 4, LC).

9. Ibid.

10. MJR to NPT, Aug. 2, 1827 (Trist Papers, UNC).

11. MJR to EWC, June 30, 1828 (Coolidge Papers, U. Va.).

12. MJR to TJR, March 2, 1827 (Edgehill-Randolph Papers, U. Va.).

13. Cornelia to EWC, May 30, 1830 (Coolidge Papers, U. Va.).

14. MJR, Oct. 2, 1833, note in MJR's hand (Edgehill-Randolph Papers, U. Va.).

15. MJR to NPT, April 4, 1827 (Trist Papers, UNC).

Index